T0323070

Open Innovation Results

Open Innovation Results

*Going Beyond the Hype and Getting
Down to Business*

HENRY CHESBROUGH

OXFORD
UNIVERSITY PRESS

OXFORD
UNIVERSITY PRESS

Great Clarendon Street, Oxford, OX2 6DP,
United Kingdom

Oxford University Press is a department of the University of Oxford.
It furthers the University's objective of excellence in research, scholarship,
and education by publishing worldwide. Oxford is a registered trade mark of
Oxford University Press in the UK and in certain other countries

© Henry Chesbrough 2020

The moral rights of the author have been asserted

First Edition published in 2020

Impression: 2

Published in the United States of America by Oxford University Press
198 Madison Avenue, New York, NY 10016, United States of America

British Library Cataloguing in Publication Data
Data available

Library of Congress Control Number: 2019941413

ISBN 978-0-19-884190-6

DOI: 10.1093/oso/9780198841906.001.0001

Printed and bound in Great Britain by
Clays Ltd, Elcograf S.p.A.

To the growing community of innovation scholars and managers, who together are advancing the theory and practice of Open Innovation far beyond what one person could ever hope to do.

Acknowledgments

This book is the culmination of many years of listening, learning, and reflection from a variety of people in industry, academia, and the classroom. Due to the positive reception of my previous work, I am frequently invited to participate in fascinating discussions. These have been wonderful opportunities to develop and test ideas and approaches to questions of innovation, and in particular, how to manage it effectively to achieve real business results. I have come to realize that there will never be a final answer to these questions, which means that I will have a job for life, if I can keep up. There are therefore many people to acknowledge in the creation of this book, and the research upon which it is based.

Let me start with my colleagues at UC Berkeley. Within Berkeley's Haas Business School, I have benefited from the thoughts of David Teece, Solomon Darwin, Robert Cole, Steve Blank, Andre Marquis, Richard Lyons, and Maria Carkovic. Solomon, in particular, has been critical in disseminating Open Innovation beyond Berkeley, and is achieving real business results with Open Innovation in his home country of India. Many current and former Berkeley students have provided excellent research assistance, including So-hyeong Kim, Ann-Kristin Zobel, Sea Matilda Bez, Chiara DeMarco, Anna Baranskaya, Nadia Carlsten, Ellen Chan, Camilo Ossa, Jean Lu, Nishil Bali, Bill Fusz, Alia Al-Kasimi, and Tania Dutta. Berkeley has been blessed with a rich crop of visiting scholars, many of whom contributed to this work as well, including Mei Liang, Marcus Holgersson, Frederic LeRoy, Neil Kay, Thomas Kohler, Tommi Lampikoski, Anssi Smedlund, Annika Lorenz, Wolfgang Sachsenhofer, Tobias Weiblen, Andy Zhu, Donghui Meng, and Bowen Zhang.

Outside of Haas, I have been fortunate to spend time each year in Barcelona at ESADE, where I even had the pleasure of a sabbatical in 2016. There I have had many wonderful discussions with Jonathan Wareham, Esteve Almirall, Ivanka Visnjic, Ken Morse, Nuria Agell, Ivan Bofarull, Marcel Planellas, Xavier Ferras, Laia Pujols, Luisa Alemany, Laura Castellucci, Elena Bou, Connie Lutoff-Carroll, Cheryl Fragiadakis, Tuba Bakici, Mehdi Bagherzadeh-niri, and Henry Lopez Vega. In the business environment around ESADE, I had excellent discussions with Xavier Marcet, Paco Sole Parellada, Pablo Rodriguez, Cecilia Tham, and Roc Fages.

Other academic colleagues have contributed substantially to my thinking along the way. I want to thank my previous co-authors with Oxford University Press, Wim Vanhaverbeke and Joel West, along with Marcel Bogers, Andrea Prencipe, Alberto Diminin, Melissa Appleyard, Janet Bercovitz, Sabine Brunswicker, Xiaolan Fu, Oliver Gassmann, Annabelle Gawer, Keld Laursen, Hila Lifshitz-Assaf, Kwanghui Lim, Ikujiro Nonaka, Gina O'Connor, Francesco Sandulli, Melissa Schilling, Scott Stern, Chris Tucci, and Max von Zedtwitz.

A third critical source of information for this book has come from managers of companies grappling with the challenge of getting results from Open Innovation. Many of these people are identified and quoted within the text of this book, and I won't lengthen this Acknowledgement by repeating all of those names. Help and advice that went beyond the call of duty, however, does deserve special mention: Ernesto Ciorra of Enel, Carlo Papa of the Enel Foundation, Mohi Ahmed of Fujitsu, Jim Spohrer of IBM, Graham Cross of Unilever, Pierre Orlewski of Goodyear, Havard Belbo of Tlab, Monika Lessl and Melanie Heroult of Bayer, Marisol Menendez of South Summit (and formerly of BBVA), Marco Waas of Nouriyon (formerly AkzoNobel), Anna Baranskaya of Renault-Nissan, Chun-cheng Piao of Daikin, and Markus Nordberg of CERN.

Another recent development is the growing use of Open Innovation in innovation policy. EU Commissioner for Research, Science, and Innovation, Carlos Moedas, has built his policy around the Three Opens: Open Science, Open Innovation, and Open to the World. And Tom Kalil, Deputy Director of the Office of Science and Technology Policy, in the Obama Adminstration, similarly brought Open Innovation into US innovation policymaking. And Arati Prabhakar, former head of DARPA, reminds me that an open, distributed innovation process has been in place inside the Pentagon for over sixty years, and is slowly spreading to energy and perhaps other departments. It has been tremendously exciting, seeing these developments unfold.

Despite all of this help and feedback, there are undoubtedly still many mistakes in this book. However, they are new and better mistakes than I would have made, had I not talked to these people. This is true of innovation in general I think. It is an inherently collaborative activity, which improves as a result of the open exchange of knowledge. So I would like to dedicate this book to the growing community of innovation scholars and managers, who together are advancing the theory and practice of Open Innovation far beyond what one person could ever hope to do. I hope that this book will challenge us all to keep going, share our experiences, learn from our mistakes, and to realize even better results.

I have also benefited enormously from excellent administrative assistance that really acts as a force multiplier for creating, disseminating, and absorbing this work. Special thanks to Anita Stephens at UC Berkeley-Haas, for over a decade of such support, to the point now where she is more of a partner than a support. Adriana Macias, also at Haas, is dragging me kicking and screaming into the digital world. Tristan Gaspi has kept a close eye on the numbers at my Center. Anna Bonet, Olga Plaza, and Rosa Vilanova at ESADE have each been helpful during my time in Barcelona.

I am also indebted to my editor Adam Swallow, and his colleague Jenny King at Oxford University Press for their thoughtful comments, support, and guidance through the manuscript's development and editing process.

My wife Katherine read through much of the manuscript, and gently exposed the gaps, errors, and incomplete thinking of earlier drafts. The book is better for her patient reading. She has been a powerful force multiplier for me in many ways, and words cannot express my gratitude to her. I am also indebted to my children, Emily and Sarah, for their patience and support during the writing of this book. I sincerely hope that they will be proud of this book, should they ever decide to read it.

Henry Chesbrough

Berkeley, California
chesbrou@haas.berkeley.edu

Contents

List of Figures

Introduction

It's been more than a decade now since the financial crisis of 2008 devastated many of the economies in the West. There have been many impacts from the crisis, but one that has not received much attention is the impact of the crisis on innovation itself. When the crisis hit, innovation budgets plunged at most companies. And as the recovery has slowly taken hold, companies have asked hard questions about whether to resume their earlier innovation spending at its pre-crisis levels.

These questions fundamentally revolve around getting results from innovation. To be sure, many of us regard innovation as a luxury good—we love innovation when times are good, but it is the first thing to be cut when times are bad. Such an attitude cannot lead to business success. Innovation activities that generate publicity, but fail to drive new revenues and more profits are not delivering the results needed to sustain innovation investment over time. Without strong evidence that innovation can achieve positive business results, it becomes hard to justify spending additional funds on innovation, even when markets are improving after a financial crisis. And another crisis will surely take place in the coming years, making it imperative to get business results from innovation—or else!

A similar perspective is needed towards Open Innovation. Open Innovation was just getting established in most organizations when the financial crisis hit. While there were indeed examples of real business results achieved from individual companies, for many organizations the concept was too new to show its full benefits. (And there was a learning curve for many organizations as well, such that the first attempts with Open Innovation did not always attain the expected results.) In the time since the financial crisis, Open Innovation has become far more widespread. A quick search on Google using the search term 'Open Innovation' obtains more than 600 million page links. This is an enormous increase since 2003, when my book *Open Innovation* first came out. At that time, using the same search term on the same search engine, there were approximately 200 page links. On LinkedIn, there are now tens of thousands of jobs with 'Open Innovation' in the title, whereas there were hardly any at all back in 2003.

Open Innovation Results. Going Beyond the Hype, and Getting Down to Business. Henry Chesbrough, Oxford University Press (2020). © Henry Chesbrough.
DOI: 10.1093/oso/9780198841906.001.0001

Most of this increase has taken place since the financial crisis. But the crisis may have impacted the way that most organizations have implemented Open Innovation. In its early days, Open Innovation was a framework that leveraged internal Research & Development (R&D) by bringing in more external knowledge to accelerate and enhance the current business (and business model), while enabling unused internal R&D to go outside for others to utilize in their business (and business model). However, after the financial crisis, some organizations employed the language of Open Innovation to reduce or eliminate internal R&D, and relied on outsourcing instead. Open Innovation was not intended as a strategy to diminish innovation investment, but in some cases this is how it has been used. And that path may deliver some short term improvement, but is likely to result in long term decline for the organization.

What is needed is a renewal of our understanding of Open Innovation, and how we can get better business results from using Open Innovation. This book is my attempt to explain just that. It begins with a paradox within many Western economies: technological advance is growing exponentially, but economic productivity growth is actually declining. Think of this as an Exponential Paradox. We discuss this paradox by introducing the need for society to engage with innovation on three critical dimensions: generation, dissemination, and absorption. Within the firm, there is a parallel situation. Many firms are not investing in and sustaining their own innovation infrastructure, which is critical to achieving superior innovation results for the business. Here too, the organization must not only generate innovation, it must disseminate it across internal organizational siloes to the internal business units, and absorb it into its business processes and business models inside those businesses.

These three facets of innovation form the conceptual underpinnings throughout the book:

1) Innovation Generation—the facet through which organizations discover and develop novel products, services, and processes.
2) Innovation Dissemination—the facet in which these discoveries move throughout the larger organization (or society), from the laboratory through to the marketplace, from the front end innovation group to the back end business unit.
3) Innovation Absorption—the facet which takes the generated, disseminated inputs from the organization (or society) and puts them to work, embedding the innovation in an organizational unit and business model that can deliver, scale, and sustain the innovation.

The plan of the book starts from innovation in general and then moves to Open Innovation in particular. In Chapter 1 we examine the Exponential Paradox within the US, and provide some evidence of this issue in many other leading Western economies. As we will see, the Exponential Paradox results from too much attention to generation, and too little attention to dissemination and absorption. In Chapter 2, we examine Open Innovation itself as a novel process. Here too, it is not enough to generate new innovation possibilities. Equal attention is needed to disseminate these throughout the organization, and to absorb them into the business units of the organization.

In Chapter 3, we place Open Innovation into context, examining the role of open science and Open Innovation in creating new knowledge, and carrying that knowledge to the market. The norms of open science that do so much to generate new knowledge do not suffice to carry that knowledge into the market. For that, different norms around Open Innovation are required. In Chapter 4, we build upon those Open Innovation norms, examining the practices of innovating organizations who try to connect the front end of their innovation processes to the back end business units that receive the outputs of the innovation process.

In Chapter 5, we focus on the less studied, less practiced branch of Open Innovation, the inside-out branch. We introduce Lean Startup practices as a new, valid methodology for applying inside-out thinking to explore new businesses, and new business models, from unused or under-utilized internal ideas and technologies. In Chapter 6, we consider how corporations can engage more effectively with startup companies, from both an outside-in and inside-out perspective. The question here is how best to engage with startup companies, particularly if one seeks to engage with many startups simultaneously.

In Chapter 7, we discuss the use of Open Innovation in smart cities, and introduce a novel context for Open Innovation, a rural village in India. Surprisingly, Open Innovation has demonstrated an ability to catalyze new economic vitality in a rural setting, with a market-based mechanism for scaling its results to many other villages. In Chapter 8, we return to the advanced economies and discuss some best practices that companies have found, in getting business results from Open Innovation. In turn, though, some of the early exemplar companies that used to be showcases for Open Innovation are now struggling to sustain these results. And there have been failure cases that indicate some of the limits or boundary conditions needed for Open Innovation to achieve its intended results.

Chapter 9 concludes with a consideration of Open Innovation in modern China. Under Xi Jinping, China has taken a different road from that of the

Western economies on the one hand, or the former Soviet Union on the other hand. This has profound implications for innovation, and this chapter particularly focuses on the tension between the decisive role of the market, and the leading role of the Party, in Xi Jinping thought. We return to the three facets of generation, dissemination, and absorption of innovation, shown in this chapter through three different industries in China: high-speed rail, automotives, and semiconductors.

As I finished writing this book, I realized that there were a number of possible journeys that a reader could take through the volume. Of course, I welcome the intrepid reader who diligently reads (and absorbs!) each and every chapter in the order it is presented. But my experience with busy managers, overloaded students, and my own sometimes-distracted children advises me that it may be wise to sketch some shorter journeys for other readers.

- For the busy manager who wants to focus on the latest developments in Open Innovation, Chapters 2, 4, 5, and 6 will provide the most 'bang for the buck'
- For those interested in innovation policy, Chapters 1, 3, 7, and 9 will capture most of the policy implications of Open Innovation, with Chapter 7 examining rural India, and Chapter 9 discussing modern China
- For my academic colleagues who are often as starved for time as most business managers, Chapters 1, 3, 5, 7, and 8 will be the right chapters to focus upon (unless they have an interest in China, in which case they should add Chapter 9).
- For the 'heat seekers' who just want the bottom line, each chapter has a handful of chapter review points, that summarize the insights of the chapter. So one could start with these reading these chapter review points, and then decide whether or not to read the entire chapter.

The publication of this book represents the generation of a set of new insights about Open Innovation. But much remains to be done to disseminate these insights, and even more must happen if these insights are to be absorbed and put to work. At UC Berkeley, I have been fortunate to have the chance to teach dozens of bright students each year, and send them off to the workforce with Open Innovation in their heads. I also have established the Berkeley Innovation Forum, which gathers more than forty companies together face-to-face two times each year, to share practices and experiences with managing innovation, including Open Innovation. With LUISS University in Rome, there is a similar group called the European Innovation Forum. And we have an annual World Open Innovation Conference that gathers together some of the best new research in Open Innovation, and solicits challenges from industry as well. We create workshops to present and discuss these challenges, with some of the most active researchers sitting alongside some of the most adept practitioners of Open Innovation. There are frequent special issues to capture the latest academic research in Open Innovation, in academic journals like *Research Policy, Industrial and Corporate Change, California Management Review, Industry and Innovation, Long Range Planning, Journal of Product Innovation Management, R&D Management*, and *Technovation*. We also provide access to more innovation management resources at corporateinnovation.berkeley.edu, and openinnovation.net. There are even Open Innovation groups on Facebook and on LinkedIn.

But much of the work of absorption inevitably falls upon the reader. Once you have opened this book, please let me know what more needs to be done to get these ideas implemented effectively inside your own organization. You can reach me at: chesbrou@berkeley.edu

1

The Exponential Paradox

Living in Silicon Valley as I do, I am surrounded by exciting new developments on a daily basis. And there is a wonderful optimism here about the power of new technologies and new ideas to help us move toward a better future. (Anyone who likes the *Star Trek* TV shows and movies will recognize this attitude immediately.)

One widespread observation from Silicon Valley is that so-called 'exponential technologies' are leading us into a future of abundance. Whether it is Moore's Law, doubling the density of semiconductor circuits every twenty-four months, or Metcalfe's Law, increasing the value of communication networks by the square of the number of people on the network, or the myriad possibilities of advancing human health through genomic data sequencing (and the cost of sequencing is dropping exponentially over time), technology is on the march. This suggests that many important items are going to become much cheaper, much more powerful, and much more pervasive, in a surprisingly short period of time.[1]

These technological advances directly affect our lives. Our smartphones today have the power of a supercomputer from the 1980s, at a price of a TV or a VCR from the 1980s. We can access information on the Web from anywhere in the world at a click. Businesses have arisen today that have achieved tremendous success by linking us all together more tightly, more quickly, and more cheaply. Medical technologies like gene sequencing have fallen tremendously, and we now have the ability to actually edit gene sequences with technologies like CRISPR as well. Indeed, the cost of starting a new business itself has fallen substantially, due to the ability to use open source software as a building block, and to house your storage in a cloud where you pay only for what you use.

Here in Silicon Valley, you cannot escape this parade of exponential possibilities, with more exciting technologies coming to market all the time. I could go on, but you surely get the point.

And yet, if one steps away from Silicon Valley and looks at the wider world, troubling signs quickly arise that suggest that all is not well in this world of exponential technology. Productivity in our economy is growing only very

Open Innovation Results. Going Beyond the Hype, and Getting Down to Business. Henry Chesbrough, Oxford University Press (2020). © Henry Chesbrough.
DOI: 10.1093/oso/9780198841906.001.0001

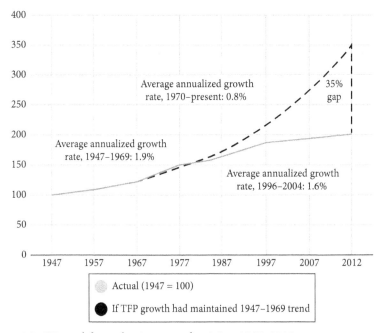

Figure 1.1 US total factor business productivity, 1947–2012

Source: Center for the Study of Income and Productivity, Federal Reserve Bank of San Francisco.

slowly, and this growth even declined in a few recent periods. Figure 1.1 shows this historic rate of productivity growth in the US. Note how much productivity has slowed in the past thirty years. This slowdown is not unique to the US—it can be found in many advanced economies, as is shown in Figure 1.2 for seven of the major Western economies.

The creates a puzzle: if all this wonderful technology is growing so rapidly, why are we seeing such a slowdown in productivity growth? The slow rate of productivity growth is the opposite of what you would expect to see in an exponential world. If the technology optimists are right, productivity growth should be accelerating. Instead, not only is it not trending up, it is actually slowing down. This is troubling. I call it the Exponential Paradox. Yet my technophile friends out here in Silicon Valley take little or no notice of this.

Productivity is what drives long term economic growth. But people don't get to eat productivity, they get to eat based on their income. And here the puzzle is as bad, if not worse. People's incomes aren't growing rapidly. In fact, they are not growing at all, they are just stagnating. As shown in Figure 1.3, their incomes are lagging the growth in productivity (which, as we just saw, is slowing down). While there are many factors involved in this process, it runs

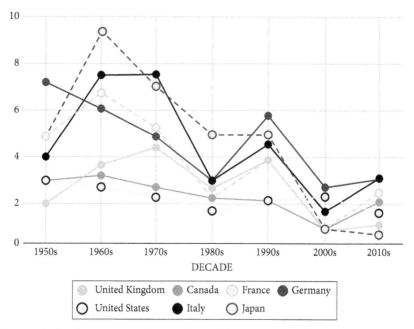

Figure 1.2 Productivity growth trends in G7 Countries, 1950–2015
Source: OECD "Productivity Trends in G7 Countries", 2017.

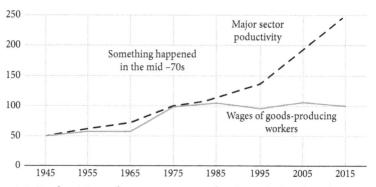

Figure 1.3 Productivity and average wage trends, 1945–2015, index relative to 1975
Source: Bureau of Labor Statistics, "Understanding the Labor Productivity and Compensation Gap",
June, 2017, volume 6.

directly counter to the technological optimists' view of a future of abundance
for us all.

Indeed, one of the sad results of these troubling trends is that most US
citizens expect that their children will not live as well as they themselves did.[2]
This is a dramatic sea change from earlier generations in the US. The

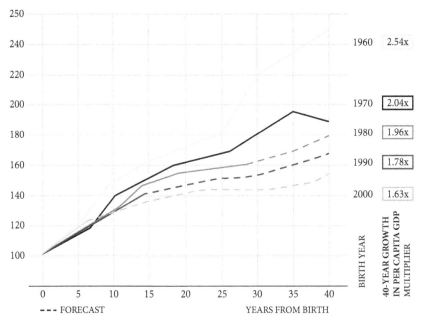

Figure 1.4 GDP growth rate by decade of birth, 1960–2000

Source: US Bureau of Economic Analysis, McKinsey Global Institute Report, "Poorer Than Their Parents? A New Perspective on Income Inequality", July 2016.

American dream was built in part on the open frontier, the chance to chart your own destiny, and the comfort that your children would likely have a better life than you did. But Figure 1.4 shows precisely the opposite. Baby Boomers born on or before 1960 have seen the economy grow at a rate of over 2.5 per cent compounded each year for them during their lifetimes. However, later generations have seen a steady decline in the growth rate of the economy in which they lived, with the most recently born confronting an economy only growing 1.6 per cent compounded annually. It is hard to see the benefits of exponential technologies in these data.

In Europe, while it varies by country, the pattern is quite similar. Countries like Spain and Italy have had extremely high youth unemployment rates since the economic crisis of 2008–9. Almost a decade later, well over 20 per cent of young people from eighteen to twenty-four cannot find work, and a significant number are leaving for other countries to try to improve their economic prospects. In countries like Germany, which is doing comparatively well economically, there are other problems. The German population is aging rapidly, reducing the growth of demand in the German economy, which slows down growth for them too. This is also happening in Japan.

Again, this is completely contrary to what one would expect, based on the promise of exponential technologies and our abundant future. Personal income per person should be increasing from one generation to the next, not slowing down.

There are some qualifications to the slowing of personal income per person. In countries like China and India, personal income per person is growing quite rapidly. Hundreds of millions of people have been lifted out of poverty in the past thirty years, an enormous human achievement, and a truly hopeful sign for our collective future. So world income is still growing, and there have been some areas of the world that are catching up, while other areas have slowed down.

But China and India's rapid growth in income faces challenges as well. The most salient of these is the so-called Middle Income trap, whereby developing economies grow to a point, but fail to reach the level of high income per person. This is due to the fact that it becomes harder to grow incomes once a country reaches a middle level of income. At a middle income level, wages have risen to the point where manufacturing is no longer based on cheap wages, while the skills and technologies needed to produce at world class levels (and thereby support high wage employment) have yet to develop. And China's one-child policy over previous decades means that China may well become old before it is able to become rich. India has more demographic promise, but faces enormous social challenges of its own (and possesses a much less developed infrastructure than China).

It's an Exponential Paradox. Technology is accelerating, while productivity growth and incomes are declining or stagnant. Something is not right. And that is what has motivated me to write this book. Before I consider some of the possible explanations for this paradox, let me share my own view, so you'll know where I'm going: the root of the problem is in how we are managing and investing in innovation, both inside individual organizations and also in the larger society. We must extend beyond the creation of new technologies, to also include their broad dissemination and deep absorption, in order to prosper from new technologies.

This has implications within organizations, and also for the larger society in which organizations operate. Innovation in most companies is treated as a luxury good; in good times, everyone loves it and wants more, but it is the first thing to cut when times are tough. We distract ourselves with the 'shiny new objects' that arise from the advance of technology. All too often, the front end of the innovation process is not connected to the businesses that are to commercialize any new technologies.

Something analogous happens within the larger society. We celebrate the achievements of an Elon Musk, a Jeff Bezos, or a Jack Ma, but we pay far too little attention to the subsequent dissemination and utilization of these advances in our society. How many organizations are really taking advantage of artificial intelligence, or data science, to name just two hot topics of the moment? The answer as of this writing is, very few. So individual companies are thriving from their use of these new capabilities, but their overall social impact is minimal to date. To realize the potential from exponential technologies, we must refocus our attention on the things that really matter in innovation (instead of simply starting another one and blithely ignoring what happens afterwards). That will require us to rethink innovation, both inside organizations and in society as a whole.

Now that you know where we're going, let us consider some of the other proffered explanations for this exponential paradox. Some thoughtful technology optimists have taken note of these troubling indications that our future of abundance may not be emerging as we would like it to. One hopeful explanation they offer for this apparent paradox is that our new technologies are impacting our lives in ways that are hard for economists to measure. So the exponential benefits are in fact real, but are not yet showing up in our economic data.

To see what they mean, consider the smartphone. It contains a wide variety of technologies that all used to be separate devices: a phone, a computer, a game player, a CD player, a camera, a video recorder and playback device, a watch, a calendar, a calculator . . . and this is before one considers the value of the millions of apps now available to download and use on the smartphone. If you add up the cost of these separate devices, you can easily go well above $10,000. Yet good smartphones can be had for $100, and state of the art smartphones can be purchased around $500 to $1000.

Measuring economic activity, the shrinkage of over $10,000 of electronics into a single device of a few hundred dollars represents a marked decline in economic output. But in reality, smartphones have greatly improved our productivity, not least because we have all of that capability in one place, right in the palm of our hand. So the economic measure, in this instance, fails to capture the full benefit of the many innovations in the smartphone.

The technological optimists use this reasoning to convince themselves that the innovation paradox is nothing more serious than a measurement problem. Once we develop better measures for economic outcomes from our amazing technological inputs, the paradox will vanish, and the true value of all this exponential technology will become apparent.

Other observers like Robert Gordon of Northwestern are not persuaded by this logic. Gordon has studied a variety of innovations since the time of the first and second industrial revolutions.[3] He argues that these revolutions have truly transformed human activity (and productivity) by replacing brute human labor with a wealth of labor-saving devices. These have resulted in lifestyles among lower- and middle-class families that would be unrecognizable to all but the wealthiest families of two centuries earlier. Human longevity has greatly advanced, nutrition is much improved (along with the average height of people), more time is spent in education now for people from all walks of life, child labor is a thing of the past in most societies, and so on.

By contrast, according to Gordon, the so-called third industrial revolution of computing has failed to deliver any benefits that rise to scale of the earlier innovations of the first and second industrial revolution. To his thinking, the ability to instantly process data, communicate around the world, access information from anywhere with just a click, all amount to improvements and conveniences in our lives. They do not by themselves enable us to escape drudge work the way the earlier breakthroughs did, and do not enable the labor-saving improvements of those earlier periods. Nor do they improve our health or increase our height.

Gordon's work reminds us that the wide diffusion of technology is necessary before the society receives any real benefit from it. Labor-saving devices only save labor if they are available to all or at least most households in the society. Nutrition and longevity for the population of people only rise when most or all people in the society have access to safe food and adequate health care.

Another explanation was recently offered by the Organization for Economic Cooperation and Development (OECD), examining 'the best vs. the rest'.[4] The OECD found that the best firms in both manufacturing and services during the period of 2001–13 continued to grow productivity at historic levels. The 'rest', however, lagged badly behind. This argues that Gordon's analysis is correct on average, but the best firms have continued the trends of the past. So the very best firms today are in fact continuing to save significant costs from their latest innovations. However, most of the rest of the firms have yet to adopt these technologies, and therefore get no benefit from them.

The OECD analysis shows us that we must absorb these technologies, and put them to work, before their impact will show up in our economic statistics. The question becomes how the rest of us can learn more from the best, to help everyone grow their own productivity more rapidly. The root of the problem is that our innovations may not be impacting enough businesses to fulfill the

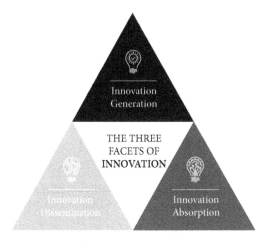

Figure 1.5 The three facets of innovation

potential they possess. For example, a recent survey of businesses by McKinsey showed that only 47 per cent of firms surveyed were using artificial intelligence (AI), even at a pilot scale. Only 21 per cent of firms surveyed were using AI technologies in multiple parts of the company.[5]

One can see this gap clearly in India. The Indian government under Prime Minister Modi has embraced the latest blockchain technology for improved access to government services for all citizens. On the other hand, more than 30 million households in India lack electrification, while a similar number lack access to clean water. This gap between the best and the rest is easily seen here, and the productivity benefits of blockchain technology will take a long time to reach those 30 million households.

This motivates the three vertices in Figure 1.5. New technology discoveries start the process of improving economic productivity. By themselves, however, only a small portion of the society might benefit from them. Broad dissemination is the second vertex in Figure 1.5, in which many or most people in the society gain access to these technologies. That helps to extend their impact further. But the real payoff only comes when the final vertex is observed, when many or most in the society put this knowledge to work in their own organizations.

We've Been Here Before: The IT Paradox

Astute observers might well note that we have seen a version of this debate not so long ago. There was an 'IT paradox' back in the early 1990s that has echoes of this more recent Exponential Paradox. Back then, as Robert Solow famously observed, 'we see computers everywhere but in the statistics'. He meant that one could readily observe companies and governments pouring billions of dollars into computers, but the economic statistics of the time showed little or no benefit to all of this investment. Either the supposed benefits of computing were vastly overstated, or we were somehow failing to record their impacts in our data.[6]

While many scholars investigated these issues, some of the most insightful work in my view came from an MIT scholar, Eric Brynolffson. In a series of papers[7] he carefully unravelled the IT paradox that Solow indicated. At the risk of oversimplifying all of this work, he came to the following conclusions:

1) Economic indicators were mis-measuring the impact of IT investment.
2) However, firms that simply spent money on IT by itself received little benefit (so the measures weren't far off here).
3) It was those firms who developed new, improved business processes that were enabled by IT investment that reaped significant benefits from that investment. Those new processes weren't always accurately reflected by the economic indicators, and here was where the measurement problem was most serious.

As Brynolffson's work showed, firms had to change their processes to benefit from their IT investments. Then, and only then, would they benefit from substantial investments in computer technology. Note how this fits with the three vertices in Figure 1.5. Firms have to learn about these technologies, and make investments in using them inside their own organizations, enabling new business processes, to get the economic benefit of their investment. In a recent article, Tim O'Reilly added a further insight: new technologies can enable organizations to do new things, rather than just improve what was done before.[8]

The logical implication of this work is that we cannot resolve the Exponential Paradox without changing business processes and doing new things once more. Only when we develop business processes that are able to generate, disseminate, and utilize exponential technologies to the full, will we be able to raise productivity growth rates and wages. And in the spirit of the OECD study of the Best vs. the Rest, we need to drive these process improvements through to the average businesses, not just the top 1 or 2 per cent.

Changing the Business Process of Innovation: Open Innovation

One of the most important business processes that must be changed, if we are to realize the economic and social potential of exponential technologies, is the innovation process. I will devote the next chapter in this book to this topic, so I will restrict my discussion here to a few key points.

Traditionally, most business innovation processes have been closed. Companies often restrict their innovation inputs to their own internal research labs, and refuse to work with external knowledge sources that they do not own and control. Equally, companies start many more projects than they finish. The result is numerous stranded projects that have no place to go, and no path forward. Not surprisingly, this impairs productivity.

The way to change these processes is to open them up. To bring greater external knowledge into the organization, outside-in processes are required. Outside-in processes encompass many mechanisms, from technology scouting to crowdsourcing to university collaboration to in-licensing to engaging with startup companies, to name a few of the more prevalent practices. And there's another kind of opening up that's needed for more pathways for stranded internal technologies: the inside-out processes. These include out-licensing, joint development agreements, spin-outs, internal startup ventures, and Lean Startup methods for discovering new business models inside large companies, to again name some of the more prevalent practices.

This transformation, however, is highly incomplete. As with many Research and Development (R&D) projects, we have started more experiments with new Open Innovation processes than we have finished. Many times, we examine the results of an innovation process experiment, such as crowdsourcing, without following the result through to an actual business result. As we will examine in a later chapter, we know much more about the beginning of the innovation process than we do about the back end of the process, where the innovation transfers to the business, and is subsequently commercialized and later scaled.

The Value of Opening Up the Innovation Process

It's worth making this change in the innovation process, as there is growing evidence that it improves business performance. Some of this evidence comes from individual firms' experiences with Open Innovation. A consumer products firm, General Mills, analyzed sixty new product introductions in a twelve-month period. They found that those which had a substantial Open Innovation component outsold the ones that did not by more than 100 per cent.[9] Procter & Gamble has claimed that its use of Open Innovation has increased its revenues by billions of dollars.[10] In the industrial sector, a recent study of 489 projects inside a large European manufacturer found that projects involving significant Open Innovation collaboration achieved a better financial return for the company than projects that did not.[11] Open innovation also improved the time-to-market it took for many projects as well.

Other evidence comes from large surveys of firms in an industry or a whole economy. A number of studies employing the Community Innovation Survey have found that organizations with more external sources of knowledge achieve better innovation performance than those with fewer sources, controlling for other factors.[12] A recent survey of 125 large firms also found that firms that employed Open Innovation were getting better innovation results.[13] We will review Open Innovation as a business process in greater detail in the next chapter. For the rest of this chapter, though, we will discuss some of the investments that society must make in order to support its effectiveness.

Supporting Open Innovation: Society's Need for an Innovation Infrastructure

While Open Innovation has been a great success for at least a few of the 'best' firms, it requires public investment to sustain that success over time, and to drive the process improvements throughout the majority of businesses in the society. Only then will the full benefit of a more Open Innovation process be apparent. To support a more Open Innovation process within firms and organizations, we need to create an innovation infrastructure within our society that invests in all three areas of the innovation infrastructure shown in Figure 1.5. We need an infrastructure that needs to generate useful innovations, starting with basic research and then extending those results to the market. It needs to disseminate those innovations widely throughout the society, beyond the confines of the earlier closed innovation process. And it needs customers, users, partners, and citizens able to absorb that knowledge. Only then can we finish the innovations we have started. Only then will the potential benefits of exponential advances be realized. Only then will the rest be in a position to catch up to the best.

This may not sound very hard to do. But doing this actually requires us to reverse some important negative social trends that have arisen over the past forty years. These trends reversed some quite positive developments that arose after World War II. So we need to revisit some of these positive developments, then trace how they were changed, and conclude with how to get them back on track. In a way, we need to go back to the future.

Revisiting the Productivity Gains of the 1940s–1970s

What if we were to flip the question behind the Exponential Paradox around? Instead of asking why productivity growth has slowed down in recent decades, let's ask the opposite question: why was productivity growth so <u>high</u> in the 1940s through the 1970s? Was something going on in society then that perhaps is no longer continuing?[14]

This is a fruitful avenue to explore, because it changes the focus away from the continued parade of exciting new technologies, and directs our attention to the larger society making use of new technologies. Brynolffson's work suggests that *how the IT technologies were used* proved to be critical to their economic benefits.

The 1940s were a truly tumultuous decade. They began by the world being plunged into the chaos and destruction of World War II. World War II had many far-reaching impacts, but one of them that directly stimulated productivity growth was the extensive mobilization of science on behalf of the war effort for both the Allies and the Axis powers. This mobilization gave rise to a number of technological breakthroughs, from the rocketry and ballistic capabilities of Germany (e.g. the V2 rocket), to the advancement of radar and sonar, to cryptography, to the creation of nuclear weapons. While these technologies did not directly advance industrial productivity, the many supporting technologies needed to create them, such as computing technologies, communications technologies, materials technologies, etc., provided a strong boost to industry in the post-war period.

Policy innovations in the aftermath of the war were also important to productivity growth. Vannevar Bush, President Roosevelt's science advisor during the war, drafted a far-sighted document for how to extend the benefits of public science in peacetime. This was called <u>Science: The Endless Frontier</u>,[15] and made the case for continued involvement of the Federal Government in the funding and support of science for the economic well-being of society. If the government led the way with continued support for basic scientific research, this could provide the basis for sustained economic growth out into the future, indefinitely, thus creating that Endless Frontier of the title. The advent of both penicillin and the polio vaccine were tangible instances of this system in action.

This approach, which had strong bi-partisan support, led to the creation of the National Science Foundation and the National Institutes of Health. The Defense Department attracted strong ongoing support for scientific research for military applications, with its Defense Advanced Research Projects Agency (DARPA) again earning strong bi-partisan support and high levels of funding.

As important as all this funding was to productivity growth, what was also vital was the way in which these funds were spent. The Federal Government could have built up its own government laboratories to spend all of the money. In the case of nuclear weapons, the government did this, though even there the government was careful to have the national weapons labs managed by outside entities like the University of California (for Lawrence Livermore National Labs and Lawrence Berkeley Labs) or major government contractors (for Sandia Labs). This meant that the government labs were better connected to the outside world, and that more knowledge likely flowed into and out of them, than would have been the case in a government managed, government owned, government staffed, government operated laboratory system.

Beyond nuclear weapons, the system of funding for science was far more distributed. The research funding agencies National Science Foundation (NSF), National Institute of Health (NIH), Defense Advanced Research Projects Agency (DARPA), etc. nurtured ongoing relationships with universities and research institutes around the country. Even during wartime, much of the research and most of the development was performed in private companies' laboratories and factories, resulting in both the creation and the transfer of useful industrial knowledge to many parts of industry. Had the research and the production of wartime technologies been restricted to government facilities, there would have been significantly greater problems transferring this knowledge into industrial uses after the war.

Another critical development in the 1940s was the creation of the Servicemen's Readjustment Act of 1944, more popularly known as the GI Bill. This bill provided funding for returning military personnel to help them integrate back into society (in direct contrast to the many problems experienced by military personnel returning from World War I). Importantly for productivity, the GI Bill supported funding for further education for the GIs, massively stimulating the higher education sector of the economy, and infusing US workers with much more knowledge and skills than they otherwise might have had. This made US workers much more capable of working with new technologies, increasing their 'absorptive capacity' for productivity enhancing investments. The US was also encouraging the immigration of top scientists from the Axis powers to the US in the immediate post-war period as well.

The 1950s continued the surge in government-supported investments that enhanced productivity growth. The Cold War had emerged out of the ashes of World War II, augmented by the Korean War that started the decade. Under the rationale of creating a network to move land-based missiles from one location to others (to reduce their vulnerability to a sudden Soviet first strike), President Eisenhower launched the National Highway system. This was a huge infrastructure project that greatly improved the quality of inter-state highways, helping the automotive industry directly, and through improved transportation and logistics, helped many, many other businesses as well.

The US had an economic and military rival in this period, though. The launch of Sputnik by the Soviet Union in 1957 shocked Americans, and prompted the country to respond by launching its own satellites. But going further, the US government greatly increased its funding of research, science, and technology, and soon expanded this increased funding to the social sciences as well. Again, this response was distributed widely throughout the society, instead of being concentrated in a few industries or a few locations.

This strong support for research, science, and technology continued into the 1960s. The Apollo moon mission became a national priority, preceded by the Mercury and Gemini missions that built the knowledge to get to the moon. The Great Society programs of the Johnson years greatly expanded the social safety, dramatically reducing poverty among the rural and elderly populations. At the same time, the Vietnam War grew to such a large size that there soon arose a conflict between 'guns and butter'. These conflicts were resolved by running the first large Federal budget deficits since World War II, shown in Figure 1.6.

Richard Nixon's administration led the US into the decade of the 1970s. Yet while his administration was Republican, his policies toward large federal funding for research, science, and technology continued, as did the strengthening of the social safety net begun in the Johnson years. In fact, Nixon launched the Environmental Protection Agency, and began to fund new research in that area.

Figure 1.6 Annual federal budget deficit or surplus, as a percent of US GDP, 1930–2017

Source: Office of Management and Budget; Nationalpriorities.org

Revisiting the Paradox

Once we flip the question on the Exponential Paradox, it becomes easier to understand why productivity growth during the period of the 1940s through the 1970s was so high. Looking back across these four decades, notice how much these various policies and initiatives noted above advanced industrial productivity! The boost in federal funding for research, science, and technology led to an acceleration in the production of knowledge. The growth in universities and the distributed pattern of performing the R&D inside industrial firms greatly increased the pace and extent of knowledge dissemination during these years. And the massive support for increased education from the GI Bill and similarly inspired initiatives greatly improved the ability of the US workforce to master new technologies and put them to work.

These policies that contributed so much to industrial productivity, however, stopped being followed, starting in the 1980s. While government funding for research, science, and technology continues, it has not kept pace as a percentage of the economy with the levels of support these activities received earlier, as shown in Figure 1.7.

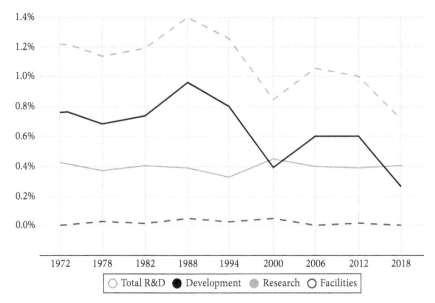

Figure 1.7 Federal R&D spending as a percent of US GDP, 1976–2018

Source: American Academy for the Advancement of Science, "Historical Trends in Federal R&D", April, 2018.

While the society enjoyed the benefits of the enhanced infrastructure created in the previous period, further infrastructure funding started to decline. Thirty five years later, we have deteriorated to the point where funding and building infrastructure is now a partisan political issue (which it was not in the earlier period). And the universities that benefited from the GI Bill began to receive less public support from the state and federal governments. This resulted in a long, steep set of tuition increases, to the point where college tuitions that were either free or easily affordable in the 1960s have reached the point where in-state tuition, room, and board easily exceed $100,000 for a four-year college degree in a public university, as seen in Figure 1.8. Tuition in a private university often is more than double this amount, greatly reducing the ability of most people to access a college education, or forcing them to take on a heavy burden of debt right at the beginning of their working lives.

At the same time, other developments have significantly detracted from improved industrial productivity across the broad swath of society. Elementary and secondary education in the US is in real crisis, with increased spending coinciding with deteriorating academic performance in the classroom. The strong support for science, technology, engineering, and mathematics (STEM) education that resulted from the response to the launch of

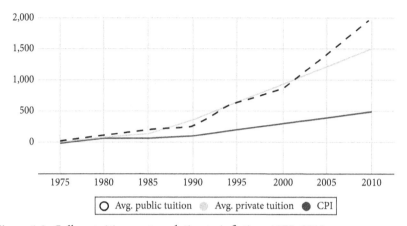

Figure 1.8 College tuition costs, relative to inflation, 1975–2010
Source: US Department of Education, "Weighing the Cost and Value of a College Decision", 2013.

Sputnik has given way to a crisis of funding and support for STEM, particularly once one considers students in low income schools who often lack access to basic scientific equipment, or female students who are discouraged from pursuing careers in STEM.

In essence, we have been living off of the fruits of the innovation infrastructure that was built in the post-war period that started over seventy years ago. We have not kept up this infrastructure in the past forty years, and our productivity data reflect the consequences of that lack of investment. The best firms are still thriving, but the rest of the firms (where most of the employment will be provided, and where the overall productivity effects will be observed) are lagging badly.

The Three Facets of Innovation Infrastructure: Generation, Dissemination, and Absorption

This suggests a different context for understanding exponential technologies, and their impact in the society. These technologies do not create value (or productivity) in a vacuum. Instead, the knowledge must be generated, it must be widely shared throughout the society, and the vast majority of the workforce in the society must be able to absorb these new developments and put them to work. Somewhere in the past thirty-five years, the earlier strong societal and governmental support that enabled all this has broken down.

The innovation infrastructure of the larger society surrounding these exponential technologies hasn't kept pace with them. If anything, the innovation infrastructure has deteriorated instead of advancing.

Critics might reasonably observe that government spending has continued at a high level, notwithstanding my observations above. It is true that government spending at the federal level remains quite high by historic standards. But the nature of that spending has shifted sharply away from knowledge-generating, disseminating, and absorbing investments, towards spending on the social safety net. (We already saw the declining spending on Federal R&D, both for defense and non-defense purposes as a percentage of GDP in Figure 1.7.) There are strong reasons to create and sustain a social safety net. But this must not be done at the expense of public investments in both visible and invisible elements in the innovation infrastructure of the society. Instead, the reduced investment in the innovation infrastructure has now led to reduced productivity growth and stagnant wages, which are reducing both the ability and the willingness to support further innovation infrastructure investment.

Investing in the Society's Innovation Infrastructure

In the mid-twentieth century, significant public funds were invested in a variety of infrastructure assets. Some of these helped to generate new knowledge, such as the formation of the NSF and NIH, along with the funds they directed to the burgeoning university sector. Other investments helped to disseminate useful knowledge. The universities were important here, because they greatly help to diffuse knowledge through publications, conferences, teaching, and not least, graduating students every year to carry their knowledge out to the society. And the Internet has enormously advanced our ability to communicate in virtually real time, across a wide variety of methods and channels.

While creating useful knowledge is vital, it is equally important to ensure that this knowledge is widely spread throughout the society. National highways also helped to diffuse useful knowledge, as they opened up new geographies for economic purposes. In a way, air conditioning performed a similar task for the southern half of the US in the latter half of the twentieth century (though this was not a public investment itself, it greatly leveraged the earlier rural electrification infrastructure of the first half of the twentieth century, which was a public investment).

There were also invisible elements that supported the diffusion of knowledge. One important element was the capability of making pensions portable, so that workers were not tied to a single employer throughout their working lives. Portable pensions enabled them to take their useful knowledge to other places, when those seemed more attractive than continuing with the same employer. A different invisible element was a relatively liberal bankruptcy law, allowing entrepreneurs the chance to launch a new business, but have the liabilities of that business stay with the business, rather than following the entrepreneur thereafter if the business should fail.

A further force that powerfully disseminated useful knowledge was the growth of the venture capital sector. While venture capital does not invest directly in basic knowledge creation, it provides powerful incentives to apply useful knowledge to important economic problems. This encourages the experimentation and risk-taking needed to discover and then scale up the commercial outputs from scientific research.

Yet another force that disseminates useful knowledge widely is anti-trust policy. Breaking up monopolies benefits consumers through lower prices, and is the usual justification for anti-trust. But there are important benefits to liberating useful knowledge as well. The decision to force AT&T to license its patents in the 1950s powerfully aided the nascent electronics industry. Instead of slowly disseminating transistor-based technology through the Bell system, hundreds of startups raced to deploy transistors in thousands of uses. The decision to sue IBM in the late 1960s effectively unbundled hardware from software, enabling the emergence of an independent software industry. Instead of having IBM drip-feed new software upgrades in years when they chose not to introduce new hardware systems, an entire industry of startups emerged to create programs, games, operating systems, and eventually, smartphone apps. The antitrust actions against AT&T in the 1980s finally broke AT&T's long-distance monopoly, setting the stage for a much more dynamic communications industry, from networks to cell phones, to today's digital multi-channel media and entertainment industry.

Creating useful knowledge and disseminating that useful knowledge are necessary to restoring productivity growth in the society. But the final item needed to restore that growth is investments in the human society to enable people to absorb, apply, and transform that useful knowledge. Without this final item, the benefits of generating and sharing technology might flow far away from the regions that created it.

Our elementary and secondary schools are not able to produce the number of students in STEM fields that our society requires. The problem is both one of quantity and also quality. In quantity, we are producing hundreds of thousands fewer students in science and technology than our society requires. In quality, the US system's students regularly place far down the rank of top countries in math and science knowledge. This results in a mismatch between jobs available and the ability of local residents to perform those jobs.

The US receives a tremendous inflow of foreign-born masters and PhD students from around the world, particularly in STEM areas. And many of these foreign-born students go on to generate new companies and new employment opportunities within the US. However, the domestic supply of scientists and engineers in the US is falling far short of the needs of the society. And more foreign STEM graduates are returning home, instead of making their new work lives in the US. The STEM problem in the US means that, as a society, the country struggles to translate the new knowledge being generated into new work for its own citizens. Instead, that work is getting done in other countries through the use of extensive global supply chains, with the US citizens often reduced to acting as consumers of the products of that knowledge.

We need to make the investments that will allow our society to fully absorb the exciting new possibilities that exponential technologies offer to us. And we need the social technologies in our educational systems to equip many more of our citizens to become digitally savvy scientists, engineers, business executives, workers, and entrepreneurs.

Shared Value Can Help Societies Absorb Innovations

Companies might determine that it is unlikely for the trends on under-investment in the innovation infrastructure of the past three decades to reverse themselves. But these trends don't have to reverse, in order for companies to make progress. Companies themselves can help move our society forward, and expand their own opportunities for growth in the process. This is a core idea in the Shared Value concept propounded by Michael Porter and Mark Kramer. Shared Value is firmly grounded in a capitalist system, but argues that a longer term, vibrant, sustainable capitalism requires companies to look beyond the short term bottom line. As the authors explain:

> The concept of shared value ... recognizes that societal needs ... define mar-
> kets. Social harms or weaknesses frequently create internal costs for firms ....
> Addressing societal needs does not necessarily raise costs for firms, because

they can innovate through using new technologies, operating methods and management approaches—and as a result, increase their productivity and expand their markets.[16]

One example of this approach comes from Nestle's coffee business. In traditional practices, where many coffee growers run small farms and face many constraints, including low productivity, poor quality, and environmental degradation, Nestle was buying on price and availability, bidding between farmers competed away most of the surplus, and the result for the farmers was a cycle of grinding subsistence. How did this change? To quote Porter and Kramer, 'To address these issues, Nestlé redesigned procurement. It worked with its growers, providing advice on farming practices, guaranteeing bank loans, and helping secure inputs such as plant stock, pesticides, and fertilizers. Nestlé also began measuring the quality of the coffee produced at the point of purchase, a change that made it possible to pay quality premiums directly to growers. As a result, yields and quality increased, as did farmers' incomes.' The spread of these practices caused the quality of coffee to rise, along with incomes, while reducing the negative environmental impact of coffee farms. Meanwhile, Nestlé's reliable supply of high quality coffee grew significantly.

The promise of exponential technologies requires a supportive innovation infrastructure from the society, and the embrace of Shared Value by companies in that society. We have been woefully inadequate on providing this. It is not enough to generate innovations; society must ensure broad dissemination and enhance the absorption of those innovations as well. Porter and Kramer advise us that companies can start to correct this inadequacy on their own, in order to grow and sustain their own businesses.

Open Innovation is one of those vital, new innovation processes that gets more value out of society's knowledge. In the next chapter, I will critically examine Open Innovation, and discuss how it too must be managed in order to get better business results, and improve productivity.

Chapter 1 review points:

1. Exponential technology is rising, while economic productivity growth is declining. This is the Exponential Paradox.
2. To improve productivity growth, innovations must be generated, disseminated, and absorbed throughout the society. These comprise the three facets of innovation infrastructure.

3. The best companies appear to be diverging from the rest. This means that the rest of these companies are not absorbing innovation effectively, which diminishes productivity.
4. Society needs knowledge infrastructure investment to sustain productivity growth over time, and to help the rest keep up with the best. We used to do this well, from the 1940s to the 1970s. New knowledge infrastructure investment is needed to address the Exponential Paradox.
5. Companies need to embrace a Shared Value approach, in order to sustain their growth in an environment of inadequate innovation infrastructure investment.

2

Open Innovation in the
Twenty-First Century

Innovation processes need to change if we are to close the gap between the promise of exponential technology, and the lagging economic results we are seeing. Not long ago, innovation was a largely internal affair. The journey from the laboratory to the marketplace took place largely within the four walls of the firm. Think of Bell Labs, IBM Research, or Xerox PARC. Each of them created important technological breakthroughs. And each breakthrough was commercialized through the company's own businesses.

In recent years, though, this 'do it all yourself' approach is increasingly hard to sustain. It costs a lot of money to support each of the many processes needed to achieve success in the market. It takes a long time to complete the journey, at a time when the world is changing more and more rapidly. And it places all the risk squarely on your own shoulders. This unpromising combination of cost, time, and risk has caused many organizations to rethink their approach to innovation. There is an alternative approach that offers a better combination of lower internal cost, faster time to market, and shared risk. It is an approach known as Open Innovation.

Open Innovation is a recent phenomenon. As recently as 2003, if you had done a Google search on that term, you would not have found any useful responses. Today that Google search would return hundreds of millions of responses. Two recent surveys of large companies in North American and Europe found that 78 percent of them were practicing at least some elements of this process.[1] Open Innovation has gone from nowhere to nearly everywhere in just over a decade.

Open Innovation is based on the fundamental idea that useful knowledge is now widespread throughout society. No one organization has a monopoly on great ideas, and every organization, no matter how effective internally, needs to engage deeply and extensively with external knowledge networks and communities. An organization that practices Open Innovation will utilize external ideas and technologies as a common practice in their own business

Open Innovation Results. Going Beyond the Hype, and Getting Down to Business. Henry Chesbrough, Oxford University Press (2020). © Henry Chesbrough.
DOI: 10.1093/oso/9780198841906.001.0001

(outside-in Open Innovation) and will allow unused internal ideas and tech-nologies to go to the outside for others to use in their respective businesses (inside-out Open Innovation).

What evidence is there that Open Innovation actually works? Let's recap some of the evidence presented in the previous chapter. Many individual companies such as Procter & Gamble have proudly proclaimed their success with their version of Open Innovation called Connect and Develop.[2] Another consumer products firm, General Mills, analyzed sixty new product introduc-tions in a twelve-month period. They found that those which had a substantial contribution from Open Innovation outsold the ones that did not by more than 100 percent. [3] In the industrial sector, a recent study of 489 projects inside a large European manufacturer found that projects involving significant Open Innovation collaboration achieved a better financial return for the company than projects that did not.[4]

Research of large numbers of companies also supports the value of Open Innovation. A number of studies employing the Community Innovation Survey have found that organizations with more external sources of know-ledge achieve better innovation performance than those with fewer sources, controlling for other factors.[5] A recent survey of 125 large firms also found that firms that employed Open Innovation were getting better innovation results.[6]

Yet I believe that most of us don't really understand Open Innovation very well. We don't agree on what it means, we don't know how best to use it, we don't think hard enough about its problems and its limits, and therefore we aren't getting the most out of it. That's a key goal of this book: to bring a more complete understanding of Open Innovation to the world, and help us all get the most we can out of this exciting concept.

Also, a lot has changed in Open Innovation since 2003. I will examine the most important developments and what they mean for industry, innovation, and policy. One theme that will emerge is that Open Innovation has spread well beyond collaborations and partnerships between two organizations (though that remains an important part of its operation) to a much broader canvas of supply chains, networks, ecosystems and public-private partnerships. Open Innovation isn't just about the firm anymore. It's also about the surrounding environment in which innovation occurs. For Open Innovation to thrive, we need to build ecosystems of innovating organizations. And to harness these ecosystems to enhance productivity growth, we need to go further, and build an innovation infrastructure to support an Open Innovation society.

Defining Open Innovation

Let's start by defining Open Innovation. Just as Eskimos have dozens of words for 'snow', there are multiple meanings to the term 'Open Innovation'. In my own view, the Open Innovation paradigm is best understood as the antithesis of the traditional vertical integration model, where internal innovation activities lead to internally developed products and services that are then distributed by the firm. I term the vertically integrated model a Closed Innovation model. Put into a single sentence, Open Innovation is a distributed innovation process based on purposively managed knowledge flows across organizational boundaries, using pecuniary and non-pecuniary mechanisms in line with the organization's business model.[7] This is an admittedly academic definition. But it basically means that innovation is generated by accessing, harnessing, and absorbing flows of knowledge across the boundary of the firm, either flowing in or going out. However, this definition is not universally accepted, a point I will return to later.

In this definition of Open Innovation, we assume that firms can and should use external ideas as well as internal ideas, and internal and external paths to market, as they look to advance their innovations. Open Innovation processes combine internal and external ideas together into platforms, architectures, and systems. Open Innovation processes utilize business models to define the requirements for these architectures and systems. The business model utilizes both external and internal ideas to create value, while defining internal mechanisms to claim some portion of that value.

Outside-In and Inside-Out Open Innovation

There are two important kinds of Open Innovation: outside-in Open Innovation and inside-out Open Innovation. The outside-in part of Open Innovation involves opening up a company's own innovation processes to many kinds of external knowledge inputs and contributions. It is this aspect of Open Innovation that has received the greatest attention, both in academic research and in industry practice. A lot has been written about technology scouting, about crowdsourcing, about open source technology, and licensing in or acquiring technology. Many scholars and industry people think that is all that Open Innovation is about. But that's incomplete. There is a second branch of those knowledge flows that is also a critical part of the concept. Inside-out Open Innovation requires organizations to allow unused and under-utilized knowledge to go outside the organization for others to use in their businesses and business models. This could result in licensing out a technology, or spinning off a new venture, or contributing a project to an open commons, or forming a new joint venture with outside parties (Box 2.1). In contrast to the outside-in branch of Open Innovation, this portion of the model is less well understood, both in academic research and also in industry practice. As

---

Box 2.1 The role of knowledge spillovers in defining Open Innovation

---

What's behind the definition of Open Innovation? The definition of Open Innovation that is based on 'purposive inflows and outflows of knowledge' hearkens back to a vibrant economic literature on spillovers that arise from the firm's investment in research and development. Because firms cannot fully specify the outcomes of this investment in advance, R&D inevitably produces outcomes that were not expected beforehand. These outcomes spill over beyond the ability of the investing firm to benefit from them, hence the term 'spillovers'.

Economist Richard Nelson observed back in 1959 that basic research generated many such spillovers, and that firms who funded this research had only limited ability to appropriate value from these spillovers. Nobel Laureate Kenneth Arrow also took note of this spillover problem, recognizing that these spillovers meant that the social return to R&D investment exceeded that of the private return to the firm undertaking the investment. Hence, he reasoned, private firms will underinvest in R&D from a social perspective. It is reasonable in this context for the public to provide a subsidy for R&D investment, in order to stimulate further R&D to move closer to the socially ideal level. Economists Wes Cohen and Dan Levinthal in turn wrote about the importance of investing in internal research in order to be able to utilize external technology, an ability they termed 'absorptive capacity'. Nathan Rosenberg asked a related question: why do firms conduct basic research with their own money, and answered that this research enhanced the firm's ability to use external knowledge.

It is important to note, however, that the specific mechanisms to enable companies to absorb external knowledge were not identified by these scholars. Nor was there any consideration of companies opting to move

(continued)

Box 2.1 Continued

---

unused internal knowledge out to the wider environment, which might enable the firm to obtain additional revenues, or lower their costs of sustaining the technology over time.

Throughout this literature, spillovers are deemed a cost to the focal firm of doing business in R&D, and are judged to be essentially unmanageable. This is the critical conceptual distinction made by the Open Innovation concept, which proposes that, in the Open Innovation model of R&D, spillovers are transformed into inflows and outflows of knowledge that can be (and should be) purposively managed. Firms can develop processes to seek out and transfer in external knowledge into their own innovation activities. Firms can also create channels to move unutilized internal knowledge from inside the firm out to other organizations in the surrounding environment. Specific mechanisms can be designed to direct these inflows and outflows of knowledge. Thus, what was unspecified and unmanageable before (a cost of doing business) can now be structured and managed in the Open Innovation model (and become sources of new opportunity, new cost reduction, a way of sharing risk, or even developing new offerings).

we'll see in a later chapter, it is this second branch of Open Innovation that provides the path to discovering new business models for unused or underused internal ideas and technologies.

What Open Innovation is Not

Notice what Open Innovation is not: it is not (only) about crowdsourcing, where someone looking for a breakthrough concept or solution submits a problem for a group or crowd to solve. Open Innovation is not (only) about managing one's suppliers better. And Open Innovation isn't (only) about open source software, and the open source methods inspired by open source software.

This last item deserves more discussion, as it is a very common misconception. The open source approach to Open Innovation ignores the business model and takes no account of the inside-out half of the Open Innovation model. It also treats intellectual property (IP) as a barrier to innovation, ideally one that should be eliminated. The work of Eric von Hippel, for example, analyzes 'open and distributed innovation', using the example of open source software as the motivating example for his analysis.[8,9] And he is far from alone in this.

There is an irony in this, because of a schism that has arisen in open source software itself. Within that community, there has been a strong disagreement between the 'free software' people and the 'open software' people. The free software people were people like Richard Stallman and others who thought 'software should be free'. Projects like the GNU operating system were constructed using a copy-left approach, meaning that any use of the GNU code must itself be shared with the rest of the GNU development community. This is very much akin to the belief that IP is unnecessary and indeed, unhelpful to innovation. Users can be expected to freely reveal their knowledge within the community, because they benefit directly from innovation advances as users of that innovation. Business models similarly have no role to play in his conception. Whatever capital organizations may require to scale their innovations, and how that capital may earn a return once it is employed, is completely ignored.

On the other hand, there is a separate branch of open source software that uses the term 'open software', which allows companies that use open software code to make additions to that code *without having to share those additions back with the software community.* Linux is a software project organized along these lines. Companies like Google and Amazon, which make extensive use of Linux, have developed a variety of extensions to that code that have deliberately been kept private, and are not shared back with the Linux community. Open software enables companies to build upon open or shared code, but to invest in proprietary extensions if they so wish.

Linus Torvalds, the creator of Linux, is squarely in the 'open' camp (rather than the 'free' camp). In fact, he is rather dismissive of Richard Stallman's evangelism for 'free software':

'He's too inflexible, too religious.... I certainly am of the opinion that *open source started working a lot better once it got away from the Free Software Foundation politics and values,* and more people started thinking about it as a tool than a religion. I'm definitely a pragmatist.'   (emphasis added)[10]

Torvalds' pragmatism is akin to my definition of Open Innovation, in which a company utilizes a business model to support investment in a project and allows that company to scale that project over time. IP is not only allowed in my view of Open Innovation, it actually enables companies to collaborate and coordinate together, confident in the knowledge that they will be able to enjoy some protection from direct imitation by others in the community. This will allow firms to invest capital to scale their innovations, should they prove to be successful, and earn a return on that capital.[11]

Both views of Open Innovation share the insight that being open is a powerful generative mechanism to stimulate a lot of innovation. Von Hippel rightly notes that users are a powerful source of innovation in the early stages of a new product. The differences between 'free' and 'open' become apparent once the initial stage of a new product is over and the innovation begins to gain traction in the market. At this point, hobbyists give way to companies that come into the market to commercialize these innovations, business models are created, and capital investments have to be made to grow volume sufficiently to spread throughout the society. As we saw in the previous chapter, the real social benefit of an innovation requires more than its generation, it also needs wide dissemination and absorption. While Linux was created by Linus Torvalds and a small community of volunteers early on, it is sustained today by the participation of companies like IBM, Google, Red Hat, and Amazon, who have built business models around Linux and have driven its usage in the enterprise.[12] The Open Innovation folks like me think you can have and should have legal regimes and business models to enable that process, whereas the free (or the 'open and distributed innovation') people don't regard this as necessary.

Now you know what Open Innovation is, what it is not, and why it's not just a glorified version of open source software. Let's turn now to see how it works, and how that has evolved since the idea was introduced in 2003.

How Open Innovation Works

My 2003 book *Open Innovation*[13] is credited by Wikipedia[14] and other observers for being the first sustained analysis of this new approach to innovation. That book was based on close observation of a small number of companies' innovation practices. It found a number of cases where what these companies were doing was contrary to the prevailing wisdom about innovation at that time. The prevailing wisdom of the time derived from the work of Michael Porter and Alfred Chandler, two very influential Harvard Business School professors.

Porter's work argued that firms would innovate more effectively by creating or increasing entry barriers, to keep other firms out of the industry.[15] Chandler argued that managing R&D was done best by managing internal R&D to create economies of scale and scope. In both professors' views, the real action was inside the firm, and the outside world was not fundamentally a part of the innovation process.[16]

In my 2003 book, I showed that this conception was no longer a valid description of the innovation activities of many leading industrial companies. In order to understand what these companies were doing, we needed to move past Porter and Chandler, to a new approach. It is helpful to visualize this transformation via 'before' and 'after' diagrams of an innovation process (see Figures 2.1 and 2.2 below).

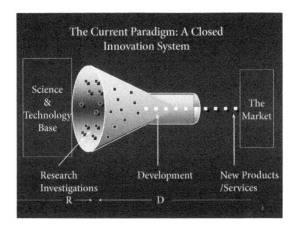

Figure 2.1 shows a representation of the innovation process under the previous closed model of innovation. Here, research projects are launched from the science and technology base of the firm. They progress through the process, and some of the projects are stopped, while others are selected for further work. A subset of these are chosen to go through to the market. This process is termed a 'closed' process because projects can only enter in one way, at the beginning, and can only exit in one way, by going into the market. AT&T's Bell Laboratories stands as an exemplar of this model, with many notable research achievements, but a notoriously inwardly focused culture. Other celebrated twentieth-century examples of this model include IBM's TJ Watson Research Center, Xerox PARC, GE's Schnectady laboratories, Merck, and Microsoft Research. (It is worth noting that each of these storied institutions has greatly altered its innovation model since my book appeared, and they no longer restrict themselves to a closed innovation model.) In other countries such as Japan, however, the closed model remains quite popular among many leading companies to this day.

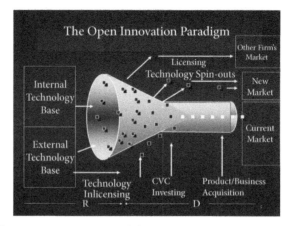

Figure 2.2 shows a representation of the Open Innovation model. The initial focus remains inside the firm, examining its R&D activities. There is still an innovation 'funnel', conducting projects from an initial ideation stage through to the market. However, there are important differences. In the Open Innovation model, projects can be launched from either internal or external technology sources, and new technology can enter into the process at various stages, the outside-in portion of the model. In addition, projects can go to market outside the initial business model of the firm, such as through outlicensing or a spin-off venture company, in addition to going to market through the company's own marketing and sales channels. This is the inside-out part of the model. I labeled this model 'open' because there are many ways for ideas to flow into the process, and many ways for it to flow out into the market. IBM, Intel, Philips, Unilever, and Procter & Gamble all provided early illustrations of some of these aspects of this Open Innovation model.

Anomalies Explained by Open Innovation

Open Innovation, when properly understood, is able to explain phenomena that the earlier closed model of innovation could not.[17,18] Open Innovation began from close observation of what companies actually are doing. Then I would step back and reflect on what they were doing in relation to what I'd read as a PhD student and what we were teaching our students. Professor Michael Porter's work on business and corporate strategy was very powerful and influential when it first appeared in the 1980s and the 1990s, and remains popular to this day. It is really a model of closed innovation, where you figured out what your key strategic assets were and you either went for low cost or went for differentiation or you found a niche. You were constantly looking for ways to compete against the other guy. In my observations of what was going on in the industry labs it was clear that a lot of Porter's model was happening, but there was a lot of other stuff going on that Porter's model didn't really explain very well. These anomalies were what led me to the concept of Open Innovation.

I spent a significant amount of time at Xerox and its Palo Alto Research Center. Some of my research there tracked thirty-five projects that started inside of Xerox's labs and got to a certain level of development, but then internal funding for all these projects was stopped. I was curious as to what happened to these projects subsequently because in many cases Xerox pro-actively encouraged the employees working on them to leave and take them to the external market. Why? Because once these people left the lab, that budget was freed up to be redeployed in the lab for something that was more strategic and promising for Xerox's core business.

One of the things I discovered was that most of the thirty-five projects, when they went outside, subsequently failed. And that was what Xerox expected. Since they didn't see the value of continuing the project, they assumed that there wasn't much value to be realized. But I found a fascinating anomaly: a few of the projects that went outside succeeded brilliantly, and actually became publicly traded companies. In fact, if you added up the market value of those publicly traded spinoff entities, it more than exceeded the value of Xerox's own market value. I can assure you that no one inside Xerox ever expected that! It is also a result that Michael Porter and Alfred Chandler would have a very hard time explaining.

So that really made me think how to better understand this, and how would you innovate effectively, whether in a large corporation like Xerox or in a small corporation or startup. How would you think about an innovation system that was more open? In the example of Xerox, their core innovation processes were doing a good job of commercializing certain technical projects that really fit well with their business model. But there were also had these other projects that didn't fit with the core but when they exited to the outside they found different business models that made them much more attractive as standalone entities.

I have come to think of these misfit projects as 'false negatives', projects that lacked value in the context of the company's current business model, but might have significantly more value if commercialized through a different business model. The root of the problem is that innovation involves a sub-stantial degree of both market and technical uncertainty. When evaluating projects under these conditions, managers will exercise their best judgment, but will sometimes commit evaluation errors. These can be 'false positives': projects that looked highly promising, and were launched into the market, where they promptly failed. Or they can be 'false negatives': projects that were stopped during the innovation process, because they were judged to be unpromising. But some of these projects that manage to continue outside the organization go on to become successful, hence the false negative label. (This concept of false negatives is also something not discussed in the previous research on innovation processes.)

Open Innovation treats false negatives as a consequence of a mismatch between a potential technology and the company's business model. This mismatch means that the false negative project needs to be managed through processes that explore alternative business models internally, or to spin off the technology outside the firm, to allow the nascent venture to locate a different business model. We will look at such processes more closely in Chapter 5. These false negatives are at the root of the inside-out part of the Open Innovation model.

A second set of new insights from Open Innovation lies in the treatment of intellectual property. In the closed model, companies historically accumulated intellectual property to provide design freedom to their internal staff. The primary objective was to obtain freedom to operate, and to avoid costly litigation. As a result, most patents are actually worth very little to these companies, and the vast majority are never used by the business that holds them.[19] In Open Innovation, intellectual property represents a new class of assets that can deliver additional revenues to the current business model, and also point the way towards entry into new businesses and new business models. Open Innovation implies that companies should be both active sellers of IP (when it does not fit their own business model) and active buyers of IP (whenever external IP does fit their own business model).

To assess the value of this insight, consider your own organization and evaluate its *patent utilization rate*. Think of all the patents that your company owns. Then ask yourself, what percentage of these patents are actually used in at least one of your businesses? Often people don't even know the answer, because no one has ever asked the question. One fact is known: about two-thirds of all the issued patents in Europe are allowed to lapse before their twenty-year expiration date, because the company didn't want to continue paying the renewal fees to keep the patent in force.[20] In cases where large companies have taken the trouble to analyze their own patent usage, the percentage used is often quite low, between 10–30 percent.[21] This means that 70–90 percent of a company's patents are not used. In most companies, these unused patents also are not offered outside for licensing either. If you have a low patent utilization rate, you might also benefit from opening up your patents to others for their use (on your terms, of course!).

The Business Model is Critical to Absorbing Innovation

As the Xerox PARC analysis and the IP discussion above show, the business model plays a critical role in the innovation process. As I reflected further upon this point, I realized that it warranted an entire book in its own right. This became the motivation for my second book, *Open Business Models*, published in 2006. Instead of treating the business model as fixed, as I did in the first book, I examined the implications of being able to innovate the business model itself. Making business models more adaptive might allow companies to obtain more value from innovation, from those false negative projects.

Had Xerox, for example, been willing to experiment with alternative business models, some of the value that resulted from 3Com, Adobe, VLSI Technology, and other spinoffs might have accrued directly to Xerox. And some of these experiments can even be done with 'other people's money'. If Xerox were willing to sell some of its technologies on an Original Equipment Manufacturer (OEM) basis, for example, those technologies might have become industry standards while being housed within Xerox. And the experiment would have been whether external companies were willing to buy the technology or not. In other cases, technologies that were licensed out went to companies that employed those technologies in very different business models. Xerox could have selectively emulated some of those models with other technologies still in its possession.

The book also presented a maturity model of business models, from commodity-type business models (offering undifferentiated products) to the highest, most valuable kind of business model, a platform business model. The platform models are more open, because they entice numerous third parties to innovate on your architecture, your system, your platform. And they often enable others to license unused technologies from you to place those into other business models. This makes continued investment in R&D more sustainable, and can even confer competitive advantage.

P&G, for example, is best known for its embrace of outside-in Open Innovation via its Connect and Develop initiative. But P&G also opens up its business model to license out many of its technologies for others to use.

This isn't as weird as it might seem, because P&G is strategic about how, when, and on what terms it licenses those technologies. As Jeff Weedman of P&G put it to me:

The original view [of competitive advantage] was: I have got it, and you don't. Then there is the view, that I have got it, you have got it, but I have it cheaper. Then there is I have got it, you have got it, but I got it first. Then there is I have got it, you have got it from me, so I make money when I sell it, and I make money when you sell it.[22]

Today, business model innovation is becoming a growing area of interest for many authors.[23] While my book was among the first to link innovation results to the fit with the prevailing business model, this is an area that is developing rapidly. However, most organizations treat R&D activities quite separately from the design and improvement of business models. This has held back progress in this area.

The good news is that some pioneering thinkers in the entrepreneurship area have created a set of processes that have the capability to explore new business models with potentially false negative internal R&D projects. This is the Lean Startup movement, initiated by Eric Ries, advanced by Steve Blank, and from a design perspective, illustrated by the Business Model Canvas of Alex Osterwalder. Because of their collective work, we know now how to design and test potential new business models. What is not well known, though, is that Open Innovation can play a powerful role to advance these new explorations, particularly inside large companies. I'll devote an entire chapter to this topic later in this book in Chapter 5.

Open Innovation: Shifting into Services

Another recent development in Open Innovation is the consideration of how innovation occurs in services. Most of the top forty economies in the OECD have half or more of their gross domestic product (GDP) from services. And many companies are witnessing a shift to services as well. Xerox now gets more than 25 percent of its revenues from services. IBM is another classic case, along with GE and Honeywell.

In some cases, what's really happening is the business model is shifting, which can turn a product business into more of a service business. For example, a GE aircraft engine can be sold for tens of millions of dollars to an airframe manufacturer. That same engine can also be leased on a so-called 'power by the hour' program to that airframe manufacturer. In the first case, it's a product transaction. In the second case, it becomes a service. And, in the second case a hidden benefit for GE is all the aftermarket sales and service, spare parts, etc., that accrue during the thirty-year operating life of the engine. With a Power by the Hour offering, all that work—and revenue—comes back to GE.

More generally for services, innovation must negotiate a tension between standardization and customization. Standardization allows activities to be repeated many times with great efficiency, spreading the fixed costs of those activities over many transactions or customers. Customization allows each customer to get what they want, for high individual satisfaction. The problem is that standardization denies customers much of what they want, while customization complicates the efficiencies available from standardization.

The resolution to this dichotomy is to construct service platforms. These platforms invite others to build on top of your own offering (the platform), so that there are economies from standardization in the platform, along with customization via the participation of many others adding to the platform. Recall that a fundamental premise of Open Innovation is 'not all the smart people work for you'. If that's the case, there's actually more value, not in coming up with yet another building block of technology, but rather in coming up with the architecture that connects these things together in useful ways that solves real problems before other people do. So that system architecture, that system integration skill to combine pieces together in useful ways, becomes even more valuable in a world where there are so many potential building blocks that can be brought together for the purpose.

Platform leadership to me is the business model side of systems integration.[24] To get others to join your platform, you need to construct a business model that can inspire and motivate customers and developers and others to join the platform. You design your model in ways that they can make money and they can create business models that work for them, even while your business model works for you. Done well, their activities increase the value of your business to you, so their money makes your business more valuable. These ideas are explored further in my 2011 book, *Open Services Innovation*.[25]

In summary, Open Innovation is a powerful approach to improve the results one can obtain from innovation. It offers a number of insights when compared to more conventional ways of approaching innovation, as shown in Box 2.2.

Box 2.2 Eight insights from Open Innovation, relative to prior innovation theories[26]

---

1. Equal importance must be given to external knowledge, along with internal knowledge.
2. The business model is critical in converting technology into commercial value.
3. Type I (false positive) and Type II (false negative) measurement errors inevitably result from evaluating R&D projects, and innovation processes should respond to these errors.
4. Knowledge flows can be managed purposively, rather than being unmanageable.
5. The knowledge landscape for firms is fundamentally abundant with useful knowledge.
6. IP management is important, nuanced, and deserves proactive management by R&D staff (it's too important to leave it to the lawyers).
7. Markets for innovation between R & D are emerging, as can be seen with the rise of innovation intermediaries like Innocentive and Nine-Sigma, and crowdsourcing providers like Kickstarter and Indiegogo.
8. All this means we need new and different metrics for assessing innovation capability and performance.

What are Open Innovation's Problems? When Might it Fail?

So far, you might think that Open Innovation is wonderful. So if it is so great, why doesn't everyone do it? And why hasn't it resolved the gap between exponential potential and economic reality that we examined in Chapter 1? Two large sample surveys, done in 2013 and 2015, reveal that in large companies, nearly 80 percent of companies are practicing at least some elements of Open Innovation.[27] But those same surveys showed that companies are not satisfied with their measures for managing Open Innovation. And, as we have already seen, Open Innovation means different things to different people.

It is high time to consider some of the problems involved with practicing Open Innovation. Academics are still publishing Open Innovation success cases for the most part, or performing large scale statistical analyses that show an innovation benefit to Open Innovation.[28] Some academics have done excellent work on crowdsourcing, to explore how best to construct a request for submissions, and whether or not to have submitting respondents collaborate or compete for the rewards.[29] With a few notable exceptions,[30] however, academics have ignored the very real problems of Open Innovation failures.

Meanwhile, inside companies one finds many who are trumpeting their successes with Open Innovation. The barriers they faced, the projects that failed, 'the ones that got away', are all swept under the rug. Many consulting firms now offer Open Innovation services for interested clients. They too are quick to trumpet positive results, while discreetly burying anything that didn't work as expected. This shouldn't surprise us, as these consultants do not want to embarrass their clients (and in the process, perhaps themselves). But we miss the chance to learn from negative experiences with Open Innovation, causing us to overlook its risks, its problems, and its true character.

In order to move beyond simply celebrating Open Innovation's successes, we can start by considering some underlying conditions that need to be satisfied. At its root, Open Innovation is about generating, disseminating, and absorbing inflows and outflows of knowledge. This recalls Figure 1.5 that we considered in Chapter 1, only now we examine it in the context of an individual organization (Figure 2.3).

As in Chapter 1, it isn't enough to simply discover or locate useful knowledge. That knowledge has to be disseminated to the right people and the right

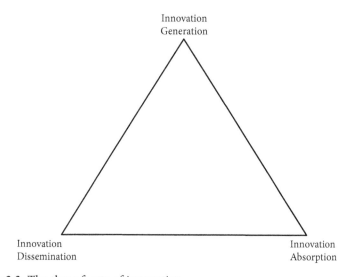

Figure 2.3 The three facets of innovation

places in the organization. And other people in the organization need to learn it, understand it, and potentially modify or extend it, in order to put it to work inside the organization. The best way to move knowledge from one person to another, even in this hyper-connected, always-on world, is to put people in close proximity, so that they interact enough to really share and transfer that knowledge. So one critical requirement for effective Open Innovation is a high level of education and skill in the workforce, combined with a reasonably high level of labor mobility from one organization to other organizations, to diffuse that knowledge broadly throughout society.

This is hard to do in some environments. In Japan, for example, there's a two-tier labor market where many people join a company once they graduate college, and they stay with that company for most of their career. There's a second tier in the market that's much more temporary, with people moving from company to company. Those people are typically in lower status jobs. Within that first tier of the market, labor mobility in Japan remains very low even today. That really impairs Open Innovation because even if you bring in external ideas, it's the same people that you had last year or the year before or the year before that, who are trying to embrace the new ideas. The idea might come in but the people with those ideas don't come in, and don't make the necessary modifications and adjustments to the new idea so that it works in the context of that company.

As we'll see in a later chapter on the back end of Open Innovation (Chapter 4), internal siloes often frustrate Open Innovation, because useful internal knowledge gets trapped in specific functions, or hoarded by defensive managers. To break through these siloes, people also need to rotate between innovation groups and business units, in order to transfer a promising innovation project into a business unit. Such a transfer often requires making the modifications and adjustments to an initial idea to incorporate it into a business unit, and take it to market. And to take advantage of the inside-out branch of Open Innovation, one or more people often need to move with the project, for some extended period of time, to effectively transplant the project outside the originating department.

Another requirement for dissemination and absorption of new knowledge is the presence of internal R&D. Some consider Open Innovation to be a rationale for outsourcing R&D. But this misunderstands the nature of innovation. To really transfer knowledge effectively in a way companies can really make use of it, you need a certain amount of creative abrasion and a certain amount of dwell time for people who are working to apply that knowledge together.[31] Open Innovation works best when you have people collaborating side by side, with people that are sharing knowledge from one organization to another.[32] These aren't people from purchasing, but instead are very talented people from your own organization. A related requirement are people who operate in a boundary-spanning role to connect knowledge from difference sources, and find ways to mash them together. This is particularly useful to overcome organizational siloes that specialize knowledge within specific functions, and restrict its access to anyone outside of those functions. Such people are sometimes termed 'T-shaped managers'.[33] This is part of the absorption process.

A well-known phenomenon in R&D that can impair Open Innovation's effectiveness is the Not Invented Here (NIH) syndrome. Organizations with strong technical histories often feature R&D personnel who are convinced that if they didn't invent it themselves, it must not be important or must not be very good. This hubris arises typically in organizations with a solid history of good technical results, and non-technical people are not able to evaluate the capability of internal R&D very effectively on their own. Open Innovation depends on internal R&D staff at many critical stages of the innovation process, and so an organization with a strong NIH culture might find many ways to subvert the Open Innovation process.

One recent paper documented the impact of NIH upon Open Innovation quite clearly. Hila Lifshitz Assaf did her doctoral studies at Harvard Business School under the direction of Karim Lakhani. She studied the adoption of Open Innovation practices at NASA, and focused particularly upon the use of crowdsourcing to generate new ideas for NASA.[34] One successful idea allowed NASA to significantly improve its ability to predict solar flares.

But Lifshitz Assaf's work went beyond this successful idea. She looked at the impact that the idea had inside the engineering organization at the Johnson Space Control Center at NASA. Internal engineers were troubled by the result obtained from outside. Their sense of identity, their understanding of their role in the organization, seemed threatened by the Open Innovation outcome. I suspect that many R&D intensive organizations responded similarly to the practice of Open Innovation in their own company.

Another issue with Open Innovation has to do with whether and how the results of externally-obtained knowledge move through a company's subsequent innovation process. Hosting a crowdsourcing challenge, and offering a prize to the winning submission, is just the beginning of the innovation journey for the hosting organization. Even excellent ideas must be adapted, modified, and customized to the specific context of the host organization. And this work must be done by internal staff, often technical staff in the organization. At the same time, the externally-sourced idea must compete for attention and priority with other ideas and projects. The internally-sourced ideas and projects usually have champions who explain, justify, and promote them inside the organization. This advocacy is critically important to advance projects through the many hurdles that any innovation project must clear. By contrast, there is often no internal technical champion for an externally-sourced idea or project. Even if an award or prize has been paid, that does not assure the idea of continued internal support through those subsequent innovation hurdles.

A different constraint emerges in potential inside-out Open Innovation projects. Many companies under-utilize their library of patents and other know-how assets. It is quite possible that some shelved internal projects might find new life in a new market, if they were allowed the chance to pursue that opportunity outside the company. Yet there are real barriers to doing this, not because of the fear that those exploring the opportunity would be wasting the company's time or resources. The real barrier is the fear that those explorers may succeed in finding a new market. Instead of celebrating this success, those inside the company who previously shelved the technology now look bad. As long as the project stays shelved, no one is at risk of being embarassed. But allowing the project out of the organization invites the possibility of appearing to look foolish. This behavioral response might be termed Fear of Looking Foolish, or FOLF (with a nod to the millenial notion of Fear of Missing Out, or FOMO).

Eric Chen and I looked at this issue in the pharmaceutical industry, when we explored the idea of recovering abandoned compounds.[35] While every pharma asserts that its critical mission is to address unmet medical needs among patients, organizational siloes strongly inhibit the process to export an abandoned compound outside the company for another group to commercialize. One pharma with 7000 research scientists working on tens of thousands of compounds had exactly two people charged with outlicensing the company's patented compounds. In some years, one compound might be licensed out, while in other years, no compounds were licensed out. Our interview subjects candidly admitted to us that FOLF was a major constraint to overcoming this.

There are more subtle problems that arise with Open Innovation as well. If one succeeds in fielding a successful call for solutions to a crowd or innovation community, one will likely attract a lot of submissions. It takes time to review all of these submissions, and the level of quality of most of them is often rather poor. Perhaps worse, if a great many more ideas enter into a company's innovation process, and the company has not invested in greater downstream capacity within the different support organizations (not just engineering, but also IT, procurement, finance, legal, etc.) to process these ideas, the wealth of new ideas can create bottlenecks and congestion that slow down the overall innovation process—instead of stimulating more innovation. Many companies that exhibit slow innovation processes do so precisely because they have overloaded the support resources that these groups need to do their work.

These are not easy issues to address. We will consider them in more depth in Chapter 4.

Open Innovation Today: Networks, Ecosystems, and Platforms

Open Innovation began as a series of case studies that examined collaborations between two organizations to open up the internal innovation process of the focal firm. Today, though, we see many instances in which the concept is being used to orchestrate a significant number of players across multiple roles in the innovation process. Put simply, designing and managing innovation communities is going to become increasingly important to Open Innovation's future. This is true both for firms, and for the larger society in which these firms operate.

Many observers have noted how firms like Uber, Airbnb, and Amazon have developed quite valuable businesses by building and scaling platforms that connect customers for various goods and services with disparate suppliers of those goods and services. These are relatively pure forms of platforms, characterized by the platform owner not needing to own any of the assets being traded.

But Open Innovation goes well beyond these pure play examples. It is actually transforming a variety of consumer (B2C) and industrial (B2B) businesses, by extending their reach and focus to the surrounding ecosystem in which they operate. Playing close attention to one's ecosystem can unlock new sources of growth for these firms. Ron Adner has a wonderful book that addresses this point at length, though not in the context of Open Innovation.[36] Let me illustrate this point with two rather distinct examples of two different kinds of community level Open Innovation across a broad spectrum of innovation activities.

My first example comes from Taiwan Semiconductor Manufacturing Corporation (TSMC), a foundry operating in the semiconductor industry. TSMC provides manufacturing services from its manufacturing facilities (foundries) to its clients, who design new semiconductor chips. The customers take these chip designs to TSMC, and TSMC fabricates the designs onto silicon wafers, and gives these back to its customers. The customers then package them into individual chips, and sell them. This saves TSMC's customers from having to invest in expensive manufacturing plants to manufacture chips. Instead, they rely on companies like TSMC to do the fabrication work for them.

Designing chips is a complex process that requires customers to use a variety of design tools, such as reference designs and process recipes. With the growth of TSMC's business ecosystem, many of the third-party companies who make these tools began to take steps to assure their customers that their offerings would run on TSMC's processes. This expansion in third party tool offerings creates more design options for TSMC's customers—a clear benefit. However, these new offerings also increase the complexity for TSMC's customers to manage, and this complexity might cause new chips to require re-designs or other expensive modifications to be manufactured correctly—a clear risk.

TSMC has addressed this risk with its Open Innovation Platform (their term, not mine!).[37] The Open Innovation Platform starts by combining the many design and manufacturing services of TSMC with those provided by many third-party companies, and *then testing all these combinations together.* TSMC then certifies to customers of those offerings that they can use these tools with confidence that the chip will turn out properly the first time through the process. TSMC's Open Innovation Platform helps its customers get their designs manufactured on the first pass. This avoids very expensive 'turns' of the chip design, whereby the chip must be redesigned in order to be manufactured properly in volume. The result is faster time to market for TSMC's customers, at a lower cost of design. So TSMC uses Open Innovation to manage a complex ecosystem of internal and external design sources, and provides a guarantee to its customers, provided they stick to these validated resources when designing their chips.

My second example comes from GE, and its recent ecomagination challenge.[38] While GE has a very large energy business of its own, with revenues of nearly $40 billion annually, the company has noticed a great deal of venture capital and startup activity in green and renewable energy technologies. Recognizing its own limits, GE sought to establish a process to tap into the potential project ideas out there that had the potential to become promising new ventures in green and/or renewable energy.

But GE did this in an open way. Instead of doing all the work themselves, they enlisted four active VC firms who had already had experience investing in this space. Together, the four VCs and GE pledged a total of $200 million to invest in attractive startup ventures. The ecomagination challenge was born. In July of 2010, the challenge was launched to the world, and everyone was invited to submit potential project ideas for consideration for startup investment.

In the process, more than 3800 venture proposals were received (they were expecting perhaps 400). As of this writing, twenty-three ventures have been funded, with five other projects receiving other awards, and even a People's Choice award was given as well. While the ventures are quite young, the VCs and GE are all enthusiastic about the experience. GE's level of enthusiasm has led them to adapt the model to the health care space (a Healthymagination challenge was launched in 2011) and also in China (a challenge was launched there as well).

And one need not be a large company to open up to the community in one's innovation process. A small firm in Florida, Ocean Optics, has instituted a community innovation challenge on a much smaller scale.[39]

This is the future of Open Innovation, a future that is will be more extensive, more collaborative, and more engaging with a wide variety of participants. Just as no man is an island, no firm will be successful in an Open Innovation world if they restrict themselves to the prescriptions of Porter and Chandler. Instead, these companies must embrace the bountiful useful knowledge that exists all around them, and find ways to identify, harness, and deploy that knowledge to advance their business—before their competitors do so.

Open Innovation offers a great deal of opportunity, for the firms that embrace it and for the larger society that sustains it. To get the most out of Open Innovation, however, we will need to pay close attention to the boundary conditions that support or inhibit effective Open Innovation. As with the previous chapter, firms must do more than simply generate a new technology. Firms must also disseminate the technology widely, across the many siloes that infest most large organizations, and overcome the fear of looking foolish (FOLF). And these firms must absorb the technology, embedding it in a business unit, and a business model, in order to scale it. In the next chapter, we'll examine the process for getting that technology out of basic scientific research. For those who want to get directly to Open Innovation results, you can skip to Chapter 4, where we will look at these issues in more depth. Chapter 8 will showcase some exemplary companies practicing Open Innovation, and will also consider some notable failure cases as well.

The innovation capabilities of organizations around the world will no longer stop at the boundaries of one's own organization. Instead an organization's Open Innovation practices will extend to suppliers, customers, partners, third parties, and the general community as a whole. This is the secret to getting business results out of the Open Innovation process. As one R&D manager explained to me, 'It used to be that the lab was our world; with Open Innovation, the world is now our lab.'

Chapter 2 review points:

1. Most companies used to use a Do-It-All-Yourself, or Closed model of innovation. Innovation in many companies today is more open.

2. Open Innovation uses inflows and outflows of knowledge across organizational boundaries to identify new opportunities, save time and money, and share innovation risks.

3. The generation, dissemination, and absorption of technology within the firm requires not only technology development, but also business model design and deployment. This parallels the innovation infrastructure we saw for the overall society in Chapter 1.

4. Open Innovation affects service industries, in addition to product and process industries. Service platforms can resolve the tensions between customization and standardization.

5. Open Innovation can be blocked by NIH attitudes, a lack of internal R&D capability, a lack of internal champions, a fear of looking foolish (FOLF), or congested support functions that lack the capacity to respond in a timely manner.

6. Open Innovation is moving beyond single collaborations between individual organizations, to networks and ecosystems of organizations, often collaborating through platforms

3

From Open Science to Open Innovation

In the previous chapters, I argued that investing in knowledge infrastructure was critical to restoring growth in productivity, and that we need to open up innovation processes to get the most value out of the knowledge available in the society. We need to generate knowledge, we need to disseminate that knowledge widely, and we need to prepare citizens in the society to absorb that knowledge. In this chapter, I will delve more deeply into these three aspects of the knowledge infrastructure, and show how to catalyze more innovation and more productivity. We will return to specific company Open Innovation practices in Chapter 4, so readers who are not interested in the scientific creation of knowledge might want to skip this chapter, and go directly to Chapter 4.

One powerful way to generate and disseminate useful knowledge is through the processes of open science. Open science shares its discoveries quite broadly, and reduces the lag time between the discovery of new knowledge and the transmission of that knowledge throughout society. Both the breadth of sharing and the speed of sharing invite broader partner participation in the discovery of new knowledge. This in turn deepens the knowledge, improves its quality, and helps its diffusion (which then leads to another cycle of discovery and diffusion).

As valuable as this broad engagement is, however, it does not assure the subsequent effective commercialization of scientific knowledge. Indeed, the norms of open science can, in some ways, create challenges that impede the absorption, or subsequent commercialization, of that knowledge.

As we discussed in Chapter 2 Open Innovation is a concept that is sometimes confused with open source software. There is indeed a connection, but there are key differences between the two concepts. In this chapter, I will show how these very differences can help to connect the fruits of open science to more rapid translation and development of its discoveries. Like open science, Open Innovation assumes broad and effective engagement and participation in the innovation process. But effective commercialization of new knowledge in Open Innovation also requires the discovery and development of a business

Open Innovation Results. Going Beyond the Hype, and Getting Down to Business. Henry Chesbrough,
Oxford University Press (2020). © Henry Chesbrough.
DOI: 10.1093/oso/9780198841906.001.0001

model. This is perhaps the key contribution Open Innovation can make to open science.

The business model creates value within the innovation system, but also enables the focal actor to capture at least some of that value. This is an important part of knowledge absorption—the incentive and ability to run experiments, take risks, and invest capital to translate scientific knowledge into commercial innovations. Relatedly, the handling of intellectual property rights becomes relevant to the ability and willingness of commercial actors to invest resources and undertake risky activities in hopes of developing a successful new process, product, or service. However, overly strong protection of IP, or prematurely assigning IP rights at early stages of scientific inquiry, can stifle innovation rather than advance it. That might enhance absorption for that firm, but at the cost of stifling dissemination of that knowledge across the wider society.

Open Science

The pursuit of knowledge is as old as the human race, but the institutions that promoted scientific discovery really arose with the Enlightenment. Prior to that time, there were individual scientists sponsored by wealthy patrons, and there was also the founding of the early universities. But the former had strong incentives to hoard knowledge, while the latter focused most of their intellectual energy on the liberal arts (divinity being the leading degree conferred by these universities during the Middle Ages).[1]

During the Enlightenment, there was something of a Cambrian explosion in scientific institutions that both generated new knowledge and disseminated that knowledge, as the pursuit of knowledge migrated from royal patrons to a much larger merchant class. This migration caused a tremendous increase in both the volume of scientific knowledge generated, and in the speed with which new discoveries diffused within society. One landmark event was the formation of the Royal Society in England in 1660, which published its *Philosophical Transactions of the Royal Society* starting in 1665.[2] Other societies soon emerged in France (1666), Berlin (1700), Russia (1724), and Sweden (1739). By 1700, there were over thirty scientific journals being published, which would skyrocket to more than 1000 journals a century later.

During this period of intellectual ferment, the norms of science also came to be established. One insightful analysis of these norms that proved quite influential came from Robert Merton's *Sociology of Science*.[3] Merton argued that science had developed norms of behavior that cumulatively contributed significantly to the growth and quality of scientific knowledge. These were packaged into an outline he termed CUDOS:

- **Communalism**: sharing discoveries with others, in which scientists give up intellectual property in exchange for social recognition gained through sharing.
- **Universalism**: claims to truth are evaluated in terms of universal criteria, and should be reproducible by others under the same conditions.
- **Disinterestedness**: the researcher's attitude is one of objectivity; such that the researcher follows the evidence wherever it goes, regardless of its implications for profit or lack of profit.
- **Originality**: research results should yield novel contributions to understanding.
- **Skepticism**: all ideas are subject to rigorous, structured community scrutiny, which curates the quality of the work that results.

With the advent of the Internet and the Web, these Mertonian norms have found expression in new institutions that again create even greater volumes of knowledge that diffuse even more rapidly. One concrete example is open source software. Open source software is a method of software development in which the code base is open for inspection to all participants. This enables the software to spread rapidly to others, and also allows common routines in the software to be rapidly applied in other contexts. In tandem, this code is tested by numerous independent developers and testers, such that software 'bugs' are rapidly detected and then fixed. According to Richard Stallman's famous dictum, 'With enough eyes, all bugs are shallow.' This has allowed open source software to produce code of high quality and reliability.

More recently, the norms of open science have been manifested in projects to expand further the access to scientific knowledge. One example of this is the Open Science Grid in the US.[4] The concept here is that wider, faster, and cheaper access to new knowledge will promote more rapid understanding and use of science. This Open Access movement has found expression in journals like the *Public Library of Science*, for finished scientific articles. It has also led to new initiatives like the Research Data Alliance,[5] for sharing the source data collected in the scientific process, so that research data and research methods that lead to new science can also be shared.

As the need to access data grows, as access to high quality instruments and high data volume grow, and as supporting infrastructures are developed to organize and manage access and the results from open access, the pursuit of science itself is expanding. This is leading to an era of 'citizen science' or 'crowdscience', where important scientific contributions can be made by ordinary people from all over the world. In astronomy, amateur astronomers are finding new stars, new exoplanets, and new phenomena. In biology, programs like FoldIt are enlisting ordinary contributors to solve complex protein folding problems. In neglected diseases, open science is finding new application. And in large, seemingly intractable problems like global climate change, open science is making inroads as well.

One superb example of open science can be found at CERN. Its name comes from the French: Conseil Européen pour la Recherche Nucléaire. While its origins were in nuclear research, CERN has made many contributions to science, from its experience as the birthplace of the World Wide Web; as contributor to grid computing initiatives such as one linking its particle accelerator to 170 labs globally (WLCG);[6] another linking several EU labs in varied disciplines(EGI)[7] and an open access repository of high-energy physics journals accessible in forty countries(SCOAP3).[8] With all this activity, CERN is nonetheless best known as the host lab for its Large Hadron Collider, which was designed to test for the Higgs boson using collisions of light particles at extremely high speeds.

CERN's history is a powerful demonstration of the power of open science when it is adopted across an entire set of institutions at large scale. From its inception, CERN made provision for the widespread access to and diffusion of its research results, and invited participants from all over the world in the project.[9] The norm of openness enabled significant achievements to be contributed by very large numbers of participants. For example, the two foundational papers that described the discovery and verification of the so-called Higgs boson each had roughly 6000 authors.[10] These papers led to the award of the Nobel Prize in Physics to the leading researchers at CERN in 2013.

Open Science Does Not Directly Result in Innovation

While open science has advanced impressively in the past few decades, not least in places like CERN, one cannot yet claim that it has simultaneously led to a similar increase in innovation. We saw the productivity slowdown in the G7 countries in Chapter 1. Indeed, there is concern within Europe that its extraordinary science base is not leading to enough industrial application of the new science.[11] This is something that those who believe that open science is all that is necessary to restore innovative capabilities need to ponder.[12] In addition to the institutions that promote open science, we may also need to consider institutions that promote the application of that science in the commercial realm, if we are to truly activate more innovation and more productivity. As stated in an earlier chapter, knowledge must not only be generated and disseminated, it must also be absorbed and put to work. Only then will we see the full benefit of this knowledge in the whole society.

There are straightforward reasons why open science by itself may not translate into new innovations. Once a new discovery is made, it is often unclear (or of less importance) to the researcher(s) how best to apply it. Understanding the behavior of a new material, or a new physical property, may say little about the best uses of this knowledge. For example, it is not at all clear how knowledge of the Higgs boson discovered at CERN could be applied commercially. To take an older example, the fundamental physics behind the principle of lasers originally developed for molecular structure studies demonstrated new properties of light. But it would take decades to put this knowledge to practical use at any industrial scale. And it turned out that the most prevalent use of this knowledge was to be found in CD and DVD players, for audio and video recording and playback. This application was quite far from the minds of the scientists who performed the foundational science that enabled this use. Moreover, applying this knowledge required many, many years of experimentation, along with substantial investments to develop and scale the devices using this invention.

Different Incentives and Contexts

The application of scientific knowledge involves different incentives, contexts, and mechanisms than those that are present in scientific discovery. In science, the fundamental questions are causal explanations of the behavior of some phenomenon. As Merton noted above, the scientist foregoes her possible claim for ownership of the fundamental discovery in exchange for complementary knowledge or social recognition and prestige. The ability to replicate and verify this knowledge is an important part of the scientific process. And open science norms facilitate this ability to replicate and verify knowledge, and diffuse it, in return for this social recognition, and to gain additional knowledge for a new cycle of discovery.

The best ways to apply that new knowledge, though, are ambiguous, and involve making judgments and taking risks in what domains to explore. This kind of applied science is not perceived to be as prestigious as 'real science'. There are no Nobel Prizes for inspired applications of knowledge. Indeed, it can be harder to publish the results of such inquiries. And it is less clear whether those seeking to apply this knowledge even want others to rapidly reproduce and verify their results, at least when the seekers are hoping to obtain an economic reward for this work.

Scientific researchers also are often ignorant of the practical context, constraints, and priorities that must be addressed in the application of new knowledge in the commercial realm. This contextual knowledge is not universal, and is often tacit, making it less able to be shared widely unless others have direct experience with the process that produced the initial knowledge. The conditions of a laboratory, where the experiment can be carefully described and controlled, give way to a messy reality, where many factors are in play in an uncontrolled fashion at the same time.

For these reasons, the investment of time necessary to create innovations from new scientific knowledge run contrary to the 'pure' academic incentives for promotion and tenure in leading universities.

There are other barriers to translating science into innovation as well. Funding is an important one. Basic scientific research is usually funded by public agencies, usually employing a peer-reviewed process. This funding typically ends when a new discovery is made and then published. There is seldom any public funding for further development and application of the knowledge. The implicit assumption is that the private sector is better positioned to allocate resources to the application of this knowledge.

The Valley of Death

The private sector will require a financial return on its investment, if it is to devote funds to a promising new discovery. This requires a careful evaluation of risk and reward. While new scientific discoveries may offer exciting possibilities, they are reported at an early stage in their development, with actual data being provided only at laboratory scale, as an initial proof-of-concept. Translating this initial proof into a new innovation at commercial scale involves substantial risks and large investments. This can create a Valley of Death between the published results of open science, and the profitable application of that knowledge. In this Valley, there is no further scientific funding available for the project, while the nascent understanding of the project discourages private capital investment.

This Valley of Death has received considerable attention in innovation policy within the European Union. A variety of initiatives have tried to bridge this gap. The latest R&D funding program, Horizons 2020, explicitly seeks to shift funding toward more commercial application of research knowledge, whereas the preceding funding program called FP7 was more focused on funding basic research. Other EU-funded initiatives include science parks, to incubate research discoveries beyond the academic stage to make them more attractive to industry, plus accelerators, Living Labs, and Knowledge Innovation Centers (KICs).

Innovation policy in the US has had better luck bridging this Valley of Death. Universities have more ability to profit from research discoveries, thanks in part to the Bayh-Dole Act, which allows universities to patent (and then license) their discoveries that were funded by government sources. And there is a growing tradition of university professors in the US taking leaves of absence to launch new startup ventures to commercialize research discoveries they have made. The resulting startups are supported by significant funding for new ventures, from venture capitalists, crowdfunding, the Small Business Administration, and angel investors. This deep network of new venture funding is far more developed in the US than it is in Europe or Japan.

Intellectual Property

Another consideration in bridging the Valley of Death is the treatment of intellectual property (IP). In open science, as Merton noted above, ownership of a discovery is explicitly eschewed, in order to promote the rapid verification and more rapid diffusion of new knowledge. Assigning IP rights during the scientific discovery process throws sand in the gears of open science, inhibiting the free exchange of ideas and knowledge that lead to faster, better science.

When applying new knowledge to create new innovations, however, IP rights have a role to play. Social recognition is no longer enough motivation for the private sector to undertake the risky investments needed to commercialize new knowledge.[13] Some degree of protection for some limited period of time is often necessary to induce private capital into making the investments of time, money, and people to attempt to introduce a new innovation.

The role of IP should not, however, be overstated. One must balance incentives for the initial innovation against the incentives to enhance and improve upon that innovation. A moderate amount of protection is a better resolution of this balance than either a regime of no protection whatsoever (which inhibits the initial risk taking and investment in an innovation), or a regime of extremely strong protection (which inhibits or slows down dissemination and follow-on innovation). Having a clear idea of where a technology might be profitably applied helps in unclogging the patent landscape, since only the foreground knowledge of the specific application would be protected, while the larger background knowledge that supports the application would remain open to the wider scientific community.

The Institutions of Open Innovation

What is needed, then, in developing innovations from open science, are a set of corresponding institutions of Open Innovation. Unlike open science institutions, these Open Innovation institutions depend on the way and the context in which innovation is being pursued. As we saw in the last chapter, the forces that support knowledge generation must be balanced with mechanisms to support the wide dissemination and rapid absorption of new knowledge. The way these forces are managed by the larger society in the US, for example, will likely differ in important ways from that translation in, say, China, Finland, or Israel.

To explicate the contribution of these institutions, some quick history of industrial R&D will help. In particular, an earlier set of institutions that promoted larger internal, vertically-integrated R&D can be contrasted with a later set of institutions that promote more distributed, more open R&D.

Closed Innovation Institutions

The state of external scientific knowledge expanded enormously during the nineteenth century. By the early 1900s, we had learned about microbes, X-rays, the basic structure of the atom, electricity, and relativity. We had also learned about a more systematic way to conduct scientific research. As Alfred North Whitehead had remarked, 'the greatest invention of the 19th century was the method of invention itself'.[14]

Notwithstanding the scientific breakthroughs realized in the nineteenth century, for most industries circa 1900, much of the new science was just beginning to be understood, and its eventual commercial uses were far from apparent. Moreover, the norms of science at that time suggested that any practical use from this science would come without much help from the scientists themselves. Emulating the norms of 'pure' science held in leading German universities, American scientists regarded the pursuit of practical knowledge as 'prostituted science'.[15] There was a large void between the science embodied in university classroom lectures, and the beneficial use of those insights in commercial practice. Moreover, universities lacked the financial resources to underwrite and conduct significant experiments themselves.

The government was in no position to fill in this gap. The overall size of government in the economy was much smaller during this period in history than it is today. And the government did not play much of a role in the research system at this time. It did pursue a few initiatives, such as the creation of a patent system, and it provided limited funding for particular inquiries in weights and measures, military materials such as improved gunpowders, and in the US, some creative funding of land grant universities for agricultural studies. But overall the government played a very limited role in organizing or funding science.

It was large scale Industry at that time that served the role of being the primary source of research funding for the commercial use of science, and industry R&D laboratories were the primary locus of this industrial research. German chemicals firms were systematically expanding their product offerings through increasingly advanced investigations of the properties of the materials they were using to create new dyestuffs. Petroleum companies were rapidly improving their yields in refining crude oil through understanding the properties of that oil. In the process, they were innovating additional new products out of this raw material as well.

Only companies of large size could afford the investments needed to support significant R&D investments. Only these companies could access the knowledge being generated through the application of new scientific knowledge. This created a strong barrier to entry that entrenched large firms, and disadvantaged everyone else. These labs generated substantial knowledge, but greatly restricted the dissemination of that knowledge.

The institutions of Closed Innovation were built around this reality. One policy grew out of economist Kenneth Arrow's insight[16] that the benefits of R&D often spill over into the rest of society. For this reason, the social return from R&D is greater than its private return to the firm performing the R&D. The implication is that society gets less R&D than it ideally wants. This led to the adoption of the R&D tax credit, to subsidize R&D spending in order to induce firms to undertake more R&D than they otherwise would perform privately.

A second institution was the primacy of government funding for basic scientific research. As a result of the mobilization of science for the world wars of the twentith century, countries chose to assign resources and coordination to government research agencies. In the post-war era, government funding for scientific research expanded tremendously, creating an Endless Frontier, in the words of Vannevar Bush's famous memo to President Roosevelt.[17]

Another institution was the expansion of intellectual property protection. Large firms could negotiate with each other for freedom to operate (such as through cross-licensing arrangements), and strong IP allowed them to erect further barriers to entry against new entrants. The creation of the 10th Federal Circuit Court for IP litigation standardized and strengthened IP protection in the US, and this set a pattern that was followed in Europe as well.[18]

A final institution in many countries was the conscious creation of Industrial Champions, companies of sufficient size and scale that they could overcome these barriers. These champions provided reservoirs of technology and know-how within the society, and also significant employment opportunities as well. They often worked closely with government agencies to coordinate investment into new, promising areas of technology.

These arrangements gave rise to considerable innovations, but they also fostered some less desirable outcomes. Perhaps chief among these were the knowledge monopolies and oligopolies that resulted. The logic of the Closed Innovation institutions was that, in order to be good in R&D, you had to be big. In order to innovate effectively in this model, one must do everything; from tools and materials, to product design and manufacturing, to sales, service, and support. The translation of new scientific knowledge would be led by the industrial champions who stood at the commanding heights of the economy. This slows down the dissemination of new knowledge, because only a very few organizations had the knowledge and resources to attempt the innovations. And these organizations could only afford to explore a small fraction of the potential applications of this knowledge. The slow speed and narrow focus of these champions similarly reduced the dissemination and absorption of that new knowledge by the larger society.

The Shift to Open Innovation

As noted above, the rise of open science has led to an abundance of knowledge in many, if not most, scientific fields. The proliferation of public scientific databases, online journals and articles, combined with low cost internet access and high transmission rates gives society access to a wealth of knowledge that was far more expensive and time consuming to reach in the Closed Innovation era. These developments are a tremendous boost to dissemination.

The norms of science have also evolved toward more interest in not only understanding the physical world, but, in parallel, applying that knowledge. While the science being done in universities continues to be excellent, it is clear that many professors (and their graduate students) are eager to apply that science to business problems. The norms of science and engineering have changed as well: there aren't many Henry Rowlands (from endnote 15 in this chapter) in university science and engineering departments anymore.[19]

The rise of excellence in university scientific research, the extension of that excellence to applying that knowledge, and the increasingly diffuse distribution of that research, means that the knowledge monopolies built by the centralized R&D organizations of the Closed Innovation era are over. Knowledge is far more widely distributed today, when compared to, say, forty years ago.

One piece of evidence that supports the greater distribution of knowledge in the knowledge landscape, for example, is the changing level of concentration in patent awards. Patents are one outcome of a knowledge generation process, and thanks to the US Patent and Trademark Office, there are good data available on who receives US patents. Of the more than 400,000 patents issued by the USPTO over the decade of the 1990s, for example, the top twenty companies received only 11 percent of the awarded patents. Relatedly, the number of patents held by individuals and small firms had risen from about 5 percent in 1970, to over 20 percent in 1992.[20]

A second indicator of increased knowledge diffusion is reflected in US government statistics of R&D by size of enterprise. Industrial research and development is one key process that generates ideas, and makes use of them. The share of industrial R&D has increased greatly for companies with fewer than 1000 employees from 1981 through 2015. While large company R&D remains an important source of R&D spending, its share of R&D spending has fallen in half, from over 70 percent of all R&D spending in 1981 to less than 35 percent of R&D spending in 2015. Correspondingly, the share of R&D conducted in organizations of fewer than 1000 employees has risen from 4.4 percent to 22 percent over the same period.[21] There seem to be fewer economies of scale in R&D these days.

The logic underlying the innovation process now is completely reversed. In an abundant landscape of useful knowledge, one can now do a great deal by focusing in a particular area, without having to do everything.

The Open Innovation Model

The Open Innovation model discussed in the previous chapter is based on a logic of abundant knowledge. It assumes that firms or innovating institutions in general can and should use external ideas as well as internal ideas, and internal and external paths to market, as they look to advance their innovations. Open Innovation processes combine internal and external ideas together into platforms, architectures, and systems. Open Innovation processes utilize business models to define the requirements for these architectures and systems. The business model makes use of both external and internal ideas to create value, while defining internal mechanisms to claim some portion of that value.

There are two important kinds of Open Innovation: outside-in and inside-out. The outside-in part of Open Innovation involves opening up a company's innovation processes to many kinds of external inputs and contributions. It is this aspect of Open Innovation that has received the greatest attention, both in academic research and in industry practice. Large research infrastructures such as CERN embody as a hub of a large network many of these practices most effectively. For example, this has been demonstrated in the successful construction and operation of the Large Hadron Collider (LHC) and in the enormous scientific output delivered from this initiative.

Inside-out Open Innovation requires organizations to allow unused and under-utilized ideas to go outside the organization for others to use in their businesses and business models. In contrast to the outside-in branch, this portion of the model is less explored and hence less well understood, both in academic research and also in industry practice. In order to further improve the scientific capabilities and commercialize the research output from projects such as CERN's LHC, new businesses and business models must be identified, explored, and undertaken. This will require a new set of institutional rules for CERN.

Open Innovation Institutional Rules

The institutions of Open Innovation differ dramatically from those of the earlier closed approach. The incentives in Open Innovation are for specialization, collaboration through markets, exchange of knowledge, intellectual property rights, and startup formation. Large firms also play a key role in Open Innovation, but that role is quite different than it was in the closed era.

Because useful knowledge is presumed to be abundant, every Open Innovation initiative begins by surveying what is already available. Instead of re-inventing the wheel, an Open Innovation project seeks to leverage available external knowledge and extend upon it. Put differently, in a world of abundant knowledge, the value in innovation migrates away from the next new piece of technology (though these can still be valuable) to new ways of integrating technologies together into new solutions and new systems. This system integration skill is of great value in a world of abundant knowledge, and is one of the most critical contributions that large organizations can play in an Open Innovation landscape.

The knowledge monopolies and oligopolies of the earlier period give way to a more distributed division of innovation labor. The universities and research institutes may function as the locus for the initial discoveries and new knowledge. But the exploration of how best to apply new knowledge, and the subsequent exploitation of that knowledge in a new market falls to other participants in the innovation chain, based on some adopted business model. Startup firms and SMEs (Small to Medium-size Enterprises) are now capable of launching research projects, perhaps with an academic researcher continuing to provide advice and support as an early employee. Later success, should the venture survive, often comes through being acquired by a large firm to augment its own internal innovation activities. Less often, a venture may achieve its own public listing of its stock through an initial public offering.

Intellectual property is critical to the transitions that technologies must navigate on their way from the laboratory to the market. The initial formation of a new spin-out venture, for example, must include some assignment of IP for the nascent organization. Any external capital provider will demand that there be some protection for the ideas being commercialized. The later acquisition of the venture will require that the acquiring firm receive all of the IP created by the venture. And so on. However, capital markets need some sense of the intended market for applying a new scientific discovery. Absent such a signal, promising science can remain stuck between academia and industry in that Valley of Death. This is one of the concerns that led to the design of the Horizons 2020 program in the European Union.

Experimenting with the New Open Innovation Institutions

With this in mind, several actors have in recent years begun experimenting with new types of institutions or initiatives to bridge this gap between open science and Open Innovation. Many are have been pioneered in Europe—perhaps because of the now-common belief among European policy makers that the EU suffers generally from an 'innovation gap' with the US, and a rising challenge from China, and so must pioneer new processes to remain economically competitive.

IMEC[22] is one of the best-known technology hot-beds in Europe. Founded in 1974 at KU Leuven, the oldest university in Belgium, IMEC has been effective over the years at combining basic academic research in microelectronics and nanoelectronics, and developing it into practical semiconductor technologies now used by many of the largest ICT and chip companies in the world. Likewise, several European governments have supported specialized national Research and Technology Organizations (RTOs) that, with private companies as customers, use new technologies to develop specific products, or solve problem. The largest and best-known European RTO is Germany's network of Fraunhofer[23] Institutes that work directly with specialized sectors of industry, from machine tools to solar power. And in 2008 the European Commission created an entirely novel Open Innovation program, called the European Institute of Innovation and Technology (EIT).[24] It gathers large consortia of multinationals, SMEs and universities into networks that, spanning the EU, simultaneously develop new commercial products from university research, and train a new generation of entrepreneurs to take these and other products to market.

Among the most interesting experiments is a new initiative by a group of big European research labs, including CERN, the European Synchrotron Radiation Facility, and the European Molecular Biology Laboratory. Called ATTRACT,[25] the initiative aims to take technologies that the labs have developed for their own infrastructure and spin them out to the market, in partnership with SMEs, multinationals, and other private investors. These include world class detector and imaging technologies, of use in health physics, high performance materials, and breakthrough ICT applications. Each of these application domains represent very large markets, with different drivers and regulatory structures. The ICT sector is the fastest-moving of the three, and new innovations can often be deployed and scaled here in short amounts of time. Materials take a longer time to scale into large markets, because the material must first be proven, and then multiple applications must be attempted, and the eventual market size will depend on the success of the various uses of the new material. The health sector is the most regulated, and market success here will require both acceptance by industry as well as adoption by both regulators and health care system administrators.

ATTRACT aims to leverage the broad scientific community engaged in research activities at CERN and other members' laboratories, with the assistance of Aalto University in Helsinki and ESADE Business School in Barcelona. The best applications for the discoveries made in areas like detection, imaging, and computation, though, will require entrepreneurial risk-taking. Substantial trial-and-error will likewise be required to develop effective business models that can create and capture value, at commercial scale. Pre-competitive research in an open domain can be blended with downstream assignment of IP rights, so that the power of open science can be joined to subsequent risk-taking in the commercial realm. European Research Infrastructures, universities, large firms, and SMEs and startups all have a role to play. Through its design, ATTRACT shows how open science and Open Innovation can be combined in order to lead to a number of potential new business opportunities through the Valley of Death into new markets.

Conclusion

The norms of open science promote the rapid diffusion of the latest knowledge, and invite broader participation in the discovery of new knowledge. This deepens the knowledge, improves its quality, and helps its diffusion (which then leads to another cycle of discovery and diffusion). However, the institutions of open science do not necessarily assure the effective absorption of new knowledge, and the subsequent effective commercialization of scientific knowledge. Once this knowledge has been generated, the rest of the innovation journey remains to be traveled, to cross over the Valley of Death. Entrepreneurial risk-taking will be needed to define the most promising applications of the knowledge generated at places like CERN, and substantial trial-and-error will likewise be required to develop effective business models that can create and capture value, at commercial scale. Pre-competitive research in an open domain must be blended with downstream assignment of IP rights, so that the power of open science can be joined to subsequent risk-taking in the commercial realm. In this way, such institutions will show how open science and Open Innovation can lead to a number of potential new business opportunities.

Open Innovation is a concept that can help to connect the fruits of open science to more rapid translation and development of its discoveries across the Valley of Death. Like open science, Open Innovation assumes broad and effective engagement and participation in the innovation process. Open Innovation distributes the innovation effort across a variety of participants, from universities and research institutes to SMEs and startup firms, to large firms. But Open Innovation institutions are required for effective commercialization of new knowledge. A process of discovery will be needed, around the world, to find and tailor the best possible models for these institutions to meet the pressing needs of the global economy. Useful knowledge must be generated, then disseminated, then absorbed and put to work. This is the path to restoring productivity growth from open science.

But all this presumes that companies understand how to employ innovation effectively. This is not the case for many organizations. In the next chapter, we will consider a largely overlooked aspect of Open Innovation, the so-called 'back end' of the process, in which the innovations that have been enhanced with Open Innovation make their way to the market. As we will see, there are many barriers and problems that must be overcome, in order for Open Innovation to deliver positive business results for the organizations that practice it.

Chapter 3 review points:

1. Open science exchanges ownership for recognition, which greatly helps knowledge diffuse rapidly among scientists and engineers.
2. There exists a Valley of Death between scientific results and commercial uptake of those results.
3. Creating new innovations out of great science requires the ability to invest, take risks, and obtain at least some ownership rights to intellectual property, to overcome this Valley of Death.
4. Society needs institutions that promote strong science, and additional institutions to promote the innovative use of that science. Here is where Open Innovation is so important.
5. New examples like IMEC and ATTRACT show how open science can be combined with Open Innovation to carry promising projects across the Valley of Death.

4

The Back End of Open Innovation

Open Innovation can really help improve business performance. Yet Open Innovation remains a process, and processes have important limitations that affect their performance. This is something often overlooked in discussions of Open Innovation. In this chapter, we will examine a number of these limitations. We will see live examples of how they impede the ability to get business results from Open Innovation. And we will consider some ways to address these limitations, so that the promise of Open Innovation can be realized.

One limitation for Open Innovation processes is that it takes time and resources to evaluate the higher amount of external information. Bringing in more external knowledge often imposes an additional burden on the internal people who must judge the usefulness and meaning of these external inputs, alongside the continuing knowledge generated by internal innovation activities. (And a dirty little secret is that much, if not most, of the external contributions are poor in quality, yet still must be evaluated.)

More inputs will mean more work, and more knowledge means that there are more possible ways to shape the projects that might use this knowledge, and there may be more possible partners with whom to collaborate. In fact, I offer this mathematical insight for my exponentially-minded friends: what grows faster than an exponential function? A combinatorial function! This insight makes the point that opening up the innovation process can introduce huge amounts of complexity into that process. This can create frustration for the staff who now have more work to do (and usually are given no additional resources to do this work).

Carried too far, this problem can become quite severe. Companies often don't account for the capacity of their innovation processes, measured in terms of the number of projects that their processes can handle at any one point in time. If companies open up their innovation processes at the beginning stages, the so-called Front End of the innovation process, and do not change subsequent steps in the innovation process, the result could simply be congestion in the innovation process. More projects come into the process, but fewer projects actually come out. Imagine a road that suddenly has twice or three times the number of vehicles trying to enter, and the traffic jam that

Open Innovation Results. Going Beyond the Hype, and Getting Down to Business. Henry Chesbrough, Oxford University Press (2020). © Henry Chesbrough. DOI: 10.1093/oso/9780198841906.001.0001

results from this increased congestion. Instead of making the innovation process more effective, too much congestion can slow down the whole process—not just for the Open Innovation projects, but for all of the projects.

Bottlenecks limit the capacity of a process. One bottleneck in the innovation process is all the shared services that projects must draw upon during their development. The procurement organization must assist project leaders to identify and then negotiate with suppliers. The quality organization must assure conformance to specifications and standards, so that the project meets the quality image of the organization. The operations organization must make or buy the quantities required. The finance organization must manage the standard costs in the projects, and the provision of credit to external customers. The sales organization must manage the interaction with those customers. The marketing organization manages the brand positioning, and regulates the use of company trademarks. All of these services are shared across multiple projects, and it is here where the congestion that can arise from more Open Innovation projects will manifest.[1]

The Human Limits of Open Innovation @NASA

There are human dimensions to Open Innovation that comprise another kind of bottleneck in the innovation process. One important insight comes from the work that Hila Lifshitz-Assaf of NYU did at the Johnson Space Center at NASA. This part of NASA embraced Open Innovation to increase its effectiveness, and Lifshitz-Assaf was able to study the resulting transformation of NASA.[2]

NASA solicited extensive external knowledge contributors to a number of problems that the agency faced in its mission of supporting and sustaining manned space flight. One important challenge was to find ways to improve NASA's ability to forecast solar flares. Solar flares are eruptions from the surface of the sun that leap millions of miles into space, throwing off increased radiation in the process. These spikes in radiation from solar flares can threaten both people and equipment in space, if they are not detected early enough to enable protective measures to be taken.

At the time of the challenge, NASA had an algorithm to predict the incidence of solar flares, but this algorithm wasn't very good. It could only predict eight hours into the future, and it had about a 50 percent chance of actually predicting a solar flare. So NASA issued a challenge to the external world, to see if anyone could come up with a better prediction algorithm. As it happened, a number of responses were received (and each of them needed to be evaluated as noted above), but one of them proved to be significantly better. And the contributor of this solution was not an astrophysicist or an astronomer. Instead, he was trained in weather forecasting, and saw patterns in the solar data that were reminiscent of what he had seen earlier in forecasting weather patterns on earth. His algorithm boosted the prediction window to twenty-four hours ahead of time (providing more time to take protective actions) and his accuracy rate was 85 percent (creating many fewer false positives). This result was a huge win for NASA going forward, as it will increase safety and reduce the chance of a calamitous event in space. So score another victory for Open Innovation, this time at NASA!

But the story doesn't end there, according to Lifshitz-Assaf. The people at Johnson Space Center who were evaluating all these external suggestions were highly technical people, well trained in their scientific and engineering disciplines. They were rocket scientists, and they had joined NASA to apply their talents to help mankind explore the galaxy. When the Open Innovation initiatives were implemented at NASA, many of these talented people had an existential crisis. As one engineer put it, 'I joined NASA to solve really important problems in space flight. But now I am evaluating the solutions of other people who aren't even part of NASA. That's not what I signed up for when I joined this place. What is my role, in an Open Innovation organization?'

This is part of the back end of Open Innovation. It isn't enough to load in a bunch of new projects and new knowledge at the beginning of the process. As noted above, that can simply result in congestion, and may do little or nothing to improve organizational performance. Issues like those identified by Lifshitz-Assaf, about the ways that Open Innovation influences organizational culture and individuals' identities, suggest that much more must be done, before one can realize the performance potential enabled by Open Innovation.

So How Do Companies Practice Open Innovation Currently?

While these problems and limitations are not often discussed by Open Innovation writers, they are well known to companies who practice Open Innovation. A large scale survey of companies conducted in 2013 by UC Berkeley and the Fraunhofer Institute[3] helps to illustrate the pitfalls many companies experience when they practice Open Innovation. My colleague Sabine Brunswicker of Purdue University (previously at Fraunhofer) and I conducted this survey.

This survey examined the Open Innovation practices of companies in Europe and North America, and the sample was restricted to companies with annual sales above $250 million and more than 1000 employees. We found that 78 percent of companies surveyed practiced at least some elements of Open Innovation, which we defined as 'the purposive use of inflows and outflows of knowledge to accelerate innovation in one's own market, and expand the use of internal knowledge in external markets, respectively'.[4] Some of the detailed results are located in the Annex to this chapter.

Our survey results also suggest that it is not easy to implement Open Innovation. There are barriers for Open Innovation that are difficult to overcome, and the siloes inside internal organization, and the company's own employees (per NASA's experience above), are the most critical areas to consider. While Open Innovation poses many new challenges to firms when adopted, it is the internal organizational challenges that are perceived as most difficult to manage. Managing the journey from closed to Open Innovation requires a range of organizational changes at various levels inside the firm. Put differently, to open up outside effectively, one needs to open up inside as well.

Exploring the Back End of Open Innovation

To explore how the initial innovation activities are linked to the 'back end' of the innovation process, I assembled a research team at Berkeley.[5] We set out to document effective ways to manage the back end of Open Innovation. As the survey results in the Annex show, this is a difficult task. Companies are far from satisfied with their current Open Innovation performance. And internal employees are the most important resource for effective Open Innovation. Yet some companies are nonetheless having real success with Open Innovation. What are they doing, and what can be learned from their experience?

To research this, we were able to interview a number of companies known for their adoption of Open Innovation. They were: SAP, Intel, EMC, and the Royal Bank of Scotland.

SAP's Embrace of Open Source

SAP is perhaps Europe's most successful software company. Headquartered in Walldorf, Germany, the company today has 96,000 employees all over the world. For many years, the company had a large internal R&D unit, but the company felt that its business units were not well connected with the research being done. 'Some of this research should have been done at a university, rather than at SAP', reported one manager. 'The researchers were publishing papers, rather than working closely with our businesses.'

To fix this problem, the company eventually decided to eliminate its separation of research from the businesses, so that the two now report into the same place, with the business units clearly communicating their needs and expectations to the researchers. This has caused some researchers to leave.

One result of SAP's global footprint is that different cultures have evolved in the different areas of the world where SAP operates. In Walldorf, which is the oldest and largest facility for SAP, the company tends to be more internally focused, more hierarchical, and less open. In other parts of the world, however, SAP collaborates quite openly. In Palo Alto, for example, SAP has a large contingent of staff who mingle easily with Stanford, Berkeley, and the denizens of Silicon Valley.

An Open Innovation success at SAP that connected effectively with its business units at the 'back end' of the innovation process came from its development of version control software. Software is constantly being revised, improved, and updated. This creates a serious problem of tracking, to make sure that the version being used is the latest, tested, accepted and supported version of the software. For many years, SAP's internal software engineering staff created tools to track the myriad versions of the company's enormous software base.

While this worked reasonably well, the outside world had the same problem of managing version control, and came up with solutions that were actually significantly better than what SAP was using internally. This was the Github repository,[6] built on open source tools for version control (the 'Git'), and enhanced with extensive resources that allow users to view each other, their previous contributions, and current activities (the 'hub' surrounding the Git tools, hence 'Github'). This expanded social view of dispersed contributors greatly enhanced collaboration, and was not available with the internal SAP tools (one internal version was called 'GitGarrett') that SAP employed.

Here is where the differing cultures worked to SAP's advantage. While it took time and concerted effort, the large internal group at Walldorf was eventually persuaded by the upstarts in Palo Alto to move their software version management control systems over to Github. The company has been quite pleased with the results, and this has helped to boost the perception of Open Innovation inside the company. It also helps that SAP's business units can see the same information that the developers and researchers use in their many collaborations. This increased transparency helps decisions get made faster in the company, and moves projects a little more quickly through the development process to the market. It even saves SAP the cost of having to maintain and update their internal version control tools. Now those costs are borne by the entire Github community, instead of a single organization.

The Back End of Open Innovation: Inside Intel

Intel is the world's largest semiconductor manufacturer, with 107,000 employees worldwide. Intel's research efforts began inside Intel's manufacturing facilities, and the company did not have a separate research organization for the first thirty years of its life.[7]

Initially, Intel focused its research on its supplier base, in areas such as photolithography. As the company's business grew, the research function gradually emerged as a separate function, with a broader remit beyond Intel's own supply base. The company has extensive collaborations with universities, including leading universities in semiconductor research such as Berkeley, KL-Leuven, MIT, and Stanford. It is also an active participant in many government consortia, including the Open Innovation 2.0 initiative inside the European Commission.[8] Today the company has laboratories in the US, the EU, and in China. Some of its current focus areas include user experience, semiconductor architecture and design, systems and SW development, security, and privacy. While Intel's primary customers are systems manufacturers, much of its research activity studies 'the customer's customer', to understand better what the needs of the market will be in these new technology areas.

In recent years, the company created a new function, called New Business Initiatives (NBI) to strengthen the connection between promising areas of new research and technology on the one side, and Intel's businesses on the other side. NBI was created to create new growth 'seeds' inside Intel, in areas that were outside the domain of its current business units. As one NBI manager explained, 'We are not primarily focused on developing new technology, but inside on developing new businesses for Intel. This means that we pay particular attention to what the new business model might be. If we don't know that, we don't have anything for our business units.'

To pursue this new business model, Intel follows the Lean Startup processes pioneered by Eric Ries (see the next chapter in this book for more on those processes). The company tries to get each business unit to define their biggest needs and issues, so that the NBI work is directly informed by these. The business units are asked to define their acceptance criteria for a new project, so that the NBI team knows what they need to demonstrate to engage the business unit.

One of NBI's insights is that the biggest risk areas should be the first ones that NBI attacks. This 'de-risks' the projects quickly, before major funds have been spent. 'We are a resource pool', said another NBI manager. 'If we transfer a venture or stop a venture, I still have a job.' This helps remove the personal risk for team members from cancelling nascent ventures. This is an important practice to improve the connection between the early stages of innovation and the later absorption of that innovation into the business. If the job of the innovation manager depends entirely upon continuing an innovation project, resourceful innovation managers will find many reasons to continue, even if the internal business shows little or no interest in the project.

At the time of our research, the NBI group had roughly forty permanent people, and utilizes a larger team of people on a project basis when required. Intel has an internal consulting pool of staff called FLEX, and external consultants are also brought in when they have relevant expertise needed by the NBI team. This allows the forty-person team to flex up when projects need more staff, without taking on more permanent employees.

In its process, the NBI group is quite selective. In a typical year, the team will evaluate 50–100 projects, and launch ten to twenty investigations. Five to ten of these investigations will be seeded as formal projects, with the expectation that one to two of them will go to market. In recent years, the NBI group has conducted seed projects in areas including mobility, cloud computing, Internet of Things, and Data Analytics.

The NBI group has its own budget for these activities, but once the project is ready to transfer to the business unit, the NBI budget is insufficient to support the work going forward. The business unit instead must devote some of its budget to the seed activity. This creates a problem that is common in many organizations, namely that the business units have little to no slack in their budgets. This means that there can be a considerable delay in the path to market for a promising innovation project, precisely because no one has the needed funding at that moment to continue its development. It is the Valley of Death problem we saw in the last chapter, here found inside a single organization between the front end and back end of the organization's innovation process. Often, the only resolution to the problem is to wait until the next fiscal year, when the new project can be included in the budget request for that year.

After some struggling with this gap in funding, Intel's senior management decided to create an additional line item budget specifically to support project transfers from NBI to the business units. As one manager explained, 'We have convinced senior management to provide additional resources without drying up the rest of our pipeline. We have done it enough times that there is now a new bucket for scaling projects. We can send the budget for the first year of the transferred venture to the BU, to help them absorb this into their plans.' This helped resolve the funding gap, until the business unit could budget for the new activity in next year's budget process.

Another organizational innovation that NBI developed was to assign one of its staff who had worked on the seed project to transfer with the initiative to the receiving business unit for a six month period. This was done to transfer the knowledge gathered in the NBI research phase more effectively to the BU. Since most of the NBI staff will be assigned to new projects after the formal transfer of an initiative to the business unit, keeping one staff member involved full time greatly speeds up the access to the project's knowledge.

This is another good practice. Once an innovation project concludes, the team who worked on that project breaks up, and each individual gets redeployed onto other work. Within a few weeks, it can be quite challenging to figure out who did what on the earlier project. New questions about the earlier project can be hard to resolve, unless there is someone available who worked on the project and knows how the work was done, and who did that work. Seconding one of the team for six months is a good way to achieve this.

A further discovery for NBI has been the importance of an external customer. If a project is able to attract strong customer support, that support really helps when trying to transfer that project to one of Intel's business units. Not surprisingly, business units like to listen to customers, and having strong customer commitment behind the project reduces the business acceptance risks of that project to the business unit. And the corollary is also important. As one NBI manager put it, 'If one of our projects is unable to attract a customer, that says something too.'

EMC's Open Innovation Back End

EMC's approach to Open Innovation started with the creation of an 'innovation network' inside the company. This network linked internal staff to the many projects underway in the company, so that more people would know about the work going on inside the company. As the Open Innovation team organizing the network saw the various projects, they began to build a road-map of what was coming next, and roughly when. When they saw gaps, they tried to solicit internal staff to address those gaps with proposals for new projects. 'It was blue sky stuff', said one EMC manager. 'We'd try to get someone interested in doing the work, and then we'd try to sell the idea back to one of our business units.'

While this was both fun and intellectually stimulating, the team had a sobering realization. 'What happened to these ideas, once we had pitched them to our businesses? Silence! This proved to be a fundamental flaw in our approach—we needed buy-in from our businesses upfront, in order to interest them in the results later', commented the manager.

Now they have flipped the process. With the support of the Executive Vice President of the company, the Open Innovation team solicits each business unit for their key needs and challenges. The team curates these, and posts them to the internal employee network as challenges. The employees self-organize into small teams to propose solutions to these challenges, and the business units help review the submissions. The winning proposals receive funding to prototype their solution, with the help of the business unit, who is now more prepared to carry it forward.

EMC is handling about thirty such projects a year.[9] Like Intel, the company has created a separate incubation fund to help projects transition from the early R&D phase in the Open Innovation network, to scale up inside an existing business unit. This helps cover the gap in budgeting during the current fiscal year, where the business wants the project, but lacks available funds to take it over until it can budget for it in the next fiscal period.

This flipping of the process has created significant new business revenue, estimated in the hundreds of millions of dollars over the past five years. This is a powerful validation of Open Innovation inside EMC. However, it is not a complete answer to the innovation challenges of the company. This process strongly biases the projects selected to ones that are either incremental to the current businesses or to adjacent markets near the current businesses. There is no funding for the so-called 'white spaces' that involve exploring distinctly new markets for the company.

One idea to address the white spaces gap in EMC's innovation activities is to employ an internal venturing model. In this model, selected staff would be chartered to form a new venture, outside the current businesses of the company. The goal of these new ventures is to develop early prototypes, and obtain early market validation, in new business areas, utilizing the Lean Startup approach. Investment readiness levels are employed to measure the progress of the new venture toward its goals. However, the back end reintegration of these ventures into the established businesses of EMC is still to be determined, since, by design, these ventures are operating in areas pretty far from those established businesses. Ultimately, some may connect to an internal business unit, while others might fare better if spun out to outside investors.

Royal Bank of Scotland's Back End Open Innovation Process

It's fair to say that the Royal Bank of Scotland (RBS) had a rough time during the financial crisis of 2008. The company had been growing through acquisition, up to the time of the crisis, but it encountered severe stress during the crisis. The British government had to step in to save the bank, and ended up with 80 percent of the company's stock.

In the years since the crisis, RBS has refocused its operations, effectively unwinding many of its acquisitions. The bank had a global footprint going into 2008, but today operates primarily as a retail bank in the UK. This has created a difficult environment for innovation to thrive.

In 2013, RBS changed its leadership team. With that change, a new approach to innovation has arisen. The company now performs personal and business banking, corporate and private banking, corporate and institutional banking. Innovation is again one of the pillars of the company's new strategy.

This shift has come at a fortuitous time. Banking is experiencing another turbulent period, due to the rise of financial technology startup companies (known as 'fintech' in industry parlance). There has been an explosion of innovation possibilities, ranging from new currencies (e.g., Bitcoin and other blockchain-enabled approaches) to new channels (most banking functions being delivered over one's smartphone) to new peer-to-peer lending models (e.g., Lending Club, or crowdfunding). Like most retail banks, much of RBS's asset base is invested in real estate, housing a broad network of bank branches. The recent fintech explosion may challenge the usefulness of all this real estate, as non-branch banking approaches seem to be gaining in the market. And the risk of disintermediation, of having one's partner take over your business at your expense, bypassing you in the process, is again a concern for RBS.

RBS has responded to these challenging circumstances by changing its innovation process. Rather than avoid the fintech challenge, the company has established an outpost in San Francisco to scout among the numerous prospective startups, and see which of them might be useful partners for the bank. The company has also been active in Israel (previously not an area of interest for RBS), again to get acquainted with the fintech community there. It even supports an incubator of new ventures in Scotland.

These outposts are small by design, (the San Francisco office initially had a staff of only two people full time) but RBS uses them to educate its senior management on the risks—and the opportunities—that the fintech world poses for RBS. The senior leadership of the bank is visiting these outposts on a regular basis. For RBS, there is no substitute for the senior leadership of the company understanding the innovation possibilities, and sponsoring the experiments, ventures, and collaborations necessary to respond.

One learning for RBS has been the need for different internal processes to pursue these opportunities. Traditionally, if RBS wanted to work with a new supplier, there was an extensive qualification process for that supplier, run by the purchasing organization. This required significant time from the supplier, which makes good business sense when many millions of dollars are being spent, and the results will be used across the bank. However, the new opportunities in the fintech world are often quite small initially, and a lot of trial-and-error may be needed to figure out how best for RBS to utilize a new partner's technology. Here, that onerous process proved to be far too onerous for fintech startup companies. One example of this was a standard contractual term that RBS asked of all of its major suppliers: an indemnification clause to protect RBS if something goes wrong with their technology. This is good business practice for established firms, but the concept of having your twenty-employee fintech partner indemnify its 40,000 employee partner if anything goes wrong is pretty silly.

One area where RBS has used its Open Innovation process successfully has been in security. Traditional security tokens ran on lithium ion batteries, which were expensive, not environmentally sustainable, and ran out of energy. RBS partnered with an external security expert, RSA, for a software-based solution. Initially this collaboration failed, but the parties kept at it, and were able to develop a successful prototype in Israel. This approach used multi-factored authentication, incorporating gait analysis as a new way to verify the user's identity. This has the potential to be highly accurate, very low-cost, and environmentally highly sustainable. RBS even worked to create an internal video to promote the new approach, contrasting the real Elvis with a phony Elvis.

Common Issues in the Back End of Open Innovation

As stated in the outset, simply loading up the front end of your innovation process will not create more business revenue by itself. One must examine the back end of your innovation process, in order to achieve positive business results from Open Innovation. In each of these companies there is an internal version of the Valley of Death that can thwart the successful transfer of a technology from the front end of the innovation process to the business unit that will take it to market. Scanning these four companies, some common issues arise that most companies will encounter in trying to cross the Valley of Death, to get business results out of their outside-in Open Innovation initiatives.

These issues include:

- people
- funding
- senior management support.

Let's take them in turn.

The people involved in the Open Innovation process must build good connections with the outside world, in order to discover and then implement new innovation possibilities for the company. Yet, in order for those possibilities to be realized, these people also need to establish strong connections to their internal businesses. This dual focus—both outside and inside—is fundamental to effective outside-in Open Innovation.

So where do you start with these people? Is it better to bring in someone with strong external connections, and have them get to know people inside the company? Or is it better to start with someone with a significant history at your company, who already knows many of the internal players, and get that person to initiate more external connections?

In all four cases, the companies chose the second approach in launching their Open Innovation initiatives. They found that, without strong internal connections, these open innovators could not effectively represent the company to possible external partners and collaborators. And, as projects get started and progress toward the market, it is vital to get support (and ultimately budget and personnel transfers) from the business units. People with deep internal networks inside the company will be more effective in gaining this support.

What can work well is to start with a well-connected insider, and then add a second person who brings strong external connections to the Open Innovation effort. So long as the two people work well together, this can give the company a window on new opportunities outside their own four walls, and still maintain the relationships necessary inside to capitalize on those opportunities. In SAP's case, the different cultures of Walldorf and Palo Alto helped to identify promising new technologies (Palo Alto) and connect them effectively to SAP's core businesses (Walldorf). This is also the path that Gore Technology has taken with the recent launch of its Silicon Valley Innovation Center: the Center is run jointly by a long-time insider and a recently-hired, well-connected outsider.[10]

Funding is another critical ingredient to getting results out of Open Innovation. A key problem shared across all four organizations is the mismatch between innovation budgets and opportunities. These large companies' budgets are set on an annual fiscal calendar, usually some months ahead of the start of the fiscal year. Once set, there isn't much room for variation. Meanwhile, innovation opportunities arise, and arise unpredictably, throughout the year. A promising initiative from an innovation team cannot continue inside a business unit unless and until there is money available to pay for it. Yet most business units lack the slack in their budgets to absorb this unexpected new project until the start of the next fiscal year.

Both Intel and EMC have reacted to this budget gap with a new pool of funds, expressly reserved to bridge the gap. The innovation team cannot tap these funds to start new projects at the front end. Nor can the receiving business units divert these funds to cover needs on other existing products and services. The bridge funds are dedicated to transferring and scaling the projects at the right time, and then the budgeting process can incorporate the new projects in the next phase of the cycle.

The attention and support of senior management is another critical ingredient for success in the back end of the Open Innovation process. Top management executives are very, very busy people, and there is a large internal market of activities demanding their attention. Often, the possibilities offered by Open Innovation are too vague, or too distant, or initially too small, to command much top management time.

The four companies here have all responded by presenting themselves as levers to advance the goals of top management. This is seen most clearly in the evolution of EMC, which went from an idealized view of the future (built from its own roadmaps) to organizing their activities based on the upfront buy-in of top management. RBS also took this approach, helping to organize study trips for top management to let them see the risks and opportunities of fintech for themselves. Once top management experiences the full context, and develops a view on how and where to proceed, the RBS outposts are then empowered to respond to their wishes. The SAP Github example provides transparency for top management, so they can see what their subordinates see. This gives them clear line-of-sight to the status of their top priority projects.

What About Entirely New Businesses?

We've discussed the problem of getting activities from the innovation groups that operate at the front end of the innovation process connected to the needs of the business units that carry innovations to market. As we've seen, there is an internal Valley of Death that exists between these groups, that bears some similarity to the external Valley of Death we saw in Chapter 3. And SAP, Intel, EMC, and RBS offer some useful practices for overcoming this internal Valley of Death.

However, there remains the problem of the 'white spaces' in linking the front end of the innovation process to the back end. These are areas where existing businesses may not know very much about the opportunities (because they are distant from their existing activities), and where top management may not yet care very much (because the initial market may be small or unclear). None of the four companies examined in this chapter have a complete answer to this problem. But EMC's internal venturing provides at least one path forward. A company will remain ignorant of the opportunities and risks of white spaces so long as it neglects to undertake any business experiments to explore those spaces. Indeed, only those who dare to try to do business in these spaces will obtain the knowledge and perspective necessary to know whether and when to proceed forward.

This is where adopting a Lean Startup approach to venturing becomes so important. A lean approach will keep the initial expenses low, and will be designed to learn the most in the shortest amount of time. It strives to identify initial customers quite early in the innovation process, and customers really help innovation units get their ideas across the Valley of Death to the internal business units. For this reason, the Lean Startup process warrants its own chapter, which will be our very next chapter.

Chapter 4 review points:

1. Innovation results depend on what you finish, not on what you start. Too little attention has been paid to the many processes and activities that are required to commercialize new innovation initiatives, resulting in congestion and frustration.
2. The Not Invented Here syndrome exists in many organizations (such as NASA), and Open Innovation is often viewed as threatening to many technical staff.

3. There exists a Valley of Death between the innovation function in many organizations and the downstream business unit that is intended to receive the new innovations.

4. Companies like SAP, Intel, EMC, and RBS have created practices to help overcome this internal Valley of Death. Money, people, and top management support are all necessary to create the mechanisms to cross the Valley of Death inside the company.

ANNEX: Selected Survey Results on the Practice of Open Innovation in Large Firms

In our survey, we differentiated between inbound Open Innovation where external knowledge flows inside the firm, and outbound Open Innovation where knowledge flows outside the firm. We also included practices that had either pecuniary or non-pecuniary compensation for Open Innovation participants. In a non-pecuniary mode of inbound Open Innovation, firms source external knowledge without monetary compensation for external ideas and contributions, such as when firms freely reveal their knowledge e.g. via donations or participation in standards. You can see these practices in Figure 4.1.

Our survey showed that inbound Open Innovation practices were far more commonly used than outbound practices. The share of projects in these companies with an inbound component was 35 percent on average. Only about 8 percent of projects incorporated outbound innovation activities.

As one might expect, not all of these practices are equally important. We asked our respondents to rate the importance of different Open Innovation practices in 2011 and the

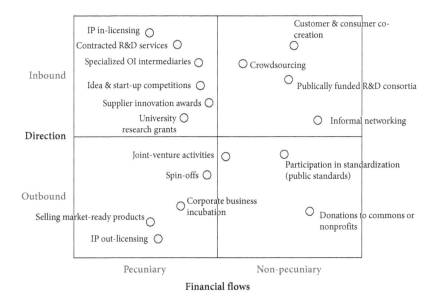

Figure 4.1 Classification of modes of Open Innovation

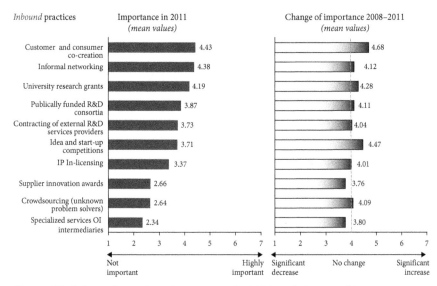

Figure 4.2 Inbound practices: importance in 2011 and change of importance 2008–11

change of their importance from 2008 to 2011. We asked them to evaluate ten distinct inbound practices and seven distinct outbound practices. To make sure that we capture a holistic picture, we included traditional practices such as R&D alliances as well as more recently emerging practices such as crowdsourcing, Open Innovation intermediaries or donations to a commons or nonprofit organization in our measurement.

Figure 4.2 reports the results for the respondents' ratings of the importance of individual inbound practices in 2011 and their changing role from 2008 to 2011. Large firms, on average, consider all inbound practices to be of modest importance (average score of 3.53 importance in 2011 on a scale from 1 = not important to 7 = highly important). On average, the perceived importance of these practices increased slightly from 2008 to 2011 (average score of 4.14 with 1 = significant decrease, 4 = no change, and 7 = significant increase).

For inbound practices, co-creation with customers and consumers was one of the top rated practices in importance (4.43 on a seven-point scale), and also growing in importance from 2008 to 2011. Informal networking and university research grants rank second and third. On the other end, crowdsourcing (among unknown innovation problem solvers) and specialized Open Innovation intermediary services are rated lowest in importance.[11] The importance of services of Open Innovation intermediaries has slightly decreased from 2008 to 2011 (score of 2.34). Besides co-creation our respondents also report a growing importance of start-up and idea competitions (score of 4.47).

Figure 4.3 reports the importance of individual outbound practices in 2011 and their change from 2008 to 2011. On average, outbound practices are less important than inbound practices to large firms (average score of 3.25 for outbound practices versus 3.53 for inbound practices). However, we notice a slightly growing interest in outbound practices over the last years. On average, they respondents report a positive change of the importance of these outbound practices from 2008 to 2011 (average score of 4.21).

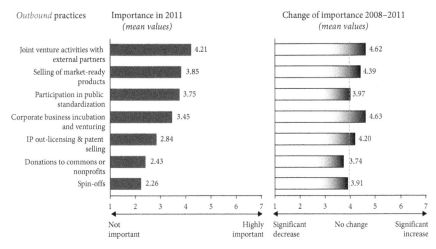

Figure 4.3 Outbound practices: importance in 2011 and change of importance 2008–11

Joint venture activities are the most highly rated outbound practice (average score 4.21), and is growing in importance over the past three years (average score of 4.62). The sale of market-ready products and participation in public standardization ranks second and third respectively. Donations to commons or non-profits and spin-offs are the least important outbound practices. Over the last three years the importance of these two practices has even decreased (score of 3.74 and 3.91 for the change of importance 2008 to 2011). In contrast, business incubation and venturing (score of 4.63)—along with joint venture activities— have been receiving somewhat increased attention from firms practicing Open Innovation.

In addition to practices, we also surveyed the kinds of partners organizations used in their innovation activities. We asked respondents to rate the importance of each prospective partner or collaboration source for their Open Innovation activities in 2011. We again utilized a seven-point scale. Figure 4.4 reports the respondent's rating of the average importance of each of the twelve Open Innovation partners.

Internal employees are considered as the most critical source by our respondents. When turning to external Open Innovation partners, we found that customers, universities, suppliers, and the final consumers (for B2B companies) are all rated above average in importance. By contrast, competitors, and communities of both kinds are rated as lowest in importance.

There are a range of challenges and constraints that limit large firms in making use of Open Innovation. To explore these particular challenges we prompted the senior executives on what they perceived as the major challenges when they started using Open Innovation. We then asked them to evaluate today's major challenges and constraints. Figure 4.5 presents the firm's view about the importance of each particular challenge when they started to engage in Open Innovation, and today.

Generally, speaking firms tend to consider internal organizational change (5.6 at start and 5.26 today) as the most significant challenge. Note that this is entirely consistent with the importance of internal employees reported in Figure 4.4 above. The management of external relationships with innovation partners is also a quite important

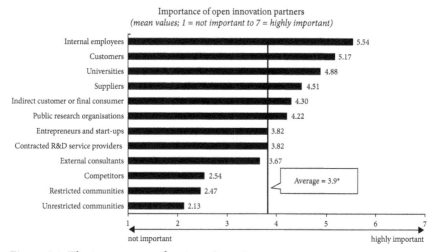

Figure 4.4 The importance of various Open Innovation partners

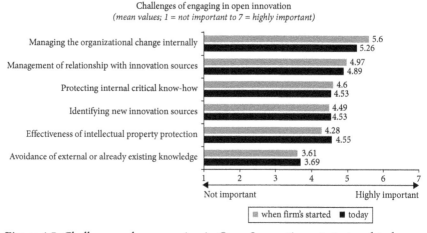

Figure 4.5 Challenges when engaging in Open Innovation: at start and today

challenge (4.97 at start and 4.89 today). Avoiding unauthorized use of external or already existing knowledge appears to be the least concern for our respondents (3.61 at start and 3.69 today).

We also investigated the firm's satisfaction with their Open Innovation performance. Respondents were asked to assess their satisfaction with their Open Innovation activities from 2008 to 2011 on a scale from 1 = highly dissatisfied 4 = neutral to 7 = satisfied. On average, the satisfaction level was 4.68 which indicate a somewhat positive view of firms towards Open Innovation. More than 44 percent of the firms assigned a score of five, and more than 16 percent assigned a score of six or seven (see Figure 4.6).

Satisfaction with open innovation performance
(Distribution of responses in %)

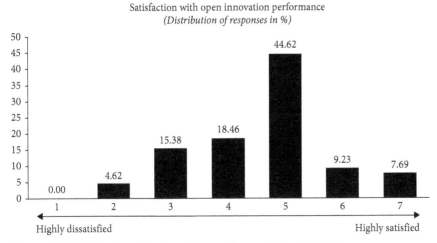

Figure 4.6 Satisfaction with Open Innovation activities 2008–11

These results show a fair amount of dissatisfaction with the practice of Open Innovation in these large firms. Even firms that are practicing Open Innovation more intensively rate their practices only slightly higher than four on average. The fact that no firm has abandoned Open Innovation, in spite of these lukewarm perceptions, suggests that firms are still learning about how to get better results with Open Innovation. Firms that report practicing Open Innovation over a longer period do report somewhat higher satisfaction with their practices. But clearly there is room to improve.

Recent academic research on Open Innovation has highlighted the roles of non-pecuniary or 'freely revealed' exchanges of knowledge. At least in large firms, though, our survey finds that these are rated among the very lowest sources in terms of their importance to those firms. And large firms appear to be more willing to receive 'free' exchanges of knowledge than they are to provide them. Open and restricted innovation communities and crowdsourcing also attract a lot of academic attention, but these too are rated as being of low importance in the survey. While we expect these sources to grow in importance over time, they start from a very low base. And firms are not all that satisfied with more established Open Innovation practices, such as working with universities and research institutes. The survey results also suggest that Open Innovation vendors of software tools, intermediaries, and other research sources need to work harder to increase the satisfaction of large companies using these resources.

5

Lean Startup and Open Innovation

Lean Startup is a relatively new concept to the world of innovation, and even more new to the world of corporate innovation. It is based upon the pioneering work of Eric Ries, in re-conceptualizing the reasons for innovation failure in startup firms. This was most clearly documented in Ries' seminal book, *Lean Startup*.[1] Ries applies the lean thinking philosophy found in the Toyota Production System to startup companies. Steve Blank has also played a critical role, as I will discuss below.

The core insight of Lean Startup is that most startup firms fail for reasons that are not the result of poor product development. Most of the time, the company is able to resolve the technical and operational challenges of developing its new product (or service) offering. Rather, *the most common reason for failure in these startups is the lack of customer acceptance for this new offering.* Yet most startups have no process to develop the market for their products, and test and validate the achievement of key milestones, in the same way that they test and validate the development of the product itself.

The traditional advice given to startups was to write a business plan that covered each of the areas of the business. Once that plan was complete, the startup was then counseled to follow the plan, update it as new information arrived, and launch the product that was specified and subsequently developed in the business plan. In essence, startups were advised to behave like small versions of big companies.

This is the exact opposite of Lean philosophy, according to Ries. Lean thinking, inspired by the Toyota Production System, is about reducing waste in an industrial process. The most wasteful use of resources for a startup, Ries observed, is to build a product that no one wants to buy. The Lean approach carefully determines the minimum set of features in a product that will compel a customer to buy the product, and then focuses the product development process on creating that set of features—no more, no less. This gives rise to a key concept in Lean Startup, the concept of a minimal viable product, MVP.

The roots of MVP go back to Agile Software Development, where the creation of complex code has gradually shifted away from a 'waterfall' model of development. In the waterfall development model, one sets a product

Open Innovation Results. Going Beyond the Hype, and Getting Down to Business. Henry Chesbrough, Oxford University Press (2020). © Henry Chesbrough.
DOI: 10.1093/oso/9780198841906.001.0001

requirement specification, freezes it, then starts the software coding. Once the code meets the spec, the process tests the software for quality and for customer acceptance, and only then considers revisions to the code for the next cycle of development. Note that there is a hidden assumption in the waterfall model: the customer knows what the customer wants (hence the specification), and we simply need to develop it for him. Note as well that there is no learning during the code development. The only feedback comes at the end of each cycle.

In recent years, this waterfall model has given way to an 'agile' model of development. In the agile model, an initial spec is developed and code is written in 'sprints' to meet the spec (often in one- to two-week cycles) and then immediately shared with users and customers for feedback. This feedback is used to refine the initial specification, and another sprint occurs. This creates an iterative loop of feedback that allows the developers to learn much more rapidly about what the users and customers really want from the software. Customers often react in surprising ways when they see actual code, and either realize new needs/benefits, and/or redefine earlier needs/benefits. It can be shown that whenever customers aren't entirely clear in advance on their needs for a complex piece of software, agile approaches will converge more quickly than waterfall approaches on a product that the customer will accept. This is the connection to Lean: agile methods use fewer resources and converge on an acceptable solution much faster than the earlier waterfall method. So there is much less waste.

One of my Berkeley colleagues, Steve Blank, has added a key concept to Lean Startup, the concept of Customer Development.[2] Just as the product must be developed, so too must a startup company identify and seek out customers willing and able to buy its offerings. While Ries' book advises startups to get market validation very early in the process, it was Blank who figured out a systematic process to do that. Blank develops a four-stage process to achieve this:

a. customer discovery
b. customer validation
c. customer creation
d. company building.

In the discovery phase, it is critical in Blanks' conception to *get out of the building* to identify customers. Using the MVP as an artifact, a startup would try to get a prospective customer to commit to buy the product. Critically, one only exits this stage when there is an actual order from an actual customer.

Note that this selling activity comes much more quickly than would be the case in a traditional waterfall innovation model. It also requires a selling capability to be available in the earliest phase of the innovation process inside the startup. It dovetails nicely with agile methods, because the customer often requires changes to the MVP before committing to buy it (and those changes often surface only after the innovator asks the customer to buy). It is imperative to make those required changes quickly, to get back to the customer and close the sale. If the customer is still unwilling to buy, the startup can either modify the product again, or try a different prospective customer for the next time.

The customer validation process starts once an initial order has been received. In the validation stage, the company seeks other customers also willing to buy. Once multiple customers and multiple orders have been received, the validation stage is completed. In this stage, the company now has multiple customers, and is looking for a common pattern that connects the customers together. The company can now identify a market segment for its product.

In the customer creation stage, the company is building a sales process, to reliably replicate the validation, and to understand the cost and time required to make a new sale in that market segment. If the cost to sell to the customer is too high or takes too long, then the startup might try a different channel of distribution.

In the company-building stage, the company now has the information needed to sell its offering, scale its business and rapidly grow its customer base. By waiting until the validation and customer creation stages are complete, the startup is less likely to waste time and money on the wrong market segments or distribution channels. Scaling too early is another way to generate lots of waste, and therefore very non-Lean.

How Lean Startup Works Inside a Large Company

The foundational work for Lean Startup originated in the context of startup companies. More recently, people have begun to apply these concepts inside large organizations. This is quite a different context than a startup context. The Lean Startup pioneers like Ries and Blank actually underplay this different context, in my opinion. Just as it was an error to tell startups to behave like small versions of large companies (e.g., writing and executing business plans), *so too is it an error to tell large companies to behave like large versions of startup companies.*

Steve Blank has an extremely useful insight about the differences between startups and large established companies. A startup is a temporary organization searching for a scalable business model, in his view.[3] A large, established company has already found that business model, and has already scaled it. So the large company is focused on executing the business model it has previously found. As we'll see, this difference between searching for a new business model and executing an existing model has many implications for why large companies cannot—and should not—simply mimic the behavior of startups.

One key difference is that a startup is really a single project organization, whereas a large company has many projects, and must allocate resources and attention across a portfolio of projects. There is no single best way to allocate resources across multiple innovation projects, but some heuristics have emerged over time. McKinsey has promoted the idea of Horizon 1, Horizon 2, and Horizon 3 time horizons, and argued that companies should allocate its innovation budget across these three horizons. Horizon 1 is the next product (in the current market), Horizon 2 is the next generation product (in the current market or perhaps in an adjacent market), and Horizon 3 is the long term (new kinds of products and/or new kinds of markets). Google has publicly stated that it follows a 70/20/10 allocation to Core, Adjacent, and Transformational projects that appears to correspond well to these three categories.[4]

A critical element of this resource allocation approach of 70/20/10 is that the company must allocate its resources to each of the three in a top-down fashion *and then have the discipline to maintain that allocation over time.* That is, the organization must not raid the funds in Horizon 2 or 3 projects to make up for any shortfall needed to fund Horizon 1 projects. If this discipline is not maintained, the likely outcome is that Horizon 1 projects will take resources away from the more uncertain, longer-term Horizon 2 and Horizon 3 projects. Over time, that misallocation of resources will diminish the growth rate of that company, as it is starving its future to fund the short term.

The reason that Horizon 1 projects tend to crowd out the other two categories comes from the many data advantages these projects have. Being closer to the core business, the customers and markets are well known. The needs of these customers are likely well understood, and competitors are similarly better understood. The data on pricing, volume, and likely rate of market uptake are based on operating history, not guesswork. All of these advantages make the business case for Horizon 1 projects seem far more credible than the 'guestimates' used to support the business case for Horizon 2 or 3 projects. This greater credibility causes many companies to over-allocate resources to the near term, incremental projects at the expense of longer-term, more potentially valuable initiatives. Note that the startup firm does not worry about these issues, since it has no core business.

A second key difference in lean processes between startups and large companies is that a large company has an existing business model, and often seeks opportunities that fit with that model.[5] The large company shuns opportunities that might disrupt its current business model, whereas a startup company has no existing business or business model to protect. The large company rightly must protect its current business, even as it seeks new business opportunities.

Rethinking Lean Startup in a Corporate Context

These differences have many implications for Lean Startup, and all of them imply that it will be much, much harder to employ Lean Startup inside a large company than inside a startup. Here, we focus on three, though there are many more in practice (and these follow the pattern described with these three).

First, consider the concept of MVP. This is a vital concept in Lean Startup, and helps to perform Customer Discovery in Steve Blank's process. Yet to a manufacturing and quality organization, MVP sounds like a 'quick and dirty' approach. These groups have worked hard (using Six Sigma, Total Quality Management, and other techniques) *to train such crap out of the process in a large company.* They will seek to eliminate this quick and dirty prototyping. Equally, they will make sure that they don't have to support something in the field that has been developed outside the normal, quality-controlled processes of the company. But this fundamental tension is nowhere acknowledged in the many writings of the Lean Startup advocates.

Second, consider the concept of Customer Discovery. This requires the developer to talk directly to customers who can make a purchase decision, in order to get direct feedback, identify needed changes, and rapidly learn and iterate to make that all-important initial sale. Every large organization I know *has a sales function that regards this as dangerous,* both to the company's sales in the current quarter or year, and to their own sales commissions. They will insist on blocking access to customers, and not distracting them with pie-in-the-sky prototypes that may never be built in volume, and worse, may give the customer a reason to delay current purchases. Again, this issue is never discussed by Lean Startup adherents.

Third, consider the procurement organization. In a large company, the procurement function is measured on its ability to cut costs, improve delivery times, and manage key suppliers. In a Lean process, developers often need to work with single-source suppliers (albeit at pilot scale) and care much more about rapid learning than the cost of an input in tiny quantities. Procurement will insist on following corporate policy on acceptable vendors, and will want to insert themselves into the negotiations with these vendors. This is a recipe for failure. No procurement organization I know is measured on its speed of learning. Any corporation that attempts a Lean Startup initiative will inevitably stumble when they involve their procurement organization in the initiative.

We could consider other aspects, like whether to use the large company brand in the early stages of Lean Startup (the brand police refuse to risk the brand on an unproven MVP)[6], or whether to use different (and often conflicting) distribution channels in the Lean Startup process. The key point here is that *a corporate context differs markedly from that of a startup firm*, so the Lean Startup approaches must be adapted with great care to a corporate context, in order to avoid the barriers noted above. One can think of the difference this way: a startup fights a battle to achieve product-market fit in the marketplace. A corporate venture fights a battle on two fronts: in the marketplace like any other startup; and a second internal fight inside the corporation to access the necessary internal resources to wage the external battle.[7]

Another way to state this is that an effective Lean Startup process inside a large corporation requires both careful bottom-up design, and thoughtful top-down negotiation. The Lean Startup people have done a good job of the bottom-up portion of this in the market, but to date they have been woefully negligent about the top-down side inside the large company. To wage this second battle, the project leader must *get upstairs in the building* (to paraphrase Steve Blank's earlier admonition).

Open Innovation's Contribution to a Lean Startup process

Open Innovation (OI) fits very well with the thinking behind Lean Startup. OI has an 'outside-in' path and an 'inside-out' path for ideas to get to the market. Like the Lean Startup approach, OI also offers the promise of less waste, and faster time to market. These benefits derive from the outside-in branch of the OI model. When partnering or collaborating with external actors on a new project, the innovating firm can 'start in the middle' rather than at the beginning. This means that the innovator uses what has already been developed and demonstrated by the collaborating partner, rather than starting the project from scratch. All of the blind alleys and dead ends that preceded that development are irrelevant to the innovator, and further development builds upon what has already been achieved. This saves both time and money in getting to market, a very Lean result indeed.

Collaborations with a university using Open Innovation follow this Lean pattern. Universities have substantial plant and equipment for performing a wide range of scientific experiments. They also have talented research staff, as well as capable support staff to manage labs, source materials, and analyze laboratory data. Open Innovation collaborators can borrow these resources, instead of having to pay for their full costs upfront—a Lean savings. In essence, you are using other people's money (and staff and other resources) when you convince a partner to collaborate with you.

Since the emergence of my book *Open Innovation* in 2003, many companies have developed sophisticated methods to search and scout for useful external technologies. One of the most famous is Procter & Gamble's Connect and Develop program, but there are now hundreds of such scouting processes in use in large companies around the world. It has been well observed that, in the earlier period before Open Innovation, the lab was your world. Today, with the advent of Open Innovation, the world becomes your lab.

However, the innovator must think carefully about the business side of the collaboration as well as the technical side. The old but famous example is how IBM's PC business was eventually hollowed out by its collaborations with Intel on the CPU and Microsoft on the operating system. It is necessary to share some portion of the gains from the collaboration with one's partner, but it is equally necessary to think through how you will sustain your position over time. This requires designing a business model of some sort. Lean Startup provides a cool way to design, develop, and test a business model. This makes Lean Startup an important addition to the Open Innovation concept.

There is a third benefit from using OI, a benefit that isn't seen in Lean Startup: the ability to share risk in the project with other parties. Some companies have created CoLaboratories, physical spaces where external parties, sometimes including customers, come and work jointly with internal staff on new projects.[8] Others utilize prize-based competitions to elicit important solutions to difficult technical problems. Others employ crowdsourcing to select the most attractive designs or products (such as Threadless or Quirky).[9] In these competitions, the innovator pays if and only if a satisfactory solution is delivered. There are no payments for trying, only for delivering a solution. What all these mechanisms have in common is that at least some of the risk of project success is borne by others, not by the innovating firm. Again, this is a very Lean result.

In the case of Threadless, there is a beautiful implementation of the Lean concept of 'make only what people will buy'. The Threadless users vote for their favorite T-shirt designs, and the company produces the top ten designs voted each week. What is really clever—and Lean—is that these ten designs have already got pre-selected customers for them, namely the people who voted for them originally! This is sometimes termed 'pre-sourcing demand'. It actually goes one step beyond the classic Lean Startup approach because in the case of Threadless the customer designs the initial MVPs to be tested.

This ability to share risk is of particular value in precisely those cases where the Lean Startup process is also helpful, namely when the customer doesn't know exactly what they want or what their real needs are. In the Lean Startup process, this will be most typical of the Horizon 2 and 3 projects. Involving partners, customers, and other third parties (like contestants in a crowdsourcing process) in these cases is a powerful way to induce useful knowledge and feedback, and expands the range of possibilities that the innovating firm might offer to its customers. Using 'other people's money' reduces the financial risk to the innovator, and aligns incentives with other involved parties to the innovation.

Inside-Out Open Innovation in Lean Startup Processes

The other branch of Open Innovation is the inside-out branch, where unused and under-used ideas and technologies are allowed to go outside the firm. This branch of Open Innovation is often overlooked or ignored, but it is particularly important for Lean Startup processes in a corporate context.

One way to utilize inside-out Open Innovation to share risk is to open up the out-licensing of one's unused and under-used technologies. Any revenue received from such licensing can offset some of the costs of innovating new products and services. More subtly, licensing to key suppliers and/or key customers can also be used in negotiations to yield better prices, terms and conditions in your business, across multiple products. It can even reduce your support costs, to the extent that licensees help pay for ongoing maintenance and support of technologies you use.

Many technologies can even be licensed selectively, so that you can retain the intellectual property protection that you want, while still obtaining additional revenues from non-competing uses of that IP. This is known as licensing out by field-of-use. A pharmaceutical company could, for example, license out agricultural uses of its compound, while retaining exclusivity for all medical uses of that compound. Or a trademark could be offered for a consumer product use, while retaining exclusive use of that mark for an enterprise application. Media content is often packaged this way, where different distribution channels have access to that content under different terms and conditions.

Inside-out Open Innovation goes even further, however. When you allow another organization to employ your idea or technology, you can observe what they do with it. In most cases, they will deploy the idea in a new market, with a different business model, in ways quite distinct from what your firm is currently doing. This can be seen as free business model research, to show you what other possible applications, markets, and business models might be for your ideas and technologies (and recall that these inside-out projects are unused or under-utilized in your company currently). Because it involved real companies selling to real customers who pay real money, you get the same validation that is achieved with Lean Startup. Only in this case, that research is done with other people's money. This is a very Lean result.

This can be particularly helpful for Horizon 3 projects, where the best applications, markets, and business models may be quite unclear to the innovating firm. At best, you can test a small number of possible business models internally on your own, even if you are skilled in using Lean Startup techniques. With inside-out Open Innovation, you can augment your own tests by observing additional business models tested and deployed by third-party licensees.

Telefonica: A Lean Elephant

One example of an effective Lean Startup process inside a large company comes from the experience of Telefonica, one of the leading telco's in Europe.[10] Inside the R&D group in Barcelona, they attempted to use a Lean Startup process to accelerate the speed with which R&D projects could move into the market.

As part of Lean Startup, the R&D group focused on the end customer of its technologies, instead of the immediate customers who packaged their technologies for the market. This was a sharp contrast to the careful organizational plans and budgets that the R&D organization had traditionally relied on for its innovation efforts. Lean Startup also required a deep cultural transformation at Telefonica and a completely new environment to foster innovation.

By 2015, the R&D team had transferred five innovation projects to the business units inside Telefonica, and had many more in various stages of development. At the same time, the R&D group was creating technological opportunities in other Horizon 2 and Horizon 3 innovation areas like: the Industrial Internet of Things, Predicting Human Behavior, Identity and Privacy, and Network Evolution.[11] At any point in time, ten to fifteen innovation projects were active and ten to fifteen ideas were in the ideation stage.

One of the goals for the Telefonica R&D organization was to de-risk innovation projects so they had a higher chance of being transferred to an operating business. Sancho Atienza Arechabala, head of Insurance Telematics at Telefonica said: 'It's difficult to transfer a R&D project to operating businesses within a big multinational company with strong local business units like us. If you try to do this before you have significant proof, it's a hard task because you're competing with a lot of people who have their own projects. Once you change the model by doing the initial go-to-market work yourself, it becomes a lot more powerful.'

Susana Jurado from the R&D team agreed: 'In the past, our innovation process was to build a prototype first to validate the technology, then we conducted a pilot where we had our first contact with customers—so you can guess what happened in most of the cases. We wanted to change that because we were facing similar uncertainties as startups were in terms of the market and the customers.' Atienza added that using conventional innovation methods at Telefonica was problematic because it took too long to find solutions for customers: 'In innovation, we are trying to get three years ahead. If you have an uncertain product and try to go the traditional route of leveraging all the capabilities in the company, it's too late for the original customer.'

Lean Startup at Telefonica started by training twenty R&D employees in Lean Startup methodologies, which were readily available through external parties, coupled with internal materials and processes. There were some initial small wins, and then they expanded to one hundred people. This generated a few more success stories, and created the internal process that modifies Lean Startup to match to Telefonica's management, funding, and processes. Today, most of the R&D projects inside the company go through this Lean approach, which Telefonica now calls 'Lean Elephants'.

Adapting Lean Startup for the Enterprise

Ian Small, who was Chief Data Officer at Telefonica, stated that although Telefonica adopted Lean Startup, the methodology needed to be adapted for a large corporation: 'When you're in a large corporation, you can't exactly do

Lean Startup because it doesn't translate perfectly—the environment you're in isn't a startup environment, there are both things that empower you and those that disempower you—your paths to market don't work the same as a startup because if you can, you can leverage 300 million customers, so you have to adapt, and those adaptations are how a Lean Startup and a Lean Elephant differ.'

Inside the R&D organization, the culture was strongly one of Not Invented Here (NIH). Many internal researchers had never interacted with a customer before. Steve Blank's admonition to 'get out of the building' was a completely new experience to these researchers. It took some time for introverted engineers to learn how to engage with ordinary people. Maria de Olano Mata noted that when internal R&D staff first interviewed customers, they would ask immediately about a woman's age and her income—topics that need to be broached carefully, and usually at the very end of the interview.

A third challenge encountered by Telefonica comes from managing the innovation budgets with the finance organization. Traditionally, the budgeting process required the R&D organization to identify specific projects, and then estimate the amount of resources each project would need for the coming fiscal year. Once a total R&D budget was agreed, and a list of projects agreed, things were locked in place throughout the fiscal year.

Lean Startup budgeting is dramatically different. Resources are kept very small in the beginning (a key part of lean thinking), and more resources are added if and only if new validated learnings justify increasing those resources. While intuitively reasonable, this is a maddening process to budget for inside a large corporation. The projects are not locked in for the full year; indeed, it is critical to Lean Startup that projects can die mid-year and other projects can start up. What Telefonica needed was approval for a pool of funds for Lean Startup projects, with the explicit understanding that the identity of those projects will change during the fiscal year.

A fourth challenge was the (in)ability to use the Telefonica brand in the early stages of Lean Elephants. There were strong arguments for and against the use of the Telefonica brand. The arguments for its use included the more realistic assessment that customers would make of the new project, if they knew that Telefonica is behind it. The arguments against its use were that brands are fragile: very expensive and time consuming to build, yet easy to damage quite quickly if something truly bad happens. The latter argument breeds risk-aversion to allowing the brand to be employed. In this case, Telefonica utilized both 'white box' brands, and a 'Telefonica Labs' brand for its early tests.

These adaptations arose from Telefonica's experience with some of its early projects: IAMMY and Thinking Things. A brief review of these projects will show why the adaptations were necessary.

IAMMY

IAMMY (I Am My Data, in Spanish) focused on helping users to control their own personal data. María José Tomé, Data Innovation Manager who worked on the project, said: 'We didn't know how we could build value for users in the field of personal data, but we wanted to start an initiative internally to explore this and work on ideation in this segment.' Tomé elaborated on the Lean Startup process: 'We tried to understand customer pain in terms of personal data related to privacy, including how customers were managing their personal data, how secure they felt, and their desire for improving how their personal data was managed in the digital world.' This process took three months, followed by the development of prototypes such as a dashboard that had different widgets that activated various services.

On the dashboard, the team used real data from select users and showed how people were able to use data related to their health, communications, social life, and navigation. 'We wanted to measure how customers were using that dashboard to determine areas that they wanted to have more privacy or more protection', said Tomé. 'The objective was not to deploy a dashboard product, but it was a way to learn from real users.'

Out of this process emerged IAMMY, a prototype/web application where people could enable their 'personal data from their phone for example, and the web app would give the user recommendations on local businesses, identify one's health status, or help the user organize contacts based on their social data'.

However, the project 'failed' for several reasons, according to Jurado: 'Although the team was amazing and got out of the building and talked to people on the street and companies that would benefit from the technology, the project didn't find a painful problem to solve. The technology was a "nice-to-have" only by that time.' The IAMMY team learned an important lesson: consumers didn't care as much about these issues as the team thought they did. The good news is that they learned this in just three months, before they had sunk much development cost and time into the project.

Thinking Things

The other Lean Startup pilot was called Thinking Things[12] and aimed to transform the market with a modular end-to-end solution for building intelligent, connected products by providing a simpler way to connect everyday 'things' and physical objects to the Internet without needing any programming knowledge or having to install additional infrastructure. The project was initially staffed with three people.

Thinking Things was a set of low-cost modular 'bricks' fitted with different sensors that connected to the cloud. These bricks were called an 'ambient kit pack' that included a communications module with an embedded SIM,[13] a module for measuring air temperature, humidity, and ambient light, and a battery module that could be charged via a micro USB drive. People could use the bricks to remotely control and manage the temperature, lighting, and humidity of their home or office, or switch on an irrigation system when no rain was forecast.

Thinking Things used open hardware developed in collaboration with Arduino (an open-source electronics platform based on easy-to-use hardware and software) and 2G connectivity available in Europe, the US, and Latin America. Thinking Things also provided an API that allowed developers to create their own Internet of Things solutions (via apps or online) and increased the possibilities of the modules.

The idea behind the Thinking Things project came from the desire to provide Internet of Things solutions that weren't that expensive to small- and medium-sized companies. Jurado said that having a problem was one of the key drivers for success of this Lean Startup project: 'The problem was already detected and there was a clear need for an Internet of Things solution that was not ad-hoc and not expensive.' Javier Zorzano Mier, Technological Expert said: 'We received many calls and talked to many people that needed a way to easily build Internet of Things solutions. Working with designers, we came up with our bricks and determined how to address a common problem in different markets.'

Zorzano discussed how the project applied Lean Startup: 'We tried to prototype as soon as possible, locate possible customers as quickly as possible, gave them the units and even tried to sell the units to them. We tried a lot of different things and defined and tested our solutions at each phase.' Customers were even brought into the Lab that was built with 3D printers and other hardware in order to help design the solution. 'That was really key for the team to design something that was what the market really needed', said Maria Olano. The team learned that the best way to apply Lean Startup and experiment with a B2B customer during the early stages was to test products or ideas with five medium-sized enterprises versus a large company to have 'the opportunity to learn rather than selling our solution to a major customer.'[14]

By 2015, the Thinking Things project had become an internal start-up where the cross-functional team was working on refining the value proposition and defining a road to market. The focus would be on testing and validating ideas with customers.

Zorzano reflected on the challenges of using Lean Startup: 'It was very hard for me. I'm extremely technical. But over time, I began talking to customers and gained experience on questions to ask or questions that were asked of me. These things were not obvious to me as a technical person. Now I meet with other colleagues of mine and when I see that they're not used to this method-ology, I ask them about their customers, what are customer needs, and I now approach the work from an evidence-based and customer-based focus.'

IAMMY and Thinking Things show both unsuccessful and more successful projects in the Telefonica Lean Elephant process. The former shows the early stage of thinking when the project was getting going, and to the organization's credit, the project was killed before too much time and resource were expended on it. This can be quite difficult inside large companies. Pet projects develop a strong internal support network, and live on long after they should have been cancelled. Thinking Things is really an early use of IoT (Internet of Things) technology, and Telefonica's Lean Elephants process is helping them find real markets and real customers in the consumer space for IoT. Consumer IoT is only now (spring 2019) finding real uses and markets. Yet in 2011 Telefonica was already studying possible early uses for it.

Scaling Up Lean Elephants

Beginning in 2014, innovation project submissions were opened up to the entire CCDO (Chief Commercial Digital Organization of 7000 people, 5 percent of the Telefonica Group, ten times the size of its R&D organization). People submitting ideas needed to be willing to lead the projects, as a way for R&D to identify, attract, and retain 'intrapreneurs' in the company. If the idea was picked, the person could spend ninety days to work on the idea with I+D without losing their existing job. At the end of the ideation phase, if things didn't work out, they could return to their prior job. 'This is a big deal for a company like Telefonica and for the types of people who work at Telefonica', said Small. 'For an entrepreneur, leaving a job for 90 days is easy to do, but for us, it's intentionally a test to see if these are the type of people we want. If they spend all their time focusing on guaranteeing their jobs, then they might not be the right people for us.'

In fact Ian Small walks the talk: in one of the regular communication mails to employees he made a point of praising the work of a lady in a discontinued innovation project where the project had been killed. Nonetheless, Small noted, her work had been superb, she was recognized accordingly and now has received a new compelling assignment. This is another critical step in managing Lean Startup inside a large company. Failure is a necessary part of the Lean Startup process, and failing early is something to recognize, rather than making it a firing offense. When people's jobs are perceived to be at risk, the resulting projects they will choose to work on become very low-risk and incremental. Instead of facing the largest risks upfront, people seek the projects where the likelihood of success (and keeping their jobs) is greatest. This is completely against the theory of Lean Startup.

In scaling the Lean Elephant process inside Telefonica, the team used three Lean Startup reference pillars to shape its innovation efforts:

1. **Start small and aim high:** the level of ambition in the innovation projects must be high. They need to bring the possibility of a global reach and the potential to make an impact in everyday life and business. This does not mean that they will burn lots of resources to start with or that they need to show full potential from day one, quite the contrary. Projects, especially at the beginning, work just with bare minimum resources, and then investment increases as the project progresses with validated learnings. More budget comes only when the uncertainty has been significantly reduced, and the market opportunity has been sufficiently validated.

2. **Iterate fast to achieve efficiency in each of the maturation stages:** this means both scaling *down* the initiatives that are too early in time, immature or unfocused, while fueling *up* the ones that show traction from external customers. Therefore, product investment decisions conducted along the Lean Elephant process rely not only on technological trends, but also on a profound understanding on which markets the digital customers will form in the upcoming years. This also greatly changes the budgeting process for these projects, from an annual process to a milestone-driven process.

3. **Fail fast, fail cheap and make sure you learn along the way:** instead of devoting large quantities of energy and resources to increase the chance of success of a few projects, Telefonica now thinks it is wiser to launch many more probes, while lowering the overall risk by minimizing the failure cost for each project.[15]

To date, Lean Elephants has been a success. The company calculates that its time to market has accelerated by a factor of 2.6. The company is conducting

45 percent more R&D projects (using the same budget level as before), while spending 48 percent less per project. The savings in cost and in time show the business benefits that an effective Lean Startup process can deliver, once it is adapted appropriately to a large company environment.

But the company knows that it is not done with changing its culture to reflect Lean thinking throughout the organization. As Ian Small observed, 'The ultimate goal is not to have 200 people sitting in a corner of an organization thinking about innovation, but to have the whole company thinking about innovation... Inside my organization, we now understand Lean Startup and the thinking, but do 140,000 other employees at Telefonica understand it? No, not yet. When we get out beyond the test phase to scale the product inside an operating business unit, and then we start talking about learning and adapting while we're in market, it's still like we're speaking Swahili.'[16]

Is this Lean Elephants approach going to be sustainable over time at Telefonica? It is still early days. As of now, Lean Elephants is also not consuming much money. If a recession were to hit Telefonica again (the company suffered significantly during the financial crisis of 2009–12), the R&D budget would likely get hit hard. It may be that the Lean Elephant approach might fare better than the traditional approach, given its lower costs. But the advocates of the traditional innovation approach will try to save their own budgets and jobs. So the Lean Elephants cannot rest on its early laurels, but will have to deliver even more business results in future.

Conclusion

Eric Ries and Steve Blank have made a fundamental contribution to the study and practice of entrepreneurship with the concept of Lean Startup. One could argue that they have done more to advance this field in the past eight years than an army of entrepreneurship academics have generated over the past two decades. As they have taught us, a startup is not a smaller version of a large company. The business plan process than governs the operations of large companies, in turn, is a poor way for an entrepreneur to launch her new business.

In this chapter, I have argued for a corollary concept: a large company is not simply a larger version of a startup. And it is an error simply to tell large companies to 'be like a startup'. This advice ignores the fact that large companies have existing businesses, have already scaled up their business models, and created processes to execute those businesses at a scale most startups can only dream of. The presence of these existing businesses and their associated processes create an entirely different context for doing Lean Start-ups inside a company.

Lean Startup processes must be adapted, if they are to work inside large companies. Telefonica's Lean Elephants approach is one example of a thoughtful adaptation. It requires a change to processes, but also to the culture of the large organization, and even the very mindset used by the organization. Open Innovation comprises an important aspect of those changes. And as in Chapter 4, one must move past the initial bright, shiny objects in the front end of the innovation process, and instead focus on delivering results to the back end of the innovation process, inside the business units and in the market, in order to sustain success. With an adapted Lean Startup approach, innovation units can find the early customers they need to engage their internal business units, and get their projects through the Valley of Death.

Chapter 5 review points:

1. Lean Startup is a new and exciting process to discover new business opportunities, and new business models.
2. Just as startups are not tiny versions of large companies, so too are large companies not simply large versions of startups. Lean processes must be adapted in large companies, if they are to be effective.
3. Lean Startup inside large companies requires careful internal negotiations with senior management, as well as getting out of the building to find customers.
4. Open Innovation can complement and extend Lean Startup processes. Both use resources efficiently, while Open Innovation leverages other people's resources and shares risk.
5. Lean Startup processes can help internal innovation projects overcome the Valley of Death inside large organizations, particularly if they help obtain new paying customers.
6. Telefonica provides a good example of Lean Startup inside a large company. It has reduced costs by 48 percent per project, increased its speed to market by 260 percent, and pursued 45 percent more chances to innovate within the same budget.

6

Engaging with Startups to Enhance Corporate Innovation

The innovation world these days is abuzz with excitement about startup companies. Large companies themselves often seek to employ collaborations with startups to advance their own innovation agendas. For example, in John Chambers' recent book *Connecting the Dots*, a man who led Cisco as its CEO for twenty-four years celebrates what startup companies can do that is hard for large companies to do. It seems like an ideal match: the energy and focus of startups, combined with the resources and scale of a large company.

Yet, nothwithstanding Chambers' enthusiasm, there are many pitfalls in these kinds of collaborations. Many past efforts of capitalizing on the complementarities between both worlds have not lived up to their expectations and were quietly abandoned. Just as there is a Valley of Death between the innovation units of companies and their downstream business units (discussed at length in Chapter 4), so too is there a big gap between external startups and corporates. This gap between the corporate and startup ways of working poses real challenges to getting both sides together. Corporations are hard to approach for startups, cultural differences often lead to misunderstandings, and different organizational clock speeds for making decisions take their toll along the way.

In this chapter, we will explore both the opportunities and the challenges of large companies collaborating with startups.[1] We've already seen in this book how it is not enough to find or access a new technology—one must transfer it and absorb it into your own organization to obtain real business results from it. That applies to corporations collaborating with startups as well. During the last few years, corporate efforts to reach out to the startup ecosystem seem to be on the increase. In its quest for speed and innovation, the tech industry, in particular, has produced a variety of ways of engaging with startups. Established models, such as corporate venture capital, are now complemented by newer models that seem to better bridge the gap between both worlds—at least in some cases. As I will discuss, there is no single best way to engage with one

Open Innovation Results. Going Beyond the Hype, and Getting Down to Business. Henry Chesbrough, Oxford University Press (2020). © Henry Chesbrough.
DOI: 10.1093/oso/9780198841906.001.0001

or more startup companies. Instead, one must choose the model that best aligns with your objectives in collaborating with them.

Startups Bring Opportunities to Corporates

Let's start with the opportunities that startups can bring to large companies in the innovation process. Producing disruptive innovation is something that startups are particularly well suited to provide. Whether it is Facebook or Tesla Motors, it is often startups, not established corporations, who come up with the 'next big thing' to create new markets and unseat longstanding incumbent firms in various industries. Nor is this limited to a few outstanding examples. Astute observers such as Rita McGrath opine that achieving sustainable competitive advantage is no longer feasible in many fast-moving industries.[2] We've already examined the rapid pace of innovation from exponential technologies as well in Chapter 1. These perspectives imply a need for large companies to move much faster than they are used to moving, lest they be left behind in the innovation race.

Recent years have seen a surge of entrepreneurial activity that moves at this rapid pace. Founders of tech ventures today are in a situation that allows them to bring their ideas to market at much lower cost than even twenty years ago. Moreover, an entire system of supporting institutions (including incubators, accelerators, legal and financial experts, financial backers, and marketing and technical consultants) is ready to help steer a new venture through its early days. Many would-be corporate partners overlook this surrounding ecosystem when they consider startup collaborations, or mimicking these startups with their own internal ventures. The presence of a vibrant support system for startups allows them to be more capable than their small size might imply, precisely because they can leverage the experience and accumulated knowledge found in this support system.

One thing startups don't need from large companies is corporate capital. Angel investors and venture capitalists are plentiful, as are startup incubators, co-working spaces, and government-funded support schemes. The US National Venture Capital Association, for instance, reports a record $70 billion of VC investment in 2017.[3] The National Business Incubator Association recorded more than 1250 startup incubators in the US and estimated that more than 7000 of them to exist worldwide.[4] Nowadays, there are also crowdfunding sites like Indiegogo or Kickstarter, that can provide seed capital and early market validation to startups, even before they have raised any outside equity capital. So there are a wealth of sources of money for entrepreneurs to tap, as they look to launch their new venture.

In addition to these supporting institutions, startup founders nowadays have access to new methodologies and tools to shape their venture. We already discussed Lean Startup methods in chapter 5. Business schools worldwide teach entrepreneurship classes, offer startup clinics, and hold startup competitions. Many graduates from leading business schools today are eschewing the conventional investment banking or consulting jobs to start up their own companies. A record 18 percent of the Stanford MBA class of 2013 decided to do so. There are at least ten different sources of startup funding available to students on the UC Berkeley campus. Research agencies, such as the National Science Foundation with its Innovation Corps program, increasingly encourage engineers and scientists to bring their basic research results to market through embracing the Lean Startup methodology we discussed in Chapter 5.[5]

There are three consequences that flow from this environment that supports numerous robust startups. First, corporations must be able to screen, identify, work with, and monitor larger numbers of startups than before. In some cases, companies want to work with lots of startups at the same time, not just one or two. This translates into a need for faster decision making by companies across many more possible relationships. (Or, if you prefer the startup parlance, corporates need scalable engagement processes to work with multiple startups.) Second, companies must develop an attractive value proposition towards startups—showing how the company can add value to startups that already have access to independent VCs, incubators, and other support institutions. As stated above, it's an error to assume that startups simply want corporate investment. Thanks to the rich ecosystem around them, any decent startup already has easy access to money.[6]

Finally, companies need to be clear on what they want to get out of their engagement with startups. That is, the company's strategic goals should determine the right model(s) of engagement they employ in working with startups. There isn't a 'one size fits all' organizational model; rather, companies must select the right model for the right kind of collaboration they want.

Traditional Models of Engaging with Startups: Influence through Equity

Let's start with some of the more traditional models that companies have used to engage with startup companies. These models include Corporate Venture

Capital (CVC) and inside-out incubators that launch new ventures, or spin-offs. Both models employ equity ownership by the corporation to achieve some degree of control over the startups.

Corporate Venture Capital

An obvious way for a company to engage in entrepreneurial activity is to finance it. Equity stakes in promising external startups allow a corporation to keep an eye on interesting technologies and markets. Their ownership stake can influence the decisions of their portfolio companies, and the company potentially might make a financial profit if the venture is later sold to an acquiring company at a high price, or goes public with an Initial Public Offering (IPO). In some cases, corporate venture corporations use their preferential insights gained as (co-) investors to fully acquire a particularly promising startup themselves. A recent example of this mode of acquiring a startup that one had previously invested in is Google Ventures' investment in Nest. Nest was eventually acquired by Google at a price of $3.2 billion.

With its initial Nest investment, Google Ventures probably intended to get a foot into the nascent Internet of Things market. Hardware plays a key enabling role in this market, but producing hardware is outside of Google's core competencies. The Internet of Things, however, is also predicted to produce unprecedented amounts of data, the mining of which is clearly of strategic importance for Google. Equipped with insights and a better understanding of the market thanks to its venture arm's investment, Google might have come to the conclusion that hardware, such as produced by Nest, was the best means to get access to this promising new data pool. As a result of this insight, Google later acquired all of Nest.

The idea of corporate venture capital has been around since the 1960s, with several ups and downs since then.[7] Most companies create a separate corporate venture entity that is exclusively funded by the sponsoring corporation. This setup is seen to provide the flexibility, speed, and freedom required by its management team to successfully operate in the fast-moving venture capital world. At the same time, however, the mission of corporate venture capital (CVC) entities is more complex than that of their independent peers in several ways. Corporate VCs not only pursue financial performance, but should also support their corporate parent's strategic goals (e.g., by backing startups making complementary products and services to those already provided by the corporation). Additionally, they should identify and encourage mutual collaboration in R&D and operations where this seems useful for the parties involved.[8]

The ties to the large company make corporate venture investments a double-edged sword for young entrepreneurs. While the large firm's technical and market insights can smooth the path to success, being bound to a big player in the industry might limit the startup's freedom to pivot and to work with or sell to competitors of that large corporation. Moreover, corporate agendas can change over time as well, such that what began as a strategic investment might become irrelevant later on. On the positive side, however, corporate backing might lead to increased credibility for the startup on the market or provide access to experts and specialized equipment of the corporation. Recent research shows that corporate venture capital funding has a positive effect on those startups that require specialized complementary assets and/or operate in particularly uncertain environments.[9]

Corporate venture capital is an important market force today, providing about 47 percent of 2018 overall venture capital invested in 2018, according to the US National Venture Capital Association.[10] In China, the role of CVC is even a larger percentage of the venture capital invested than in the US, with CVC players like Alibaba, Tencent and Baidu accounting for as much as half of total VC investment in some years.

However, CVC's potential to harness the innovation potential of startups is limited by the aforementioned boundary conditions under which it makes sense for startups to accept corporate investors. CVC processes take time for corporations to execute—in scanning potential investment candidates, in due diligence prior to making an investment, in the monitoring costs of the many board meetings of the startup, and in discussing possible exits for the venture. The time required slows down the ability of corporations to keep pace with startups, and particularly limits corporates' ability to work with multiple startups at the same time. Put differently, CVC doesn't scale well across multiple startups.

Inside-out Corporate Incubators

Not all smart ideas and promising technologies are found out in the wild—in some cases, they are born in the corporate environment, but do not fit with the current core business or business model. To profit from such cases of 'misfit' internal innovation projects (also known as false negatives, as we saw in Chapter 2), corporate incubators have emerged as a means to bring them to market as new companies. Much like independent incubators, corporate incubators provide the nascent venture with funding, co-location, expertise, and contacts. The intention is to provide the founding team with a startup-like environment in which radical innovation can grow better than in the slow and bureaucratic parent organization. If successful, the grown-up spin-off will be able to conquer new markets independently or be reintegrated as a separate division. As we saw in Chapter 5, Lean Startup processes are a rigorous, effective way to explore outside the company's current business to discover new business models.

These corporate startup incubators, in general, have a mixed track record. Many resources, including expensive equipment and customer access, can potentially be shared. And having an internal incubator can allow projects that lack a natural home inside one of the business units to continue development until the market opportunity becomes clearer. On the downside there is a risk of overprotection through corporate backing, which might increase the likelihood of later failure. Further, close ties to the mother corporation often prevent incubator-based startups from pursuing partnerships with their parent's competitors or from developing competing products that might disrupt the parent company.

An early example of corporate incubation took place in Xerox's PARC research facility, which opened in 1970 and spun off successful companies such as 3Com and Adobe. The Lucent New Ventures group is a similarly successful example. Established in 1997 to commercialize non-core inventions from its Bell Labs, the hidden gem was sold by Lucent in early 2002 in an attempt to fill its urgent need for cash.[11]

More recently, in mid-2014, Bosch launched its 'Startup Platform' corporate incubator.[12] This incubator is designed to take up ideas from corporate research or other parts of the organization that would drop out of the standard innovation process due to their lack of relevance for Bosch's established businesses. To pursue a promising idea, the originating team transfers to the incubator where it receives complementary services, coaching, and funding. It can also reach out to get support from established Bosch units and specialists as needed. The incubator is intended to facilitate early market exposure and pivoting for the startup and to shield it from corporate complexity.

After a Bosch startup successfully spends its early days in the incubator and gets traction on the market, the goal is to integrate it back into an existing business unit or create a new unit inside the company to commercialize it. Spinning it off or selling it to another corporation is a secondary option for 'real' misfits, but in general the idea is to drive corporate innovation by reintegrating startups once they have their products and business model ready to be scaled up.

The inside-out incubators have an important role to play in a healthy corporate innovation process. They provide more opportunities for technical staff to see their projects tested in the market, even when those projects aren't well connected to the company's core business. But like CVC, launching each of these companies and reviewing their subsequent progress and deciding whether to fold them in or spin them out—all this takes a lot of meetings and time. It doesn't scale easily either.

Lightweight Models of Engaging with Startups: Built to Scale

Recent years have seen the rise of new ways in which large corporations engage with startups that do scale. These new models are different from previous models in that corporate ownership is not typically involved. In addition, the programs are tailored to allow the corporation to engage with a larger number of startups at the same time. The programs are designed to act as complements to existing startup support ecosystem offerings and do not provide an incubator-like level of services. The result is a more lightweight governance process that lets corporations move faster in working with startup firms. More subtly, companies relinquish control over these startups, while retaining influence over their development. This is the secret to how companies can move much more quickly in working with startups. These are processes that are ready to scale. Breadth, rather than depth, is the focus here.

The Startup Perspective

One error in many corporate initiatives that seek to engage with startups is a failure to understand the perspective of startup firms when they contemplate a corporate collaboration. At the early stages of a collaboration, startup firms worry that companies will steal their ideas. At later stages, startups are often frustrated by how long it takes for the corporate partner to make critical decisions that are necessary for the startup to succeed.

For startups, engaging with a large corporation is greatly simplified if a startup program is in place that anticipates and responds to these concerns. With the program, the corporation establishes an interface that is designed to work with nascent companies and to meet them halfway on these concerns. It forgoes many of the bureaucratic processes usually encountered in relationships with large corporations, such as lengthy vendor qualification processes or strict certification requirements. Instead, the corporation establishes a simpler process that is intended to create proofs of concept (POCs). This project-based approach focuses the activity, reduces the risk to the corporation, and does not influence the future course of the startup the way a corporate venture capital investment would. These characteristics address some of the fears that prevent startups from collaborating openly.

There are two types of these lightweight startup programs: one (outside-in) serves to identify existing startups' technology and evaluate its usefulness for the sponsoring corporation; the other one (inside-out) seeks to establish the use of the corporation's technical platform by other startup businesses.

Outside-In Startup Programs

In this model, the focus is on making interesting startup products or technologies available to the sponsoring organization by enabling multiple startups to elaborate and deliver on their ideas. The corporation profits from a head start over its competitors and can extend its existing business into 'hot' areas by profiting from external startup innovation. The format allows the corporation to pursue multiple interesting approaches in parallel via each of the many startup companies it incubates, which leads to faster mutual learning and a more thorough exploration of a new market space for the sponsoring corporation than it could hope to do if it relied only on its own resources.

AT&T Foundry

AT&T Foundry is a good example of such a process. This program was launched by US telecom giant AT&T in 2011 and today comprises five co-working locations (four in the US and one in Israel).[13] The Foundry acts as a proxy that interfaces between the complexity of AT&T's regular organization of 270,000 staff and the dynamic startup world.

The working mode of the Foundry is designed to be as close to the startup way of doing things as possible. The process starts with a Call for Proposals in various problem areas. Potentially interesting startups who respond to the call get the chance to pitch their idea at a Foundry event. In roughly 10 percent of cases, this pitch results in a joint project with the Foundry and its scope and goal are recorded in a two-page project document. Each Foundry hosts an attorney or contracting team experienced in working in the fast-paced environment to take care of contracts and paperwork quickly.

The Foundry model is built for speed. Each project is given a fixed deadline of twelve weeks to create a POC. AT&T does not take equity at this stage, nor does it claim any IP from the startup. No confidential disclosure agreements are signed. To meet this deadline, a joint team of Foundry employees, additional AT&T experts, and startup founders gets together to work towards the common goal and deliver a useable POC that can be presented to a regular AT&T business unit.

In perhaps 80 percent of the cases, the POCs that result from the Foundry process are rejected by AT&T's businesses. In these instances, the entrepreneur leaves the Foundry, with the knowledge that it has gained from the collaboration, and still owning all of her IP and equity in her venture. In the cases where the business units *are* excited, the traditional contracting process starts. Only then does the startup's role change into that of a regular technology supplier of the receiving business unit, with the NDA, vendor qualification, and other processes that this requires.

One example of this process came from a startup named SundaySky. During a Foundry pitch session to present its technology of inserting personalized coupons into video streams, the idea came up to employ the same technology for a personalized video bill for AT&T wireless customers. So SundaySky came to the Foundry. Then, twelve weeks later, a joint prototype was presented and used to convince AT&T executives of its potential. Customers could now have access to a personalized audio and video explanation of their individual telephone bill. In the pilot, 85 percent of pilot customers found it useful and the video reduced support costs on AT&T's side. These facts required an experiment to demonstrate the validity of this idea. And AT&T was able to get this experiment done in twelve short weeks. Many companies would need twelve weeks just to decide whether or not to do the experiment! Meanwhile, the startup can still pursue its initial intended market for its technology, and now its reputation is enhanced by a key reference customer, AT&T.

Another example is that of Intucell, a four-person startup that claimed it knew how to massively improve reliability and speed in AT&T's wireless network—only that it did not own the equipment needed to prove that point. One twelve-week Foundry project later, the technology had been proven and is implemented in all of AT&T's networks today. Speed and reliability went up 10 percent, while tower overloading was reduced by 30 percent.

In both of these examples, a few more months were needed by regular AT&T units and the startups to fully flesh out the final product that originated from the Foundry prototype and bring it to market. This time span, however, remains much faster than AT&T's usual innovation cycle.

Intel has explored this approach in wearables technology. The company realized that wearables technology was accelerating, but it did not know what kinds of chips these products would need. To enhance its own learning, Intel invited fifty companies into its own incubator, where it could collaborate and learn with them at close quarters. Its experience has been documented in Andre Marquis and Manav Subodh's book *Hypershift*.[14]

Inside-Out Platform Startup Programs

Outside-in startup programs try to harness a new technology for the corporation and put the startup into the role of a supplier. The platform model reverses this logic: here the goal is to get startups to build their products using corporation-supplied technology to expand the market for the corporation, an inside-out Open Innovation approach. Platforms have become an attractive model of innovation nowadays. Platform innovation occurs when an ecosystem of companies produces complementary innovations and thereby strengthens the common platform.[15] Ideally, a large corporation can position itself as a platform leader and take profit from every innovation that is sold on the platform—think of the app economy, which was enabled by the Apple iOS and Google Android operating systems and gives the two corporations a 30 percent revenue share of every app sold.

SAP Startup Focus

A good example of this inside-out approach is software vendor SAP. SAP's traditional business was as a leading enterprise software provider, producing software solutions that help large companies run their business. However, when the company released its new product HANA in late 2010, something was different. This product was built on a revolutionary in-memory technology that could process enormous amounts of data at incredible speed. To its credit, SAP realized that such an improvement in speed would likely result in many new opportunities to employ its technology, and that it couldn't find all of these on its own. It needed to attract lots of startup firms to use HANA in their offerings, to serve their markets in new, faster ways. SAP wanted to become a platform company that could attract lots of startups to use HANA.

Against this backdrop SAP decided to launch Startup Focus at its Sapphire customer conference in Spring 2012. SAP leaders thought that they needed to attract at least one hundred developers to use HANA by the time of its Fall conference six months later, and then needed to attract more startups after that. This meant that SAP couldn't work closely with one or two startups. It needed to develop a standardized approach to achieve the required scale of activity and applications within a short period of time.

It worked. Within two years, more than 1500 startups had signed up for its Startup Focus program. And 60 percent of these startups were operating in areas that previously SAP was not serving, such as genomics, sports analytics, and targeted advertising. Meanwhile, the cost and risk for SAP in any individual startup's failure was very low. Every new startup only required a slight increase in support interactions, as well as some additional time-limited access to a development system in the Amazon AWS cloud.

It turned out to be a good thing that the Startup Focus initiative got going so fast. It took SAP eighteen months to negotiate its first HANA platform deal with SAS, another large software vendor. In the same 2012–13 timeframe, almost 1000 startups were added to the SAP program. The presence of so many startups added vital energy and credibility to HANA, at a time when it had not yet been adopted by any other large software companies. And the presence of lots of startups helped to convince large companies that HANA was for real, before SAP had many internal customers for it.

One could argue that the high-control tactics of equity investment and joint ventures would have backfired here. SAP needed to attract lots of startups quickly, so picking out a few for direct investment might have been seen as 'playing favorites' among the startups. If one or two startups had received an investment from SAP, the other startups might wonder why they did not as well. Indeed, the customers or investors of these startups might ask, 'why didn't SAP invest in you too?' to all the other startups in the program. To achieve scale, and to achieve it quickly, it was better to eschew such investments. To put it differently, SAP needed to let the market tell it where HANA could be best utilized, and SAP knew that it didn't know enough to place bets on where that might be.

Figure 6.1 below shows the combination of more traditional models with some of the new, more scalable modes of engagement with startup firms. The primary question a corporation needs to answer is which goals it wants to

	Direction of Innovation Flow	
	Outside-In	Inside-Out
Equity Involvement	Corporate Venturing Participate in the success of external innovation and gain strategic insights into non-core markets. Startup Program (Outside-In) Insource external innovation to stimulate and generate corporate innovation.	Corporate Incubation Provide a viable path to market for promising corporate non-core innovations. Startup Program (Platform) Spur complementary external innovation to push an existing corporate innovation (the platform).

Figure 6.1 Typology of corporate engagement models with startups and their key goals

achieve through its engagement. Does it want to insource entrepreneurial creativity (outside-in innovation) or utilize startup agility to push its own innovations to the market (inside-out innovation)? Is it looking for the insight, control, and upside potential provided by an equity stake, or is diversification of risk a key requirement? Figure 6.1 illustrates the goals behind the four models along these two dimensions.

The Equity Divide

The two more traditional models discussed here involve asset ownership, whereas the two newer models do not. Corporate venture capital, the first equity-based option, buys influence in interesting startups external to the corporation. The second one, corporate incubation, creates new startups as spin-offs from one's own internal 'misfit' ideas or technologies. Both types of engagement bring along organizational costs in addition to the nominal amount of the investment itself. These additional costs of equity could be summarized as: search and information costs (including the due diligence preceding the investment decision); bargaining costs (including negotiations with founders and further investors); and monitoring and enforcement costs (such as regular board meetings and governance activities).

In the case of corporate venture capital, these costs might be justified if the target startup is particularly instrumental in pursuing long-term goals that are directly relevant to the corporation's strategy. With an equity stake and a board seat, the corporate venture arm has access to first-hand insights and gets a say in the future direction of the venture.

In case of corporate incubation, the reasons to place equity also might be strategic, but is also supported by financial motives. Here, the corporation's R&D department has already come up with a technology or idea that, for whatever reasons, does not fit the current core business. The costs it took to accomplish this invention have already been incurred, and a chance to generate future revenues (instead of writing off the R&D already spent) might be more than welcome. The options here are to sell the intellectual property to another corporation[16] or to invest some additional money to bring it into a marketable stage in a spin-off in the corporate incubator. Strategic considerations, such as the potential to take the new venture back in as a new business unit in the future, are what drives this choice.

In the two non-equity models, by contrast, the question of control is secondary. The overall aim of these models is to help the corporation move faster in order to respond to opportunities emerging in its environment. Individual startup companies here are less important to the company, but collectively act to shift the corporation's market position. Increasing the number of programs available for the corporation (outside-in programs) create more options for the corporation to consider. Startups that populate the corporation's technical platform make the overall platform more capable and more attractive to the corporation's customers.

At a higher level of abstraction, the traditional models of startup engagement are based on a logic of control. Large companies often desire the ability to control an initiative from beginning to end. Yet this control comes at a real cost: it takes substantial time and effort to evaluate, execute, and monitor each startup engagement, potentially making the large company slower to move, and slower to adapt to changes in their environment. The newer models trade off this logic of control for a logic of influence. If startups engage with us on our terms, using our technology and our platform, we can win without controlling them. This is particularly true if and when we need lots of startups to engage with us. Large companies would do well to consider when a logic of influence better serves their strategic objectives in working with startups, instead of insisting upon complete control over the startup in all cases.

Chapter 6 review points:

1. Startups can be a powerful, effective ingredient in achieving your corporate innovation strategy. But startups worry that corporates are going to steal their ideas, and anyway are too slow in their decision-making.
2. Startups welcome corporate capital, but often their real needs are access to a corporation's latest tools, technologies, channels, and customers.

Large companies have multiple resources with which to engage startups. It isn't just about money.

3. Traditionally, large companies have deployed equity-based models of engagement, such as corporate venture capital. CVC has a role to play, but takes significant time and effort to manage. Equity-based models provide control, but don't scale.

4. Newer models of engagement with startups use a logic of influence, so that large companies can move faster and work with many more startups at the same time. These models relinquish control, but are built to scale.

7

Open Innovation Results in Smart Cities and Smart Villages

Throughout this book, we have examined the role of generation, dissemination, and absorption in getting real results from Open Innovation. In this chapter, we consider these issues in the context of the public sector. More particularly, we will explore how Open Innovation has—and has not—led to beneficial results for those employing it in the public sector.

The Promise of Open Innovation in Smart Cities

One of the first acts of the Obama Administration in 2009 was to sign an Executive Order that expanded access to public data maintained by various agencies of the Federal government. Competitions were launched. Citizen contributions were solicited. Intermediaries were hired with the task of connecting citizens with solutions to agencies who had need of them. Hackathons were organized to enlist citizen contributors. The www.data.gov website was created. Code for America was launched. The federal government even used the Open Innovation label for many of these initiatives. The focus of much of this work was on a concept called Smart Cities.

Smart Cities rested on a strong conceptual foundation. Scholars like Richard Florida have documented the growing importance of cities to innovation.[1] The critical mass of people, the growing diversity of people within cities, and the density of connections in those cities create a fertile soil for innovation. The acts of early Obama Administration were intended to extend and build upon these insights, to create a more accessible, more open, better understood government for its citizens.

The enthusiasm of the Federal government in that period was matched by a similar excitement within many leading cities in Europe and North America. The Smart Cities movement sought to enlist the population of these fertile seedbeds of innovation, to make local services and local decisions more available, more open, and more transparent to the citizenry. Cities such as

Open Innovation Results. Going Beyond the Hype, and Getting Down to Business. Henry Chesbrough,
Oxford University Press (2020). © Henry Chesbrough.
DOI: 10.1093/oso/9780198841906.001.0001

Amsterdam, Barcelona, or Copenhagen were leaders in this Smart Cities movement, along with New York, Boston, and San Francisco in the US.

There was another impetus for Smart Cities: the vendors of advanced information technology saw it as a powerful way to increase public spending on their products and services. Much of the 'smarts' in Smart Cities were going to come from better IT equipment, better networking, better applications, and better data management. Companies ranging from Cisco to IBM to Microsoft to Oracle and SAP could make a strong case for their wares to the excited managers of public IT budgets in the name of Smart Cities. Upgrading the cities' infrastructure would pave the way to realize the benefits of Smart Cities, and boost their sales in the process.

One particular example of how smarter infrastructure could help citizens benefit from innovation came from an app developed in Boston. This app tracked the flow of traffic in Boston and provided citizens with information on where there were traffic jams, and where traffic flowed smoothly. Interestingly, whenever the app detected a slowdown of traffic in a consistent place, where there was no known repair or other physical barrier present, the app would generate an alert to the road crews of the city. It was likely that there was a large pothole there, and this was what was slowing down the traffic. That detection could issue a ticket to the road repair crew, and quickly fix the pothole before it grew even larger. The result would be fast, efficient, effective government.

Other promising applications for more intelligent infrastructure including smart parking, and smart lighting. Smart parking would increase revenues for the city, by directing drivers to available parking spaces, while reducing the time spent circling in downtown areas in the search for such spaces. Smart lighting would use sensors to detect the presence of people near streetlights, and supply lighting whenever people were present, increasing safety and reducing crime. However, if no people were around, the amount of light would be much less, saving power and money for the city. Again, fast, efficient, effective government.

Little or No Results from Smart Cities

Since the time of this initial enthusiasm, however, it is fair to say that Smart Cities hasn't really delivered the results that it promised. In a series of papers reviewing the activities of eight different metropolises in Europe and North America, Esteve Almirall and Jonathan Wareham of Esade Business School and their colleagues document an initial wave of positive activity, followed by disappointing results.[2] They find that although many worthy experiments were implemented with the best intentions, the overall results from these efforts for citizens in those cities have been modest at best. While there is now more smart parking (which happily pays for itself via the extra revenue provided), and a bit more smart lighting (sadly, there is little or no additional revenue provided by this), these eight cities are not noticeably better off as a result of their involvement and investment in Smart Cities. In some places like Barcelona, the effort has even been discontinued, to be replaced by initiatives that seek to provide more social and economic inclusion for citizens, without any further investment in technology.

Almirall, Wareham, and their co-authors offer numerous reasons for this disappointing result. But in the context of this book, we can view the results through the generation/dissemination/absorption lens. Though there were a number of technological possibilities generated by Smart Cities (generation), these did not spread very widely at all beyond a small number of developers and enthusiasts in the target cities, and did not extend much beyond those target cities (dissemination). Even within the target cities where these actions were taken, the vast majority of citizens were completely unaware of their existence. The developers, in turn, found very few users willing and able to download and actively engage with their apps (absorption).

As of this writing, there are still hardly any 'killer apps' that are driving citizens to access and download Smart Cities applications. Indeed, it is hard to locate these apps on iOS's AppStore and Google's Play. And apps that are popular in one city are not much used in other cities, greatly limiting their ability to scale beyond a local market. So as a result, there was only a very limited amount of diffusion, with no scaling of results from one city to many others. And very little of this has been absorbed into these cities, with the exception of more, smarter parking.

There is a new, second generation of Smart Cities development that is emerging now that is more promising. Part of this greater promise is that cities are now taking steps to connect developers with more information about the context of each city's activities and processes, so that the developers can make more thoughtful apps that reflect this deeper context. This new approach to dissemination will help developers create more effective and more useful responses. An unfinished challenge is getting a common data format for cities' data to be shared widely, such that apps for one purpose in one city can easily access the relevant data in another city to run similarly well there. Some thoughtful city IT leaders are seeing their roles evolve to data access facilitators, to enable this improved absorption.

In sum, we see in Smart Cities the pattern that we have observed throughout this book: the generation of new technological possibilities by itself creates little or no business or social value. For that value to be realized, these possibilities must be widely disseminated throughout the society, and then must be absorbed into the business models and practices of a great many people in that society.

We turn now to an even newer initiative, that applies some of these technological possibilities in a more challenging economic environment. It too will require generation, dissemination, and absorption, in order to achieve a lasting social benefit.

Smart Villages: Scaling Down Open Innovation to the Village Level

While Smart Cities initiatives are transitioning to a second generation of development and absorption in advanced economies in the West, a new venture seeks to take Open Innovation concepts to get better results in a very different setting—a rural village. Unlike the major cities of Europe and North America, rural areas lack the density, the wealth, and the infrastructure to benefit much from the Smart City offerings. And while more than half of the world's population now lives in cities, that still leaves just under half of the world's population who still live in rural areas. What can Open Innovation concepts do here?

Traditional rural development approaches focused on the lack of income and wealth in rural areas, and sought to improve lives by injecting government and philanthropic aid into these areas. The intent was to build skills, improve the local economy, and unlock a virtuous cycle of rising income, leading to better living standards, leading to more education and better skills, inaugurating another cycle of improvement.

However, a recent critique of these aid-driven approaches to rural development have found that they are not achieving the results that are intended. Instead, traditional aid programs have often led to unintended consequences, negative outcomes, and reduced economic growth, according to economist Dambisa Moyo, author of *Dead Aid: Why Aid is Not Working and How There is a Better Way for Africa*. Aid, Moyo argues, 'has failed to deliver the promise of sustainable economic growth and poverty reduction ... it has not lived up to expectations. It remains at the heart of the development agenda, despite the fact that there are very compelling reasons to show that it perpetuates the cycle of poverty and derails sustainable economic growth.'[3]

One of the biggest problems with traditional aid is that it instills dependence. Finite, limited aid programs that address specific goals can help alleviate important problems, but much aid in low-income countries is pervasive and essentially continuous, writes Moyo. 'Without the inbuilt threat that aid might be cut, and without the sense that one day it could all be over, African governments view aid as a permanent, reliable, consistent source of income and have no reason to believe that the flows won't continue into the indefinite future. There is no incentive for long-term financial planning, no reason to seek alternatives to fund development, when all you have to do is sit back and bank the cheques.'[4]

Aid can also harm otherwise successful local businesses and, paradoxically, create the need for more aid. Moyo cites the scenario of a mosquito-net maker in Africa who employs ten people who altogether support as many as 150 people.[5] An influx of free mosquito nets from a well-intentioned aid program helps some people in the area but puts the net-maker out of business and makes the 150 people his business was supporting suddenly dependent on aid.

Furthermore, aid is often provided based on what donors and policymakers believe the targeted community needs. 'So aid dependency only further under-mines the ability of Africans, whatever their station, to determine their own best economic and political policies', according to Moyo.[6]

Yet, 'more than US$2 trillion of foreign aid has been transferred from rich countries to poor over the past fifty years', writes Moyo.[7] One reason: aid programs are frequently evaluated in the short term, which is largely irrelevant to their effect on the target region's long-term problems. 'Aid effectiveness should be measured against its contribution to long-term sustainable growth, and whether it moves the greatest number of people out of poverty in a sustainable way. When seen through this lens, aid is found to be wanting.'[8]

Is there a better way to unleash the economic potential of rural areas?

The Smart Villages Experiment

The Smart Villages initiative[9] focused on the development of a Smart Village in the village of Mori, in the state of Andhra Pradesh (AP), India. The chief minister of the state, N. Chandrababu Naidu, recently completed a series of visits to rural villages in his state of 60 million residents, 35 million of whom lived in rural areas. Chief Minister Naidu sought to create a new policy mechanism to address the many unmet needs of his constituents in AP. In consultation with outside experts, including professors from UC Berkeley's

Haas School of Business, he decided to launch an experiment called Smart Villages. According to Professor Solomon Darwin, 'A Smart Village is a community empowered by digital technologies and Open Innovation platforms to access global markets.' As will be seen, this initiative was primarily funded by private organizations, with the state government providing leadership and a supporting role, but only a small portion of the money. This approach promises to increase the scalability and economic sustainability of the initiative to meet the needs of rural people in India.

The initiative began in the summer of 2016 in Mori Village. There are many unmet needs of rural villagers in India, and this initiative seeks to create a positive virtuous circle, to lift skills, incomes, and open markets, so that empowered villagers can escape the trap of rural poverty that imprisons so many in India and elsewhere.

Villagers' Needs

Mori's 8000 residents are spread across the village's 1316 acres. Many of them work in the rice, coconut, and textiles industries. Others process cashews or farm shrimp or mangoes.

Life in the village presents residents with constant challenges, including lack of access to basic resources such as health care, sanitation, and clean water. For example, there are approximately 800 total toilets in the village, leading to open defecation, which leads to active mosquito breeding. In turn, the mosquitoes spread malaria and dengue, a virus that is a leading cause of illness and death in the tropics and subtropics and for which there are not yet any vaccines to prevent infection.[10]

Healthcare access in the village is limited and, for many villagers, cost-prohibitive. One Mori resident described the situation: 'Healthcare is expensive. Since we are uneducated, we cannot question what the local village doctor says. Several people in villages like ours choose to approach godmen [spiritual healers] to cure their ailments. I have heard of cases where people's health has gone the detrimental route due to improper diagnosis, poor care, and lack of proper healthcare facilities.' Although Mori does have a small clinic, the nearest hospital is 25 kilometers away from the village. Limited access to care in rural areas is not unique to Mori: in fact, 80 percent of health care providers in India are in or near urban centers.[11]

The lack of good economic opportunities also presents villagers with challenges. For example, one villager described his work: 'I used to work as a daily wage worker in gruesome conditions at a textile mill, where, working full-time, I earned 30 Rupees [approximately 45 U.S. cents] a day.' Furthermore, mechanization and automation have destroyed many jobs in the handloom, pottery, handicraft, and goldsmith industries.

In the agriculture industry, farmers must cope with unpredictable access to water for irrigation, making it difficult to plan and produce good yields. Mori has a system of gates that release water through canals to farmers, but farmers say the water is not released when they need it, and sometimes no water is available. In addition, the village's lack of cold storage facilities means a large share of what food farmers do produce ultimately goes to waste. Farmers also lack access to current information on market prices for their crops and, as a result, often sell for less than they could. Thin margins mean farmers—80 percent of whom lease rather than own the land they farm—often struggle to make any profit after paying for supplies such as seeds and fertilizers.

Some farmers would like to grow higher margin crops, and the environment is well suited to growing lentils, peanuts, sesame, and avocado. However, knowledge of how to farm these crops is limited, as is access to education and information to increase the knowledge base. Furthermore, harvesting these crops is labor-intensive, and emigration makes finding a sufficient number of workers difficult. Compounding the labor shortage are government programs. For example, a jobs program in Mori employs residents to dig canals, perform maintenance work, and other tasks. Although this program provides some value to the village, it is not a source of sustainable, demand-based employment growth. It also discourages residents from going to work for farms, where they would earn lower wages for more physically demanding work.

Other farmers harvest shrimp, a high-margin product, from man-made ponds in the village. Salt is added to the water in these ponds for the shrimp, which increases the salinity of the soil in the village. Excess salts in soil hinder the growth of crops by limiting their ability to take up water.[12] Digging the shrimp ponds, which must be deep in order to be effective, also draws seawater into the aquifer, further salinizing the soil and reducing yields for other crops, such as rice. Although shrimping near rice fields is banned in order to prevent salinization damage, according to a survey of villagers, it is still practiced.

These and other village conditions have caused many residents to leave, seeking better lives in some of India's large cities and in the Middle East. Back in villages like Mori, emigration creates shortages of not just labor but also of educated and skilled workers. With opportunities lacking at home, many of the people with the most potential to improve village life are leaving. This trend exacerbates many problems, including the lack of teachers and local doctors. One doctor explains: 'There is urgent need for doctors, yet very few are willing to work here. My family is still living in the city. They are unable to settle here due to a lack of basic education, healthcare, and sanitation facilities. My income here is also meager in comparison to what I would have gotten by working in city hospitals or as a private medical practitioner.'

Previous Rural Development Initiatives

Mori and other villages in India have received government aid, such as through the jobs program described earlier. Another aid program is implemented at schools, where all children receive free lunches to help encourage attendance. Although these programs help villagers in the short term, they do not lay the foundation for sustainable economic development. The jobs program does not, for example, improve villagers' knowledge or skills. Free school lunches do help nourish students who may otherwise go hungry, but such a wide-ranging program is not sustainable without government funding. Creating economic opportunity for parents to feed their own children would help both the village and the government, which could reduce expenditures on aid while improving villagers' lives.

Many companies have long histories of giving to villages in the developing world, but charitable donations often have no connection to the companies' missions or core competencies, such as when an oil company contributes money to promote health and wellness initiatives. As a result, the effects are not sustainable, and the companies have no incentive to expand their efforts. In many cases, governments and companies have not involved villagers in the design of their aid programs; as a result, the programs often did not address villagers' actual needs (Table 7.1).

The Smart Village Project

The meaning of the term Smart Village follows the definition developed by Professor Solomon Darwin noted above. Specifically, Darwin states that a Smart Village meets six criteria:

- An ecosystem: the village leverages its resources, as well as those of surrounding villages, distant places, and other entities to generate revenue and lower its costs and risk.

Table 7.1 Comparison between development-led aid and Smart Villages approach

Development-led Aid initiatives	Smart Villages Initiative
During the period of substantial aid, local prices often become inflated, pushing many basic items out of reach for already poor residents.	Minimal staff in village, minimal impact on local prices.
Village residents acquired little or no skills that might help them be more productive.	Strong focus on skills development and training.
Residents were still kept away from larger markets, so much of the value that they produced was captured by middle-men.	Digital technology platforms enable direct linkage to local, regional, national and even international markets.
Corruption was endemic, reducing the amount of money that actually reached the local residents, and creating political barriers that last long past the end of the aid itself.	Digital technology platforms enable much greater transparency and reduce opportunities for corruption.
There was no way to scale any success beyond the immediate rural area.	Companies contributing talent and resources are looking to expand their markets, will scale once they understand what villagers want, and are willing to pay for.
Once the aid ended, little economic benefit remained.	The business models for the village and for the companies are sustainable, so market capitalist incentives will sustain the activities in the village.

- An economic development platform: the village allows external businesses access to its resources in order for both the business and the villagers to profit.
- A brand: the village creates an identity and becomes known for its unique value.
- A community: the village is a self-organized network of people who collaborate by sharing ideas, information, and resources to build a strong ecosystem. If and when projects fail, the community remains and rebuilds itself.
- A business model: the village creates value for its people and others outside the village by utilizing lean and cost-effective state-of-the-art technologies. The village captures some of the value it creates for itself.
- A sustainable unit: the village operates using a triple-bottom-line approach, focusing on people, profit, and the planet.

This definition underlies the design of the Smart Villages initiative. While Chief Minister Naidu strongly supports the initiative, he is not providing the majority of the funding for it. The target recipients are the villagers themselves, and the digital technologies are the delivery vehicle for the services in the initiative. Note that, unlike Smart Cities, there is little public investment in infrastructure, beyond digital connectivity in the village.[13]

The Role of Open Innovation

Open Innovation is based on the concept of harnessing knowledge flows from the outside in one's own innovation processes, and allowing unused knowledge to flow outside for others to use in their innovations, as we saw in Chapter 2. In a rural setting like Mori village, the participating companies are seeking to innovate new products and services for the 'bottom of the pyramid',[14] and to uncover effective business models to serve these people. Mori village is a classic testbed for these companies to use in their explorations. These villagers have many needs and few resources. This makes it hard for companies to know what products and services they will be willing and able to buy.

But if companies can identify these needs, it is likely that many, many other villages (40,000 in AP, more than 650,000 throughout India, and millions more across the developing world) will have similar needs, and be able to buy as well. The hypothesis for this experiment is that the needs of villagers in Mori village are likely to be similar to the needs of other rural villagers in Andhra Pradesh. When companies learn how to serve these needs profitably, they will have a market incentive to scale these solutions to other villages through private markets, without need of government support.

The pilot stage of the Smart Villages project succeeded in attracting more than forty companies and organizations to Mori village. These companies are not providing charity, however. They are making small business development investments to learn about the needs of rural villagers for products and services they can provide. Importantly, these investments will reveal what villagers value enough to pay for it directly with their own funds. This is a kind of business model discovery that we see in Lean Startup approaches to business model innovation, explored in Chapter 5 of this book.[15]

These companies are providing resources to the village for little or no money upfront from those villagers. But each participating company sees an opportunity to expand their sales to rural villagers, as a result of the Smart

Villages initiative. It is not another round of corporate charitable donations to the poor. It really is an example of Open Innovation, both for the companies and also from the perspective of Chief Minister Naidu. Previous approaches were government-led, with less input and support from the private sector. Moreover, what private sector participation there was, was primarily charitable, rather than business-driven. The Open Innovation approach is potentially more scalable, and sustainable.

There is a further ecosystem effect that is emerging in the Smart Villages project. About half of the forty companies are based in India, while the other half are international companies. The presence of one company in the village makes it more attractive for subsequent companies to also locate a person in the village. The result is a vibrant ecosystem of possible products and services for local villagers. Note that no single company or organization could martial all these disparate resources. It takes an ecosystem of organizations, all seeking to understand villagers' needs and their willingness to pay, to obtain this Open Innovation ecosystem. The experience in Mori village is thus a Proof of Concept, part of the generation phase of the experiment.

Dissemination of Smart Villages

The Smart Villages program did not include monies for disseminating the initiative to other villages in Andhra Pradesh, nor did it include monies for disseminating it to other states in India. However, there was significant thought given to dissemination nonetheless. The main avenues for dissemination were three:

1) The participating companies themselves were often willing and able to carry the initiative to other villages.
2) Local government officials, working under the government of Chief Minister Naidu, were sometimes willing to disseminate the initiative to other villages, particularly if the particular official had responsibilities in those other villages as well.
3) Local non-governmental organizations (NGOs) sometimes promoted the Smart Villages initiative to other communities and local universities, and served as a resource center for those who wanted more information.[16]

Part of the design was to recruit volunteers from each village to act as a guide for the Smart Villages team in each village. This volunteer would be trained by the staff, and would also liaise with the local government official responsible for that village. In this way, Smart Villages created a local presence in each village, without introducing many of the economic distortions that Dambisa Moyo wrote about in her critique of development aid in Africa.

As of this writing, the Smart Villages initiative is now active in over 400 villages in Andhra Pradesh, which is roughly 1 percent of all of the villages in that state, so the dissemination phase of the process has only just begun. There have also been feelers from three other states in India who are interested in launching the initiative as well. So the program is starting to develop outside of Andhra Pradesh.

Further dissemination, though, will depend in part on the success of the program in improving the lives of villagers. Are they able to absorb the results of the initiative?

Absorption of Smart Villages in Rural Settings

To date, the results of the Smart Villages initiative have been varied, but overall quite encouraging.

One important event was when Google chose to install its Google Free Space Optics technology in Mori village. Every villager was connected to the Internet at a low, affordable cost. Local interns and local Google personnel provided training on how to use the Internet, so that villagers could master the opportunities. This provided a wealth of information and communication services to villagers, as well as new sources of entertainment. Villagers could even apply for jobs, or bill for their services electronically and receive wire transfers.

One small but symbolic achievement was the expansion of the local textiles industry in Mori Village. Mori village is known for the high quality and unique design of its saris, but in the past the market for these saris was inevitably quite local, and reached through middlemen who appropriated most of the value. With the advent of access to the Internet, local sari makers were finally able to bypass these middlemen. Their sales of saris in the village grew ten-fold, while the price obtained by the sari makers also expanded by five times over the traditional price. This made a noticeable impact on the incomes of these sari makers. That in turn helped to validate the utility of the Internet in the village, as the textile makers shared the stories of their improved fortunes with others. This early success was critical to absorbing the experiment in the village.

Another success occurred in cashew processing, another local industry in Mori village. The ability to bypass middlemen, and also to obtain faster, more accurate market information for their crops in regional and national markets in India allowed cashew processors to expand their production ten-fold. Again, this helped to validate the use of the Internet in the village. More stories were shared among the villagers, and this success inspired other farmers to test what this new Internet could enable for their crops.

Yet there have also been problems. Change in rural villages is hard, and there is a serious question of whom should bear the risk for employing new technologies if the results are less than satisfactory. Few villagers are eager to be the first to try a new technology, even at no financial risk, if it puts their livelihood at risk. A farmer takes a huge leap of faith entrusting the year's entire crop to a technology he's never seen before. Failure is devastating to them financially. Introducing a product or service that the village doesn't need or doesn't comprehend how to use erodes trust in the entire initiative.

A challenging experience came through the use of the Internet to sign up to an e-commerce company's services. An Indian company called StoreKing provided inventory replenishment for rural shopkeepers, so that they could re-stock their wares by ordering online from StoreKing, instead of having to leave their shops to travel to restock. For many rural merchants in the Smart Villages initiative, this was a 'killer app' that made the Smart Village initiative very attractive.

Due to the positive response that StoreKing was receiving for its online service, the company decided to waive its sign-up fee to stimulate even greater adoption. While this was great for new merchants, it also had the effect of prompting those who had already paid the fee to ask for refunds. The company denied these refund requests, telling customers that they would instead receive credit that would be reflected in their StoreKing account. However, these customers were also told that the local master franchise was no longer a part of the StoreKing organization, and it was that master franchisor who would be the one responsible for providing this credit. StoreKing declined to take responsibility or resolve the refund issue, and the villagers were left empty-handed.

This had other effects. The Smart Villages intern who had helped these villagers sign up for the StoreKing service, who was an 'outsider' in that village, was held personally responsible for the corporation's failures by the local merchants. He was held responsible, despite having no connection to the company. The villagers considered the intern and the corporation to be one and the same. In fact, he was threatened seriously enough that he no longer felt physically safe in certain parts of the village.

In another pilot program, a rice paddy cutter was introduced to farmers by video. Farmers could purchase the equipment directly, with no middleman, for significant cost savings. But the delivery of the device was late, farmers had already lost their patience, and the delivered equipment's physical character-istics (color and other minor details) did not match what the farmers saw on the promotional video. The farmers suspected they were being tricked or cheated. The farmers wanted to go directly to the police to file a fraud complaint against the manufacturer.

As these latter examples show, some of the forty participating companies chose to address the opportunities in the initiative through a franchising approach. A local villager (or someone who lived nearby) would be appointed as the local franchisee for the company. If the franchisee performed well, then the absorption worked well. But situations where the company and the franchisee disagreed, or where the company changed a policy towards the villagers without allowing any retroactive adjustments, created friction.

The distribution channel issue is one that also negatively impacts absorp-tion. Being able to utilize the Internet to do direct marketing has the practical effect of eliminating middlemen who are increasingly superfluous. Yet these people are often well connected in their communities, and also with local government officials. Their imminent removal from the supply chain leads to hostility to the point of withdrawing political contributions to officials who won't 'protect' them.

There is something of a corollary issue with some of the local government officials. While many of the officials in Andhra Pradesh have been strong and effective supporters of the Smart Villages initiative, others complain that their traditional role of helping local business people obtain jobs and favors is vitiated by the new access to the Internet. These officials have many ways they can delay and frustrate the advance of Smart Villages, if they see no benefit for themselves in its deployment. These issues greatly affect the ability of rural villages to absorb new possibilities arising from Smart Villages.

In sum, the Smart Villages initiative is showing real promise. The concept has been validated, not least by the decision of forty independent businesses (about half of whom are based in India, the other half are international firms) to participate in the project. The dissemination of the concept is underway now, with expansion occurring both within Andhra Pradesh and also in other states in India. And the absorption is also taking root, as villagers in industries as diverse as textiles, retailing, and farming are realizing higher incomes and greater sales—and then telling their neighbors. But there are signs of resistance as well, owing to the negative impacts of the initiative on certain groups that previously thrived in the village system, as well as the go-to-market franchising strategies of some of the companies who participated.

The Contribution of Shared Value

Another perspective that informs the design of this initiative is that of Shared Value. Shared value, as Mark Kramer and Michael Porter define it, does not involve a company sharing the value it has already created; that is, it is not redistribution. Rather, 'it is about expanding the total pool of economic and social value'.[17] That is, shared value is an approach to innovation in which companies look for ways to grow and sustain their own businesses and create societal value by addressing society's needs and challenges.

By way of explanation, Kramer and Porter contrast the shared value approach to the fair trade movement, which focuses on paying higher prices to farmers for the same crops, thus reducing the profits of coffee roasters, a form of redistribution. 'A shared value perspective, instead, focuses on improving growing techniques and strengthening the local cluster of supporting suppliers and other institutions in order to increase farmers' efficiency, yields, product quality, and sustainability. This leads to a bigger pie of revenue and profits that benefits both farmers and the companies that buy from them.' Kramer and Porter cite studies of cocoa farmers in the Côte d'Ivoire that indicate fair trade increased farmers' incomes by approximately 10 to 20 percent, but shared value investments increased their incomes by more than 300 percent.

Indeed, at least one example of shared value has already arrived in India. Kramer and Porter explain: 'Thomson Reuters has developed a promising monthly service for farmers who earn an average of $2,000 a year. For a fee of $5 a quarter, it provides weather and crop-pricing information and agricultural advice. The service reaches an estimated two million farmers, and early research indicates that it has helped increase the incomes of more than 60 percent of them—in some cases tripling incomes.'

For companies, the first step in pursuing shared value opportunities is assessing their products and services in terms of how they address or create societal needs, benefits, and harms. Companies can also identify sources of shared value by changing their perspective on their relationships with suppliers. 'The traditional playbook calls for companies to commoditize and exert maximum bargaining power on suppliers to drive down prices—even when purchasing from small businesses or subsistence-level farmers', according to Kramer and Porter. However, marginalized suppliers' productivity and quality levels often stop growing or begin to fall. Companies can reverse this trend, thereby ensuring access to inputs and potentially reducing the total environmental impact of their products, by helping suppliers gain strength. We saw one example of this in Chapter 1, with Nestle's experience with coffee growers.

Companies that fail to build shared value in their markets will sooner or later find their ability to grow to become impaired. Companies must seek to grow the pie, in order to be able to sell more of their own wares over time. And companies working in Mori village possess extremely useful skills and knowledge that can help grow this pie, whether it is Ericsson helping to manage water with sensors, or Hiro delivering health care through its specially designed bicycles, or IBM providing farmers with better weather data to help them know when to plant, when to fertilize, and when to harvest.

Chapter 7 review points:

1. The dimensions of generation, dissemination and absorption apply in the public and social sectors, as well as in the private sector.
2. Smart Cities initiatives have generated a lot of possibilities, but to date have not delivered much social or business value. Much of the fault lies in not in the generation of technologies, but in the lack of dissemination and absorption of these initiatives beyond a narrow circle of specialists.
3. Open Innovation can play a critical role in addressing the needs of rural villagers by enticing profit-seeking companies to engage in business development research in rural markets. These companies, if successful, become agents of dissemination and scaling via markets.
4. Smart Villages is a promising new initiative for addressing the needs of villagers in poor, underdeveloped rural settings. However, the three dimensions of generation, dissemination, and absorption apply here as well.
5. To date, Smart Villages has achieved some degree of dissemination, and a limited degree of absorption. Smart Villages has created winners and losers. The latter can sometimes organize to thwart dissemination and absorption of new innovations like Smart Villages.
6. Shared Value provides a logical framework for companies to use as they evaluate opportunities to engage in under-served markets, such as those addressed by Smart Villages. Companies that fail to consider Shared Value may be limiting their growth, or even their continuing license to operate, in emerging markets.

8

Open Innovation Best Practices

If you have made it this far into this book, it is clear by now that innovation requires a lot more than simply creating or finding a cool new technology. In this chapter, we will briefly examine some of the Open Innovation practices at leading companies that demonstrate an entire innovation system at work, from generation to dissemination to absorption. That system indeed starts with a variety of mechanisms to create or search for promising new ideas and technologies. But that system continues with the thorough dissemination of that technology within the organization, and concludes with ways to integrate the technology into one or more business units in the company, who then take it to market.

By reviewing these examples, we can also discern some underlying principles that support and sustain Open Innovation inside these organizations. We can similarly discern some boundary conditions that are needed to sustain Open Innovation. If these conditions are not present, Open Innovation may not deliver its promised results inside the organization.

Procter & Gamble's Connect and Develop

One of the earliest and most successful collection of Open Innovation practices emerged at Procter & Gamble in the early 2000s. P&G had confronted a financial crisis in the year 2000, fueled by a series of missed financial targets that drove its stock price from over $150 to just $54 in a matter of months. The company replaced its CEO with an internal leader from its beauty care business, A. G. Lafley. Lafley had seen how Open Innovation had helped to grow new business in the beauty care segment, and felt strongly that a similar approach would pay dividends across the whole company. Connect and Develop was born.

As documented in a 2006 *Harvard Business Review* article by Larry Huston and Nabil Sakkab of Procter & Gamble,[1] Open Innovation has helped achieve significant cost savings and time savings. The Pringles Print initiative is one excellent example of these savings. P&G wanted to offer Pringles chips with

Open Innovation Results. Going Beyond the Hype, and Getting Down to Business. Henry Chesbrough, Oxford University Press (2020). © Henry Chesbrough.
DOI: 10.1093/oso/9780198841906.001.0001

pictures and words printed on each chip. Instead of investing internal time and money to research edible dies and food-based printing techniques, they found a bakery in Bologna, Italy that had an ink-jet method for printing messages on cakes and cookies. P&G worked with the bakery to adapt this technology to the Pringles application. They got the product developed at a fraction of the cost, and got it to market in half the time it would have taken internally.

P&G also created new brands from in-licensing technologies from other companies around the world, resulting in products like the Crest SpinBrush, Olay Regenerist, and Swiffer Dusters. The latter two are now billion dollar brands for the company, even though the base technologies originated outside of P&G.

P&G is also getting money from licensing its technologies to other companies. One example of this is its joint venture with Clorox for the Glad brand. P&G contributed its manufacturing technology, while Clorox contributed the brand and the product, and together they created a partnership that has lasted over a decade. And the Glad business is itself another billion dollar brand.[2] More generally, P&G adopted a policy for every new patent in which the internal businesses had nine months to employ that new technology in a new product. If no business did so, that patent was then offered outside to others to license it. This created new incentives for the internal businesses to evaluate the new technologies more carefully. 'Use it or lose it' was the label one internal manager used to describe the program.

When Lafley saw the growth impact of Open Innovation, he mandated that at least 50 percent of P&G's innovations would come from outside P&G within five years. At the time of this mandate in 2002, the percentage from outside was roughly 10 percent. So this was a real stretch goal for the whole company, but they did get there by 2007.

The company has had serious growth challenges more recently, which I will discuss later in this chapter, when I consider the boundary conditions needed for sustaining Open Innovation.

P&G Best Practices

1) Utilizing P&G's brand marketing to turn external technologies into billion dollar brands. P&G doesn't have to discover it, to profit from it.
2) Making unused internal technologies available for others to use (including competitors), and creating other billion dollar brands. Use it or lose it policies can cause internal organizations to pay more attention

to newly patented technologies that they might otherwise discount or ignore.

3) If you're not going to use the new patent yourself, allow others to license it instead. This will stimulate greater internal consideration (point 2 above), bring in additional, high-margin licensing revenue, and identify new business models for deploying that technology that you might not have thought of.

GE Ecomagination

GE[3] is in real trouble these days, but for many years the company was an exemplar of numerous innovation best practices. One of these practices was its use of Open Innovation in the green and renewable energy markets, a program it called the Ecomagination Challenge. GE had a very large (nearly $40 billion at the time) energy business already, but its primary customers were utilities and power generation companies who bought large installations capable of generating megawatts of power. Meanwhile, there were a number of new technologies emerging in green and renewable energy that produced kilowatts of power, often 'behind the meter' in residential or commercial sites. GE had no presence here, and indeed, knew relatively little about the market. Thus it issued an Ecomagination Challenge, to attract entrepreneurs with ideas for new renewable energy businesses to start. If GE liked the idea, it would offer an initial investment to the entrepreneur. It set up a $100 million pool of capital for these investments.

GE could have done this on its own. But it realized that there was a network of VCs who already had extensive experience investing in this area, and that GE might learn a lot from collaborating with them. GE also realized that it knew very little about the daily realities of small startup companies, and that these startups would need a lot of coaching, mentoring, and other services that VCs provide. So GE persuaded four other VCs to invest a second $100 million in the Ecomagination Challenge, creating $200 million in investable funds.

More than 3800 responses to the challenge were received, ten times more than GE expected. It took time and effort to review these proposals, and that review was aided by the comments of 70,000 people who logged into the challenge to vote for their favorite ideas. GE even chose to create a People's Choice award, for the most popular idea among the external commentators. GE's internal R&D team led GE's technical review of the proposals, and they learned a lot about this new world.

Eventually, GE funded seventeen ventures, and its partner VCs invested in some others, resulting in twenty-three new ventures. GE also found an attractive acquisition that it would not have known about, except for the Challenge. And GE also realized that its community of 70,000 commenters was itself a potential asset for the company. So when the challenge concluded, GE created the new position of Community Engagement Manager, to sustain the community's interest and participation in renewable energy technologies.

Following this experience, GE initiated other challenges in other parts of its business, including transportation and healthcare, and also did a challenge in China. This shows that GE found a lot of wisdom in the crowd, and that even a very large and (at the time) successful firm could learn a lot from outsiders.

GE Ecomagination Best Practices

1) When exploring new business areas, ask outsiders for their ideas.
2) Let other outsiders see those ideas, and see which ones they like best.
3) Let your internal R&D staff learn by vetting these outside ideas.
4) In new business areas away from your core business, sometimes it's better to invest alongside those who know the lay of the land.

Enel: Open Innovation and Sustainability = Open Innovability

Another example of effective Open Innovation practices comes from a leading energy company headquartered in Italy, Enel.[4] Utilities traditionally are built for stability, not innovation. But back in the decade of the 2000's, Italy and Europe created some attractive incentives for renewable energy investments. Enel chose to create a new entity, Enel Green Power (EGP), to bundle its various renewable activities together, and spun this out to the public stockmarket. Francesco Starace, a longtime Enel executive, was appointed CEO of the new company.

EGP soon realized that, like GE with its renewable energy products, the renewable market was a very different market from Enel's traditional utility markets. The technologies were less mature, and new approaches often appeared. The size of power generated was smaller, the speed of decision-making needed was much faster, and the financing of the ventures required flexibility and creativity. EGP adapted to these new conditions, and became very successful in a short period of time. In fact, it became so successful that, in 2014, Starace was invited to become the CEO of all of Enel, and EGP was folded back into the company.

Once inside all of Enel, Starace did not simply revert back to a traditional utility company leader. Instead, he boldly declared that fossil fuels were the competition for Enel (not other utilities), and that the company's future depended upon renewables. One epochal moment that illustrated this bold new thinking was when Starace invited members of Greenpeace to meet with him and his top executives to discuss the company's renewable energy plans. (Only a couple of years earlier, Greenpeace had 'invaded' Enel's headquarters in Rome, unfurling a banner that proclaimed that Enel was the Enemy.) The company began to sell off nuclear plants and close down coal plants, while opening and greatly expanding renewable energy plants. Enel also launched new experiments with micro-grids to deliver power to remote locations that were forced to rely on diesel generators, and invested in a unique solar-thermal plant in the US that employed solar to start the process, and geo-thermal sources to sustain power generation.

Under the leadership of Ernesto Ciorra, formerly a marketing consultant (and also a published poet), Enel has adopted a policy of Open Innovability that combines Open Innovation activities with a sustainability mission. This involves Enel expanding its engagement with both startup companies and universities. Enel now engages startup companies in bootcamps in four locations around the world, and shares the results with its business units internally. It has also streamlined hundreds of individual university research projects into a more strategic set of focused relationships with twelve leading universities around the world. Enel's new network of collaborations in various hotspots (Europe, Silicon Valley, Israel, Boston) has positioned it to be where many of the latest breakthroughs in renewable energy are taking place. Enel now knows more about renewable energy, from more sources of new technology, than it ever did before. The company is well positioned to lead its customers into a new, greener energy environment.

Enel Best Practices

1) Sometimes, new technologies require new business models to succeed. Inside-out open innovation spinoffs (like Enel Green Power) focus more on new business models that the parent company would have struggled to implement internally.

2) Creating facilities in technology hotspots around the world promotes engagement with startups at an early stage. Go where the startups live, don't make them come to you.

3) Environmental sustainability is critical for a better future for our society. Open Innovation is a powerful way to execute that vision, hence Open Innovability makes a great deal of business sense.

Bayer: A Comprehensive Approach to Open Innovation in Pharmaceuticals

Bayer is one of the most advanced companies in the world in its innovation activities. This is not surprising, as some business historians believe that Bayer was the first company to create an internal R&D system back in the mid-nineteenth century.[5] In modern times, the pharmaceutical industry has seen a number of technological shifts, from chemistry-based approaches to biological approaches to genomics approaches. As the science base has shifted, the sources of new technology have also evolved. Initially, the sources of new technology came from inside the firm. Later, university research became an important source of new possibilities. Then young biotech companies became a vital part of the innovation ecosystem. Today, startups and VC firms have joined these disparate sources, such that any broad line pharmaceutical company needs to employ an 'all the above' strategy for developing and accessing new ideas and technologies.

Bayer is one company that has risen to this challenge. The company maintains a strong internal R&D capability, spending more than 14 percent of sales on R&D in 2017. The company also extends its access to new ideas and technologies by extensive collaborations with a number of universities, as we also saw with Enel. The company increasingly works closely with VCs to identify promising new trends in the pharma industry. It organizes hackathons for its own staff and also for outsiders, to explore areas away from its current activities. And it often acquires young biotech companies to increase its portfolio of new drug therapies.

Managing these different sources of ideas and technology requires a variety of organizational approaches, as shown in Figure 8.1.[6] Some approaches can be managed through arm's length arrangements, such as an incubator. Bayer opened such an incubator in its Mission Bay facility in San Francisco, CA. We saw this also in Chapter 6 when we examined organizational approaches to startups that were scalable. Others require assets to be transitioned from one

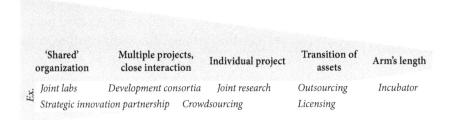

'Shared' organization	Multiple projects, close interaction	Individual project	Transition of assets	Arm's length
Joint labs	*Development consortia*	*Joint research*	*Outsourcing*	*Incubator*
Strategic innovation partnership	*Crowdsourcing*		*Licensing*	

Figure 8.1 Range of organizational approaches at Bayer

Figure 8.2 Mapping objectives to research activities at Bayer

organization to another, through licensing or donation. Bayer actively licenses compounds from both academic research hospitals in earlier stages of development, and from biotech firms in later stages. Still others require more extensive, ongoing interaction as one moves to the left in Figure 8.1, whether that be through joint research projects, a development consortia, or a strategic innovation partnership.

As can be seen in Figure 8.2, Bayer has developed a set of discrete processes for the different tasks across the range of Open Innovation activities.

Figure 8.2[7] shows four discretely different kinds of collaboration for Bayer, from insight activities which are only loosely coupled to its innovation processes, to more engaged modes like workbench, access, and development. Workbench activities involve contracting out part of the development process to others, while access requires transfers of money, rights, and knowledge. The most intensive mode is development, which is where the many sources of knowledge come together to develop a new drug. Figure 8.2 also shows higher levels of project risk moving from left to right, along with more organizational involvement rising from bottom to top.

Bayer Best Practices

1) There is no 'one size fits all' approach to Open Innovation. Instead, the specific oragnizational approach must be matched to the goals of the project.
2) Broad pharma companies like Bayer employ an 'all the above' approach to tracking new sources of innovation and bringing the most promising ones to market. This involves mastering a range of practices, from crowdsourcing to research collaborations to licensing and development.
3) Internal managers of Open Innovation must become adept at multiple types of collaboration, in order to achieve their innovation objectives. Over time, this role is becoming professionalized at Bayer.

Quirky: Building Off of the Crowd

Sometimes one can learn more about Open Innovation by studying situations where it fails than one can learn from simply studying the success cases. Quirky is one such situation. The company was founded in 2009 by serial entrepreneur Ben Kaufman, and raised over $150 million in funding.

The really cool thing about Quirky was how it found its ideas. It invited individual inventors to submit their ideas for products to the company via the company's website. If the company selected the inventor's product for commercial development, the inventor would receive a portion of the revenues as a royalty. Moreover, others in the Quirky community who helped to improve and develop the product would also participate in a smaller amount of royalty payments. In turn, Quirky would handle the further development, merchandising, distribution and advertising to promote the product. In effect, Quirky outsourced the initial concept development for all of its new products, while building a strong marketing and distribution capability to sell all those products. This model celebrated the individual inventor, and rewarded his or her ingenuity by paying out these royalties.[8]

The company attracted a lot of attention and publicity with this model. Ideas came from many different people from different walks of life, and a wide array of possible products were proposed to Quirky. The company also had some big 'hits', with products like its PowerPivot (a flexible multi-outlet plug extenstion cord) generating millions of dollars in revenues. In addition to attracting a lot of venture capital financing, the company signed a partnership with GE for manufacturing and marketing some of its products as well (GE also invested in the company). So Quirky was well-backed and well-connected. And it was practicing a particularly expansive model of Open Innovation, by relying on its external community for all of its product ideas.

Yet it all came to tears. By 2015, the company filed for bankruptcy, and founder Kaufman was forced out of the company. In this case, Open Innovation clearly didn't work, and it wasn't for lack of money or top management support. So what happened, and what does this say about Open Innovation's ability to help companies innovate?

There is some debate about why Quirky failed. Kaufman was clearly an 'idea guy', who was less skilled in the operational aspects of growing a venture. In the language of this book, he was great at generation, and less skilled at dissemination and absorption. And Quirky's business depended (as many consumer product businesses do) upon having at least a few hit products every year. So one might interpret Quirky's failure as one of execution, with little or no implications for Open Innovation more generally.

But I think that interpretation is perhaps too kind to Open Innovation. If the business needed hit products, who better than the Quirky community to supply them? In truth, for every idea that became a PowerPivot, there were hundreds or thousands that were poor or marginal ideas. And every one of these needed to be reviewed by someone within Quirky. Kaufman had to staff up quite a bit to handle all the submissions he received—yet most of these submissions were of poor quality. This has been found in many companies who have tried crowdsourcing. While my academic peers praise the merits of crowdsourcing, the empirical truth of it is what Quirky learned: most crowd-sourced ideas that are submitted are terrible.[9] Yet every submission needs to receive a response (ideally within two to four weeks of receipt), and it takes time and effort to review every, single, idea, no matter how bad. This is not acknowledged enough by many Open Innovation enthusiasts.[10]

Another lesson from Quirky's experience is that the individuals who submitted ideas for products did not submit any kind of business model with those ideas. So Quirky had no process at the beginning of its work to ensure that the ideas it received would utilize the marketing and distribution capabilities it was slowly building. This is another issue faced by many organizations trying to practice Open Innovation: there is little or no economic value for an idea or a technology until it is commercialized through a business model. Or, to put it differently, the same idea will generate two different economic outcomes when placed in two different business models.[11] Quirky's process ignored all this, and solicited ideas from all comers, regardless of whether the submitted idea connected to Quirky's commercialization process.

Quirky Lessons Learned

1) Crowdsourcing is no panacea for Open Innovation. There may be a few good ideas that come from a crowdsourced process, but the vast majority of submitted ideas will be marginal or poor.
2) Crowdsourced ideas usually lack any connection to the business model of the receiving organization. There is no mechanism for dissemination or absorption. This means that there is a high risk that the idea will fail to create any economic value, even if the idea initially seems quite positive.
3) Open Innovation companies with lots of money and a committed CEO at the top can still fail, if they cannot build a process to connect the front end of their innovation process to the back end of that process (as we saw previously in Chapter 4).

CERN's ATTRACT Initiative: Whether and When IP Rights Help Commercialize Science

CERN is one of the world's leading scientific research organizations. Its acronym comes from the French (Conseil européen pour la recherche nucléaire), and the facilities for the organization sit at the border between France and Switzerland. It is perhaps best known for its discovery of the Higgs Boson, a result that yielded a Nobel prize in Physics in 2013 for work reported out of the facility. CERN employs a staff of roughly 3000, with more than 12,000 external users who participate in research projects from their member, associate, or observer countries.[12]

As we discussed in Chapter 3, though, this superior scientific resource won't create innovation by itself. To commercialize the enormous science base that exists at CERN, new kinds of institutions will be needed that extend beyond the open science community that is well established there. This will require some sense of what business applications may be found for the many technologies at CERN, along with enough development of the technology in practice that a business or an investor can evaluate its feasibility and attractiveness for those applications. And there is the delicate question, in a substantial open science community, of what intellectual property rights these technologies will receive, and when. All of this is involved in the launch of ATTRACT.

The ATTRACT Initiative

The ATTRACT initiative (breAkThrough innovaTion pRogrAmme for the deteCtor/infrastructure ecosysTem) seeks to combine both the specific R&D needs and the commercialization potential of some very advanced, world-class detector and imaging technologies that are being developed at CERN. It aims to do this through a collaborative, Open Innovation approach, particularly the inside-out branch of Open Innovation.

The ATTRACT initiative explicitly seeks to create institutional structures to support the downstream commercialization new technologies out of CERN. Initially, three key areas of commercialization have been identified:

- breakthrough ICT technology and applications;
- high performance materials and applications;
- health physics technology and applications.

Each of these application domains are very large markets, with different drivers and regulatory structures. The ICT sector is the fastest-moving of the three sectors, and new innovations can often be deployed and scaled here in short amounts of time. Materials take a longer time to scale into large markets, because the material must first be proven, and then multiple applications must be attempted, and the eventual market size will depend on the success of the various uses of the new material. The health sector is the most regulated, and market success here will require both acceptance by industry as well as adoption by both regulators and health care system administrators.

The industrial partners engaged by ATTRACT will play a critical role in the commercialization of detector technologies in each of these sectors. The industrial partners are the players who can bring a deep understanding of each business context to the researchers, so that the subsequent technology development addresses key requirements of each sector. In the free exchange of knowledge that a place like CERN has established within its culture, it is also quite likely that there will be extensive cross-fertilization of context across the different participating industry sectors.

ATTRACT has given careful thought to the necessary IP arrangements to continue the open science culture that CERN has successfully created, while simultaneously providing sufficient IP rights to potential commercial partners to motivate them to take the investment risks necessary to move technologies into the market. The key structures here include:

- Broad, royalty-free access to the substantial background knowledge that exists in the research community, so that enterprising commercial partners can proceed in confidence with their projects, confident that they will not be 'blocked' by assertions of IP rights by another party from within CERN.
- Discovery of one or more useful contexts to apply this knowledge will result from the extensive interplay between CERN research scientists and engineers on the one hand, and industry engineers and developers on the other. Given the large number of CERN scientists and engineers, and the similarly large number of industry developers, the participants all agree to forego filing for protecting knowledge being created at this early stage. This will promote more rapid exploration of possible applications, and enable a much larger group of participants to engage in the process.
- Once specific applications are identified, industry participants are free to proceed to seek protection for the subsequent foreground knowledge created privately by participating firms who build upon the results in each ATTRACT project. Only those who participate and contribute directly to the project will have deep understanding of the work that was done, which will give them a head start in any downstream application development. Such work would, however, have to be done at their own site, away from ATTRACT.[13]
- ATTRACT has been awarded an EU grant of €17 million, to be spent on one hundred different technology projects out of CERN. This seed money will support early development work to create initial prototypes that can be shared with industry. This further development will reduce the technical risk of each project, and permit a more considered response from industry for each technology. Critically, no IP rights are assigned at this stage, so enterprising technologies and entrepreneurs can explore a wide range of possible applications.

The successful commercialization of CERN technologies will require a number of 'small wins' to be realized early in the process. These small wins are not the eventual payoffs of the new technology, but they are the first tangible demonstrations of commercial value for these applications. Large firms are often disadvantaged in pursuing these small wins, as the initial revenues are so small as to be irrelevant to the large firm's financial performance. But small firms and startups can focus on these smaller revenue streams quite effectively, and therefore they play a critical role in bridging the Valley of Death between Research and Development described in Chapters 3 and 4.

CERN Best Practices

1) Great science doesn't automatically translate into great innovation. And the best use of a new technology is often far from obvious. So create structures where scientists and industry engineers can exchange ideas and collaborate, without (yet) asserting IP rights.
2) The best applications for the discoveries made in areas like detection, imaging, and computation will require entrepreneurial risk-taking. Substantial trial-and-error will likewise be required to develop effective business models that can create and capture value, at commercial scale. Here, some IP rights will need to be assigned. But these should not block the background IP upon which the larger organization relies.
3) Small sums of money can usefully de-risk promising new technologies, without giving away IP rights prematurely. This will make it easier to cross the Valley of Death between science and innovation. This is a useful role for both public funding and also non-profit funding.[14]

The Curious Case of P&G's Growth, and Open Innovation

The rise of Open Innovation was closely linked to the success of Procter & Gamble back when my *Open Innovation* book first came out in 2003. While P&G wasn't one of the main case studies in the book, they publicly promoted their Connect & Develop innovation process around this time, and soon came to embrace the Open Innovation model. (Even today, *Open Innovation* is prominently displayed on P&G's Connect & Develop page on its website.)[15] Even the bonus programs of top executives at P&G, including support functions like legal and finance, included a component for the adoption of Connect and Develop.

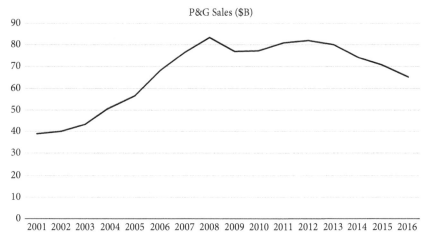

Figure 8.3 P&G sales history, from 2001–17 (P&G annual reports)

P&G's embrace of Open Innovation sustained over time. By 2006, P&G proudly touted its success with Connect & Develop, culminating in a well-received, broadly disseminated article in *Harvard Business Review*.[16] In 2008, then-CEO A.G. Lafley co-authored *The Gamechanger*, a book which portrayed his role in opening up the P&G innovation process and company culture.[17] In this book, he praises Connect & Develop, and takes much of the credit for successfully bringing it to P&G. Subsequently, then-CTO Bruce Brown co-authored another HBR article on the 'innovation machine' at P&G that had 'tripled its success rate with innovation'.[18]

What makes this a curious case is to compare P&G's business results to its enthusiastic embrace of Open Innovation and its public proclamation of its innovation proficiency. Figure 8.3 shows P&G's revenue history, from the start of Lafley's tenure at P&G to the most recently completed fiscal year.

As the graph shows, P&G revenues grew quite nicely during Lafley's tenure as CEO at P&G from fiscal 2001 through fiscal 2009. Open Innovation seemed to really help. Not only did overall revenues grow significantly (P&G revenues were stagnant throughout most of the 1990s), but there were a number of successful brands that P&G had established through its Connect & Develop process, such as:

- **Olay° Regenerist**: world's top selling skin cream
- **Olay° Regenerist Eye Roller**: Olay's #2 global seller
- **Olay° Definity Eye Illuminator**: packaging innovation wowed consumers

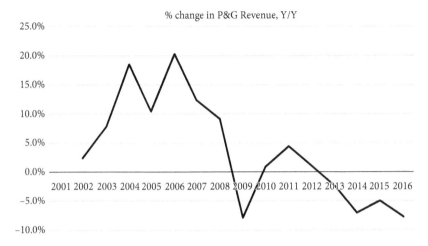

Figure 8.4 Change in annual revenues for P&G, 2001–17 (P&G annual reports)

- **Swiffer Dusters®**: market leader sold in fifteen global markets
- **Mr Clean® Magic Eraser®**
- **Clairol Perfect 10™**: 2010 Product of the Year, Consumer Survey of Product Innovations
- **Oral B Pulsonic® Toothbrush**
- **GLAD® Forceflex® and GLAD Press'nSeal®**[19]

The Great Recession clearly impacted revenues at P&G, starting in 2009. But there is more going on here than a deep, protracted recession. A casual perusal of these great examples shows that most of them were created more than a decade ago in P&G. Besides Clairol Perfect 10, what has Connect & Develop done for the company lately?. Why hasn't Open Innovation sustained growing revenues for the company?

The failure for revenue to grow at P&G can be seen more dramatically by looking at the annual growth percentage from one year to the next. Figure 8.4 shows that result.

To state the obvious, P&G's revenues have slumped badly since Lafley stepped away as CEO in 2009 and the Great Recession hit. At this point, the company had scaled up its Open Innovation processes, and had drilled its management team extensively in how to collaborate with others in the innovation process. And the external collaborators seemed pretty satisfied: of the more than 1100 external collaborators P&G worked with through Connect & Develop, more than 600 of them had done multiple collaborations with

P&G.[20] This suggests that the partners were happy enough with their first experience of Connect & Develop to try it again with P&G.

So, right at the time when P&G had mastered Open Innovation, had developed an extensive network of satisfied external partners, and had scaled this process across its businesses around the world, growth essentially stopped. Curious!

What makes this case more curious is that P&G's Board of Directors brought Lafley back to the CEO role in 2013! Presumably, the goal was to revive the growth magic that Lafley had created during his first period as CEO. As Figures 8.3 and 8.4 show, though, this hope did not materialize. Lafley subsequently stepped down again as CEO in July 2015, and retired from being Chairman of the Board in June of 2016. Activist investors have noticed this anemic growth, and launched a proxy fight to join the Board to find new sources of value. What happened to the growth benefits of Open Innovation? If a master practitioner like P&G, led by a sage like A. G. Lafley, cannot sustain growth with it, what does that mean for the rest of us?

Also curious is the fact that this erratic performance has gone unremarked by academic scholars of Open Innovation, myself included! We took note of the P&G successes in the early 2000s, but have largely ignored the more recent struggles the company has had with continued growth.

I don't have a smoking gun that isolates the single point of failure with Open Innovation at P&G. I do know of a number of organizational transitions, though, that collectively reduced the focus on Open Innovation, in favor of other priorities. Let's review some of the transitions:

- CEO and Connect and Develop champion A. G. Lafley steps down as CEO in 2008. An insider, Bob McDonough, takes the reins.
- Other key insiders in the Connect & Develop program during the glory years, like Gil Cloyd, Larry Huston, Nabil Sakkab, and Jeff Weedman, all retire.
- McDonough's tenure is disappointing, as P&G's business suffered in the Great Recession. Lafley was brought back out of retirement in 2013 to be CEO again, only to retire once more in 2015.
- In 2016, the Connect and Develop team was merged with the Mergers and Acquisitions team, under a single manager.
- In 2017, Nelson Peltz of Trian Partners launches a proxy fight to reshaped P&G's Board of Directors. $100 million is spent on the contest. Though Peltz narrowly lost the vote, he was appointed to the Board for 2018.

So what happened? My own sense is that the company has lost at least some of its belief in the value of Open Innovation. Many of the key people in the early years of the program are no longer with the company, and their skills and beliefs in Open Innovation do not seem to have transferred to those who replaced them. The Great Recession really scrambled consumer product markets for a number of years, and this downturn clearly demanded P&G's attention of its top management, perhaps to the detriment of Open Innovation. The more recent proxy contest also took the focus off of innovation, and instead highlighted cash flows and near term profitability improvement.

The other point to make is that other consumer product companies noticed the success of Connect & Develop, and began to imitate that process inside their own organizations. I have personally spoken to a number of these companies, including Nestle, Unilever, Kraft, Del Monte, SC Johnson, Clorox, General Mills, and Kelloggs. When P&G began its Open Innovation activities, it was clearly in the lead among its industry. By the time Lafley returned to the CEO role ten years later, everyone had noticed, and most had copied P&G. Perhaps the low hanging fruit of the early 2000s for P&G was mostly picked, while any new fruits available had to be obtained in a more aware, more competitive Open Innovation environment by 2013, when Lafley returned to the CEO role.

P&G Lessons Learned

1) Open Innovation isn't just a set of practices or tactics. It stems from a mindset and belief. New managers can quickly adopt the practices, but may not comprehend the underlying formula, and why it works.
2) Competitors can adopt Open Innovation too. One cannot stand still in the innovation race, one needs to keep experimenting, keep improving, and keep focused.
3) Open Innovation leaders need to anticipate the downturns, as well as managing the upside. Innovation programs often get hit hard in recessions, so OI managers must be ready with their rainy day plans to respond.

Some effective principles for practicing open innovation
As the examples in this chapter demonstrate, Open Innovation goes well beyond crowdsourcing technology or products, or working with a university,

or partnering with a startup. It's a different mindset, a focus on how you get the most out of the assets and knowledge that you have and how you can benefit from the assets and knowledge that others have. It's a much more open, distributed mindset towards innovation. Underlying this is the belief that we live in a world of abundance, where so much useful knowledge already exists that it is worth becoming skilled at seeking out, engaging, disseminating, and then absorbing this knowledge. It is also a belief that we live in a world where speed and agility matter. Letting unused ideas and technologies sit on the shelf is not only wasteful, but may cause companies to miss out on hidden value they already possess.

But Open Innovation is not a panacea. It has certain requirements that are necessary in order for it to deliver business results. One requirement that emerges in this chapter is the role of leadership. For a lot of companies, the move to Open Innovation emerged out of some kind of crisis, a moment when the company realized that business as usual was no longer going to work. In that moment, these companies felt a need to try something different, and that impulse led to the adoption of some of these open approaches, often with great success.

Some of those companies were celebrated as examples of effective Open Innovation. Many of these same companies have experienced subsequent turnover in top management and in the CEO role, and growth seems to have suffered as a result. Top management support seems to be a boundary condition for success, and even successful programs can falter when there is a change in leadership that has priorities other than Open Innovation.

As you leave this chapter, my advice is to focus more on the principles of Open Innovation shown in Table 8.1, instead the various individual best practices detailed in this chapter. These practices will need to evolve, as customers change, as competitors advance, as new technologies and opportunities emerge. The principles, though, and the thinking behind them, are likely more enduring—and therefore more useful to you when you must confront your next challenge.

Chapter 8 review points:

1. Open Innovation can be a powerful engine for growth, if properly managed.
2. Open Innovation can be valuable as a tool to enable environmental sustainability, as seen by Enel and GE.

Table 8.1 Principles of Open Innovation[21]

Closed Innovation Principles	Open Innovation Principles	Chapter Examples
The smartest people in the field work for us.	Most of the smartest people work someplace else (Joy's Law).	P&G, GE, Bayer, Quirky
To profit from innovation, we must discover, develop and ship it ourselves.	External innovation can help create value, while internal R&D and a business model are needed to claim a portion of that value.	GE, Quirky, Enel, Bayer, ATTRACT
If we discover it ourselves, we will get to market first.	We don't have to originate the research, in order to profit from it.	P&G, Enel, Bayer
If we are the first to commercialize it, we win.	Building a better business model is better than getting to market first.	Quirky, Enel Green Power
If we create the most and best ideas in the industry, we win.	If we make the best use of internal and external ideas, we win.	Bayer, ATTRACT, P&G, Enel
We should control our IP, so that our competitors don't profit from our ideas.	We should profit from others' use of our IP, and we should buy others' IP whenever it advances our own business.	P&G, Enel, Bayer, ATTRACT

3. Even organizations who embody effective Open Innovation practices can have trouble sustaining growth over time. Both Qwirky and P&G have struggled with this.

4. Open Innovation requires a certain mindset to sustain growth over time. Following the practices alone may not keep the company ahead of its competitors. Following Open Innovation principles may prove more enduring.

9

Open Innovation with Chinese Characteristics

In the final chapter of this book, we turn to innovation in the world's second largest economy, China.[1] In the forty years since the rise of Deng Xiaoping to the leadership of the Chinese Communist Party (CCP) in China, the country's economic has grown enormously. While there are considerable trade tensions today, if one looks back over forty years one cannot fail to be impressed by an economic miracle. A poor, backward nation of over 1 billion people has surged to the point where its economy will soon be the largest in the world. Perhaps more importantly, hundreds of millions of people have been lifted out of poverty during that time. Various health indicators like lifespan, height, and even diabetes from much richer diets, all point to China's incredible rise in living standards. It is a monumental achievement, and the world is better for it.

China provides a unique business environment, due to its huge population, its very large economy, and the unique role of the CCP in the governance of the country. Its unique factors suggest that existing theories of Open Innovation may not be readily applicable to the context of innovation in China. In particular, state-owned enterprises (SOEs) in China not only enjoy the support of the government and the Party but also enjoy substantial scale advantages. Unlike the former Soviet Union, the CCP has embraced markets, and market prices, as fundamental tools of resource allocation in the society. Private property is also allowed, and thousands of individuals in China have now become billionaires. Marx and Lenin would likely not be pleased.

On the other hand, unlike the United States and most of Western Europe, the CCP chooses to play a leading role in the choice of which industries to target for government support and investment. And more recently, the Chinese government has been pursuing an 'indigenous innovation' policy that aims to meet certain technology goals by 2020 and 2050, with the intention of creating Chinese dominance of tech markets that are typically the domain of companies from Japan, South Korea, and the United States.[2]

In one chapter, we cannot analyze all of this in detail. Instead, we will examine the role of Open Innovation in China, and examine how Open

Open Innovation Results. Going Beyond the Hype, and Getting Down to Business. Henry Chesbrough, Oxford University Press (2020). © Henry Chesbrough.
DOI: 10.1093/oso/9780198841906.001.0001

Innovation has played out in different industries inside China. Much of the debate about China's innnovation policy has been at the level of the overall economy.[3] But there is much that can be learned from examining innovation within specific parts of the economy. We will pay particular attention to three different industries: high-speed rail, automotive, and semiconductors. We seek to explicate 'Open Innovation with Chinese characteristics' by examining Chinese innovation across three different industries: high-speed rail, semiconductors, and automotive. Because the role of the CCP is so important, and is so different from innovation policymaking in the West, let's start with some background on the CCP's approach to innovation.

Xi Jinping Thought and Open Innovation

China's ruling Communist Party enshrined President Xi Jinping's political thought into its constitution on October 23, 2017, putting him in the same company as the founder of modern China, Mao Zedong.[4] Xi's thought is a set of very inclusive ideas that have a number of social, economic, political, military, and foreign relations aspects (the speech was three hours in length). Within these many and varied aspects, a critical central tension emerged from this speech: Xi Jinping's thought includes a commitment to the 'decisive role' of market forces in resource allocation, while at the same time insisting that the CCP exercise overall leadership over all areas of endeavor in every part of the country.

> We must see that the market plays the decisive role in resource allocation, the government plays its role better, and new industrialization, IT application, urbanization, and agricultural modernization go hand in hand. We must actively participate in and promote economic globalization, develop an open economy of higher standards, and continue to increase China's economic power and composite strength. (from Xi's speech at the nineteenth national congress)

In another part of this same speech, the role of Open Innovation was also quite salient.

> Openness brings progress, while self-seclusion leaves one behind. China will not close its door to the world; we will only become more and more open. We should pursue the Belt and Road Initiative as a priority, give equal emphasis to 'bringing in' and 'going global', follow the principle of achieving

shared growth through discussion and collaboration, and increase openness and cooperation in building innovation capacity. With these efforts, we hope to make new ground in opening China further through links running eastward and westward, across land and over sea.

'Bringing in' refers to outside-in knowledge flows in Open Innovation. It includes foreign direct investment, but also includes accessing external knowledge through university-based research collaborations, inward licensing of technology, Chinese venture capital investment in startup ventures outside China, reverse engineering of externally developed products, and following the technical literature. 'Going global' refers to the inside-out knowledge flows in Open Innovation. This includes exports of indigenously developed technologies from China-based companies. But it also includes external licensing of Chinese technologies, spin-offs of Chinese companies, Chinese venture capital investment in China-based startups that export outside of China, and the rapidly growing contribution of Chinese research to the technical literature. And all of this technology is propelled outside of China in part by the massive infrastructure initiative known as the Belt and Road Initiative.

One can look at Xi's speech as a unique blend of innovation policies that amount to 'Open Innovation with Chinese characteristics'. While the basic tenets of Open Innovation are being pursued, they are being pursued in the unusual institutional context of China. China is a rapidly developing economy, with a rapidly growing industrial base and a similarly evolving technological capability.[5] China has now achieved a tremendously large domestic economy, which has become the seedbed for substantial indigenous innovation.

As Chinese firms reach the technological frontier of many different industries, there are new innovation challenges to address, because there are fewer external firms left to learn from. In the Chinese context, the October 2017 Congress made clear that the CCP will also play a critical role in programming significant amounts of capital for future industrial development. One sign of this unusual role was the stipulation in the Constitution that the top thirty enterprises in China would incorporate the CCP in the highest levels of their leadership. This was written directly into the Constitution. This role for the Party has no counterpart in market capitalist economies. This is something that is completely new to Open Innovation in both theory and practice. The Party thus seeks to obtain the many benefits of Open Innovation, while guiding the economy forward at the same time.

How will this all work? Can it work? Let's consider this tension between CCP guidance and market signals from the perspective of three different industries in China: high-speed rail, automotive, and semiconductors. That might provide some insights. At the end of the chapter, we will return to Open Innovation, and what it might contribute to China's further innovation capabilities.

Variation in Innovation Performance across Chinese Industries

The three industries we wish to consider are the high-speed rail industry, the automotive industry, and the semiconductor industry. The first thing to notice from these three industries is that they vary in their innovation performance over the past twenty years. State guidance has helped Chinese companies gain ground in high-speed rail. In the case of high-speed rail, Chinese firms now dominate the domestic market, and are now competitive with the leading suppliers of high-speed rail technology around the world. In the automotive sector, though, while the overall industry has become the largest country market in the world, the capability of Chinese companies remains well behind that of the world's leading auto companies. The semiconductor industry falls somewhere in between the other two industries, but here too the capabilities of Chinese companies are behind those of the world leaders.[6] So by choosing these three industries we can observe three different levels of innovation performance in China.[7]

Within each of these three industries, there are at least three types of important innovation actors. The first type is the state-owned enterprises (SOEs). The second type are the privately-owned companies (POCs), which, given the relatively recent opening of the Chinese economy from the time of Deng Xiaoping, are often still run by the founders of the company. The third type are foreign companies operating in China, often with R&D activities that are performed in China. Let's examine how these three types of companies interact, across these three different industries.

The Chinese High-speed Rail Industry

The early years of high-speed rail in China were distinctly unsuccessful.[8] The country began investing in high-speed rail in the late 1990s, but none of the designs proved to be commercially viable. Collaborations with foreign firms were numerous, but these were fragmented and ultimately not very productive. The foreign firms, in turn, had a substantial technological lead, particularly firms like Kawasaki in Japan and Siemens in Germany.

This all started to change in 2004, when the Ministry of Railways transformed its industrial development direction to 'introduction, absorption, and re-innovation'. In a bold move, the ministry committed to a very ambitious 'four vertical and four horizontal' high-speed railway network planning roadmap in 2004. This network amounted to 12,000 kilometers of high-speed passenger-dedicated railway network lines—equivalent to all of the high-speed lines that were operating in the world at that time. This was an enormous boost to global demand for high-speed rail.

The ministry knew that China's indigenous technology could not achieve this ambitious goal on its own. So China's government opened its domestic high-speed train market to foreign companies, creating a tender process for this very large, attractive opportunity. The ministry went to considerable lengths to encourage foreign players to participate, including holding open the deadline to get Siemens to join. However, China also wanted to upgrade the technological capabilities of its domestic train manufacturers as a result of this tender, so that they might manufacture at least some of the trains demanded in China in the future. The Ministry of Railways therefore proposed strict principles to foreign players entering the Chinese high-speed train market via joint bidding with Chinese partners. These joint bids required extensive technology transfer from the foreign companies to the domestic partners, who were two domestic SOE players: China South Railway (CSR) and China North Railway (CNR). Four leading international companies participated in these transfers and bidding: Siemens, Kawasaki Heavy Industries, Alstom, and Bombardier.

The foreign companies likely calculated that though there were risks from this technology transfer, the huge market on offer easily justified running the risks. Moreover, they knew that they enjoyed a significant technological lead over CSR and CNR. Indeed, the earlier high-speed train designs from these two firms were noticeably inferior to the best designs in the West. It seemed unlikely that the domestic Chinese suppliers could catch up and overtake them this time around. So they all participated in the tender in hopes of serving the new demand created by the four vertical and four horizontal railway tender.

As it happened, though, the two Chinese SOEs became surprisingly adept at absorbing the new technologies from these Western companies. Why did these firms, who previously struggled to master earlier generations of technology, overcome this history for this new tender? One difference with this iteration of technology transfer was that this time the firms consciously linked with universities, research institutes, and government agencies to receive, understand, and then exploit the combination of the technology advantages from the four foreign companies. In other words, they were much more open this time around than they had been with earlier tenders. At the same time, the Chinese government made a number of institutional investments to increase university research funding for this work.

Within two to three years of the completion of the initial tender, both CSR and CNR were making CRH380A trains, which were as capable as any available in the West, and at much lower prices. In later rounds of procurement, the central Rail Ministry bought exclusively from these Chinese suppliers. This support was allowed under WTO rules, due to China's status as an emerging economy. These transformative efforts were further promoted by the central government through the establishment of the CRRC via the merger of CSR and CNR, to form a large volume SOE giant with global competitive advantage, producing at global scale. Siemens, who won the design competition in the tender, received the contract to provide the first train and to transfer its technical knowledge. Because of the rapid absorption of knowledge by the Chinese suppliers, though, Siemens did not manage to sell any more of its trains in China.

Today the government offers attractive contracts with China's CRRC as part of its policies like One Belt One Road, Made in China 2025, etc. This will create a strong pull for Chinese high-speed rail technology to be exported in many new markets, which will extend the lead now enjoyed by the CRRC, which today is not only a cost leader but also a formidable technology company as well. And its expertise extends beyond the trains themselves, to designs for bridges and overpasses, mountain terrain, wet terrain, and also to train stations.

The high-speed rail industry shows how the CCP can work with market forces to achieve technological leadership in a cutting edge industry like high-speed rail. By promoting technology introduction through Open Innovation, the Ministry of Railways played the role of the orchestrator to secure the dominance of two major SOEs in the domestic high-speed rail industry, and facilitated the dissemination and absorption of high-speed rail technology by Chinese domestic suppliers, who in turn were more open to external knowledge and technologies than they had been previously. By forcing the later merger of the two SOE providers into the CRRC, the Ministry achieved both technology leadership and tremendous scale economies in both high-speed rail and in complementary capabilities such as railway network construction, bridge spans for railways, etc. The Chinese Ministry is now further concentrating its global competitive advantages via outbound Open Innovation efforts like the One Belt One Road Initiatives. This will allow the CRRC to further increase its scale and further reduce its costs of providing high-speed rail technology at home and abroad. And the new Asian Infrastructure Investment Bank, founded by Chinese capital, will help finance the purchase of Chinese high-speed rail technology.

This example shows how China can leverage Open Innovation, both outside-in and inside-out, to achieve industry leadership. It similarly shows how the Party and market forces can align to obtain this result. This successful result may suggest why China is increasingly confident of its innovation path, and in its unique combination of Party governance and market forces. It represents the triumph of Xi Jinping thought, and likely underpins some of the thinking in his 2017 speech.

However, the picture is not so rosy in the other two industries we will now examine.

Automobile Industry

In a similar path to high-speed rail, the Chinese government required foreign automakers to transfer technology through joint ventures (JV) with Chinese partners in the 1990s in return for access to the Chinese market.[9] Every foreign manufacturer who wanted to sell its products in China had to create a JV with a local Chinese partner. This would require the foreign partner to transfer technology to the JV partner, and to jointly build automotive factories in sufficient quantity to serve the rapidly expanding Chinese market. Today, the Chinese market is the largest market in the world by unit volume.

More than twenty years later, though, the market response in the automotive industry has not been what the government intended. While the volume of cars produced in China has grown enormously, creating lots of manufacturing jobs in the process, the technological capabilities of the Chinese producers in the industry still lag well behind those of the foreign companies.[10] Chinese car-makers have made so much money selling these foreign brands that the joint ventures have dampened their incentive to compete against their partners.[11] While the foreign manufacturers have transferred significant technical know-ledge to their Chinese partners, they have successfully maintained a technical edge by not transferring the latest, state-of-the-art technologies.

Consumers in the Chinese market are free to choose the car they prefer. As incomes have risen rapidly in the society, the car has become a symbol of wealth and success. This has caused many Chinese customers to buy foreign brands manufactured in China by joint ventures. These foreign brands continue to dominate the market, and maintain a technological edge over cars designed and produced by domestic Chinese firms. Among the domestic Chinese automotive producers, the largest volume companies lag the world's best companies by the largest amount, while the smaller companies are closer to being globally competitive.[12] In contrast to high-speed rail, Chinese car consumers are satisfied with 'good enough' technology for the broad middle of the market, while the foreign companies sell their own cars directly to the most demanding, high end car customers.

In this industry, the guiding role of the Party and the decisive role of the market have pointed in different directions. A heavy government hand can inhibit innovation by restricting the free flow of ideas on which innovation thrives. For example, China now requires that electric cars have batteries that are made in China, not imported. The intent is to stimulate faster development of domestic battery technology. But the policy result to date has been disappointing. Jochem Heizmann, the president and chief executive of Volkswagen Group China, said 'At the end, this [policy] limits competition, this limits innovation.'[13] The decisive role of the market in China (comprised of millions of individual vehicle purchase decisions by consumers) has favored foreign makers, to the disappointment of government officials.

The auto sector continues to be highly fragmented and hyper-competitive in part because of a lack of openness and local protectionism.[14] There are more than one hundred registered automakers in China, far more than even the world's largest car market can support. The fragmented production network, and marketplace make it exceedingly difficult for any single Chinese company to emerge as a large player. There is an even larger number of automotive suppliers of major components and subsystems, where much of the actual product innovation is occurring in the automotive sector, both inside and outside of China.

Furthermore, the most innovative parts of the Chinese automotive sector are those that are furthest from the guidance of the CCP. Domestic privately-owned companies (POCs) and foreign multinational companies (MNCs) are the primary sources of innovation in the industry.[15] The result is a two-tiered market, where the bulk of sales and employment come from the stable but technically lagging SOEs in China, while the majority of profit and innovation in the industry are coming into the industry from the POCs and MNCs. These latter firms are much less subject to Party guidance and control, yet they are the ones leading the industry into the future.

Here the tension between the leading role of the Party and the decisive role of the market becomes a contradiction. In order to have more innovation, the market forces (and the POCs and MNCs) need to have the leading role, and the Party must take a back seat.

Semiconductor Industry

The Chinese semiconductor industry has been characterized as a tale of two very different segments,[16] in a pattern that echoes that of the automotive industry above.[17] The SOEs provide the bulk of sales and employment in the industry, and virtually all of this output is consumed in the domestic market. However, the SOEs lag the state of the art in the industry by two to three generations of technology.[18] One measure of this lag is the line-width of the chip designs manufactured in the chips. Chinese SOEs today are building and shipping products with line-widths that were shipped by foreign companies three to five years ago. These are quite acceptable in the growing electronics market in China, but lag too far behind the best in the West to enable much export outside of the country.

There is a second segment in the Chinese semiconductor industry, though, that is shipping products of the same line widths as the global leaders. This segment consists of the POCs in the semiconductor industry. Most of the output from the POCs is exported outside of China to international customers, as part of the global supply chains used by these customers. The POCs in the Chinese semiconductor industry have been the primary source of introducing new technological innovations into China.[19]

There is a further segmentation in semiconductors between firms who design chips (design houses), and firms who build those designs (manufacturers, or 'fabs'). The design segment is driven by creativity, with low capital requirements, and a premium for clever design and fast turnaround. There are many hundreds of these companies in China, none of whom are SOEs. The fabs, by contrast, are quite capital intensive, since each new fab facility costs billions of dollars to build. In addition to capital, there are many permits needed by fabs from the government for land use, energy and water access, transport logistics, etc. Here, the SOEs fare better, due to their strong relations with governments. But even here, POCs have made strong inroads, and have been faster to adopt the latest technologies, in comparison to the SOEs.[20]

The semiconductor industry has recently emerged as something of a strategic battleground between China and the West. Many foreign governments have become unwilling to allow their firms to share their most advanced technology with Chinese firms for reasons of national security. This has reduced the ability of the government and SOEs to employ outside-in Open Innovation to advance their internal technologies. One response by China has made semiconductor chip development a key plank of its Made in China 2025 drive to bolster its strength in technology against more developed global rivals.[21]

However, as is the case in the automotive sector, the demand structure in China for semiconductors is quite heterogeneous. Semiconductors are designed into tens or hundreds of thousands of products, based on price and product requirements and availability. The semiconductor industry is global, and benefits from technical standards that allow many of its technologies to inter-operate. These standards don't require products to be customized for specific regions, allowing those products to serve a global market.

The top players in the industry earn most of the economic profit, while other competitors lose money. Deficiencies in the technologies of Chinese SOE manufacturers have also limited their ability to export. The Chinese POCs, by contrast, export the majority of their output outside of China. And the most innovative parts of the Chinese semiconductor industry, the key sources of new technology, are the POCs and MNCs that lie furthest from Party guidance and control. So the situation in the automotive industry closely parallels the situation in the semiconductor industry, with the partial exception of the fabs, which do require more capital, more government permits, land and water rights, etc..

Can China Have It Both Ways?

China clearly seeks to continue its phenomenal growth trajectory of the past forty years. For most of those years, it grew by copying the technologies of leading firms in the West. It has now caught up to these technologies in many areas. As it approaches the technological frontier in many industries, its companies must provide more innovative products and services in order for the economy to keep growing. This requires a close examination of the tension discussed at the beginning of this chapter.

Xi Jinping thought aligns well with the situation in the high-speed rail market. This market is driven by infrastructure development, where governments play a critical role in authorizing, funding, and sometimes operating the high-speed rail systems. The market can be thought of as a government-to-government business. Here, the role of the Party is well suited to guide the market, since the market is constituted by other governments seeking the benefits of high-speed rail. And the Chinese government has installed more miles of high-speed rail than the rest of the world combined.

Moreover, most of the state governments in the One Belt One Road initiative require financing assistance to pay for the high-speed rail technology. The Party can help here by connecting the Chinese rail authorities to the Chinese finance ministry and the Asian Infrastructure Innovation Bank, so that there is a smooth path for the successful sale, financing, export, installation, and operation of high-speed rail technology. The CRRC today is a market leader in high-speed rail innovation today in the volume of its sales, the low cost of its technology, and the growing capability of its technology in relation to its competitors.

Perhaps entranced by the success of the high-speed rail industry, Xi Jinping thought pays insufficient attention to the role played in China by privately owned companies (POCs) in innovation. POCs are the unsung heroes of Chinese innovation in many markets, including both automotive and semiconductors. In automotive, POCs companies like BYD are developing highly advanced technologies, and even attracting Western investors like Warren Buffett. In semiconductors, POCs like SMIF and the many design houses in Shanghai and Shenzen are well ahead of domestic SOE competitors.

Outside of our three industries, the pattern of strong POCs outperforming weaker SOEs continues.[22] Full or partial POCs such as Alibaba, Baidu, Huawei, and Tencent Holdings dominate the Chinese tech sector. The government's level of involvement varies from company to company, often in inverse proportion to a firm's capabilities. China's biggest tech POCs have become emblems of national pride. They have demonstrated increased prowess in leveraging China's market scale and their own R&D to produce innovation-led growth.[23] In doing so, they have developed the capability to adapt continuously to stay on top of their competition. Alibaba, for example, ranked seventh among the world's most innovative companies in a recent KPMG survey, beating even Samsung Electronics.[24]

The Party aligns well with SOEs, but poorly with POCs. It is likely that politically connected SOEs command too much Party attention, and receive too many resources, relative to their innovative capabilities. POCs in the same industry as a result receive too little, too late. This stifles the emergence of indigenous innovation in China—one of the avowed policies promoted in the party congress of October 2017. It similarly reduces exports outside of China, because the most capable exporters lack the political and financial muscle that their SOE competitors have.

There is a separate opportunity and challenge for the Party in dealing with foreign MNC players that possess strong technological capabilities. These organizations are eager to participate in the Chinese market, and to harness the talents of Chinese engineers and researchers. Some of them, such as Apple, have built substantial businesses within China. Others, such as Google and Facebook, are largely excluded from competing in the Chinese market. This deprives the Chinese market (and Chinese consumers) of the market discipline that arises from strong foreign competition. Part of the decisive role of the market requires developing and maintaining healthy competition to promote choice for consumers, reward effective strategies by producers, and discipline lax or weak performance by producers. (It should be noted that these attributes are also under threat in the West, albeit for different reasons, mostly due to the monopoly strength of many digital giants in their economies.)

Achieving and sustaining innovation across major Chinese industries will require much more than simply utilizing the SOEs to seize control of the commanding heights of the Chinese economy. If the Party plays a very strong role, this will advantage certain concentrated industries like high-speed rail, but may disadvantage many more Chinese industries.

However, there is another path available to the Party: embrace and promote Open Innovation more fully within and outside the country. Such a policy will increase the sources of useful knowledge available to innovative organizations like POCs in the country. It may also help strong POCs increase their exports to other country markets, deepening the expertise of these firms, strengthening their positions in global supply chains, increasing their economies of scale, and improving their cost and technology positions. Such a policy, though, would require the Party to look beyond their strong relations with the SOEs, in order to realize this result.

The Party has another role to play. Innovation creates both winners and losers in the economy. While the decisive role of the market will strengthen the successful companies, the society also needs to support and re-train the workers in those organizations that lose out. This may be an area where the CCP can outperform the fragmented safety nets in countries like the US. Similarly, the CCP can direct successful companies to establish businesses in less developed parts of the country, and spread the fruits of industrial development more evenly across different geographies in the country. The CCP can help the rest to learn from the best, enhancing economic productivity.

Once China achieves developed country status under the WTO, Xi Jinping thought may face a further tension between the leading role of the Party and China's obligations to foreign players in its markets under WTO rules as an advanced economy. Giving POCs the leeway they need to keep up with their competition, through the greater use of Open Innovation in China, and welcoming foreign MNCs into the Chinese economy, would be one effective means to address these pressures.

We see this possibility in the words of Party Chairman Xi Jinping, in his speech at the nineteenth Party Congress:

> Openness brings progress, while self-seclusion leaves one behind. China will not close its door to the world; we will only become more and more open.

It will take time to see if the CCP can manage the tensions within Xi Jinping thought to the benefit of the whole society. This chapter's discussion of three industries in China suggests that the Party will need to be flexible in its policy approach, and open in its thinking. Not every Chinese industry can be expected to follow the successful path of high-speed rail, and the POCs deserve more attention and support than they have heretofore received. The SOEs, in turn, might be receiving too much support.

If we step back and think about the first chapter in this book, we saw that innovation had to be generated, disseminated, and absorbed, before it really brought material benefits to the larger society. The Party would be well advised to support all three facets of innovation, particularly the dissemination and absorption, in order to continue China's economic success of the past forty years. Policies that provide retraining for displaced workers and that spread innovation activity to less developed geographic regions can help realize the opportunities that innovation can offer to the larger society. If the Party focuses primarily upon the initial generation of new technologies, coddles its SOEs, and ignores the most dynamic and innovative participants in its industries, the growth rate in the future in China is likely to suffer.

Chapter 9 review points:

1. Open Innovation in China is greatly affected by the powerful role of the Chinese Communist Party.
2. Xi Jinping thought introduces a tension between the 'decisive role of the markets' to allocate resources and stimulate innovation across the economy and 'the leading role of the Party' to guide the development of innovation in the most important industries. This tension plays out differently in different industries in China.
3. In high-speed rail, the tension has been adroitly managed, creating an organization with world class innovation capabilities that is a peer with the best of the rival firms in the world.

4. In automotive and semiconductors, however, the tension has been more problematic. The state-owned enterprises are well aligned with the Party, while it is the privately owned companies and foreign companies that are driving innovation.

5. The Party has the option of focusing less on the generation of new technologies, and more on the dissemination and absorption of these new technologies. This is a more promising path to sustain and grow innovation capabilities in China.

Notes

1. The Exponential Paradox

1. Peter Diamondis of Singularity University is perhaps the most prominent advocate for the impact of exponential technologies upon society. His 2012 book with Steven Kotler, *Abundance: The Future is Better Than You Think* (New York: Simon and Schuster), is a great introduction to this thinking.
2. See the Pew Center for Research, http://www.people-press.org/2011/01/20/section-2-views-of-long- term-future-past/, and also http://www.pewsocialtrends.org/2010/12/20/baby-boomers-approach-65-glumly/. These attitudes are hardly what we would expect in a society blessed by exponential technologies.
3. Robert Gordon, *The Rise and Fall of American Growth* (Princeton University Press, 2016).
4. https://oecdecoscope.wordpress.com/2017/01/25/the-best-vs-the-rest-the-global-productivity-slowdown-hides-an-increasing-performance-gap-across-firms/. The OECD further added that lagging firms may have fewer incentives to catch up to the best, owing to reduced market contestability, or increased market power of the best. Note, though, that the OECD did not provide any data on the distribution of 'best practices' in the first and second industrial revolutions that Gordon analyzes. It is likely that there were significant discrepancies between the best and the rest back in those times as well.
5. See Irving Wladavsky-Berger's post in the *Wall Street Journal*, https://blogs.wsj.com/cio/2019/02/08/the-current-state-of-ai-adoption/?guid=BL-CIOB-14751&mod=hp_minor_pos4&dsk=y (last accessed February 7, 2019). Note that the McKinsey study oversampled large firms and excluded small firms. So even this 21 percent figure is an inflated estimate of the use of AI across all companies.
6. Robert. M. Solow, 'We'd Better Watch Out', *New York Times*, July 12, 1987, Book Review, No. 36.
7. Brynjolffson's work on the IT paradox resulted in numerous publications in the 1990s. Perhaps the most accessible of these are his articles with Loren Hitt, 'Paradox Lost? Firm-level evidence on the returns to information systems spending', *Management Science*, 1996, and 'Beyond the Productivity Paradox', *Communications of the ACM*, 1998.
8. See O'Reilly's post on Medium: https://medium.com/the-wtf-economy/do-more-what-amazon-teaches-us-about-ai-and-the-jobless-future-8051b19a66af.
9. Personal conversation between Mike Helsel and the author, October 15, 2014.
10. http://news.pg.com/press-release/pg-corporate-announcements/pg-sets-two-new-goals-open-innovation-partnerships; last accessed November 2, 2017.

11. See J. Du. B. Leten and W. Vanhaverbeke, 'Managing open innovation projects with science-based and market-based partners', *Research Policy*, 2014.

12. See for example, K. Laursen and A. Salter, 'Open for innovation: the role of openness in explaining innovation performance among UK manufacturing firms', *Strategic Management Journal*, 2006.

13. Brunswicker and Chesbrough, 'A Fad or a Phenomenon: Results from a Survey on Open Innovation', 2013.

14. See Stephen Cohen and Brad DeLong's 2016 book, *Concrete Economics* (Harvard Business Review Press) for an extended institutional history of US infrastructure. This book goes all the way back to Alexander Hamilton, to trace the origins of central government support of economic infrastructure.

15. Vannevar Bush, 'Science: The Endless Frontier: A Report to the President', US Office of Scientific Research and Development, 1945.

16. Michael Porter and Mark Kramer, 'Creating Shared Value: How to Reinvent Capitalism—and Unleash a Wave of Innovation and Growth', *Harvard Business Review*, Jan.–Feb. 2011: pp. 63–70.

2. Open Innovation in the Twenty-First Century

1. Brunswicker and Chesbrough, 'A Fad or a Phenomenon: Results from a Survey on Open Innovation', 2013, and Brunswicker and Chesbrough, 'The Adoption of Open Innovation in Large Firms', *Research-Technology Management*, 2018.

2. See L. Huston and N. Sakkab, 'Inside Procter & Gamble's new model for innovation: Connect and develop', *Harvard Business Review*, 2006.

3. Personal conversation between Mike Helsel of General Mills and the author, October 15, 2014.

4. See Du. Leten and Vanhaverbeke, 2014.

5. See for example, Laursen and Salter, 2006.

6. Brunswicker and Chesbrough, 'A Fad or a Phenomenon: Results from a Survey on Open Innovation', 2013.

7. See H. Chesbrough and Marcel Bogers, in Chesbrough, Vanhaverbeke and West, *New Frontiers in Open Innovation* (Oxford University Press, 2014), p. 1.

8. Eric von Hippel, *Democratizing Innovation*, MIT Press, 2005. This book discusses Open Innovation in quite some detail, but does not cite my 2003 book at all. There also is no discussion of a business model anywhere in his book.

9. Jim Euchner of the IRI has usefully distinguished Open Innovation from what he calls 'open source innovation', with the latter corresponding to von Hippel's treatment of the concept. See Euchner, 'Two Flavors of Open Innovation', *RTM* July–August 2010, pp. 7–8.

10. Torvalds' frank comments are quoted in Steve Lohr's book *Go To* (2001), p. 215.

11. In a paper with Ann Kristin Zobel and Ben Balsmaier (2016) we actually ran a test of whether IP protection impaired or enhanced innovation collaboration. Using data from photovoltaic solar panels, we examined the behavior of hundreds of

startup companies in this industry, and compared their collaborative activity before and after they received their first patent. The 'free software' camp would argue that collaboration is easier before startups stake out their IP claims in the form of patents. The 'open software' camp would disagree, arguing that having some IP protection allows companies to collaborate more, secure in the knowledge that they have at least some protection for their technology. In this instance, the empirical analysis supports the Open camp, rather than the Free camp.

12. It is worth noting, for example, that the Linux Foundation that governs the Linux kernel these days is comprised of companies like IBM, Intel, Oracle, Dell, Nokia, and others. Membership on the Board requires an investment of $500,000, well beyond the financial capacity of any hobbyist. These inconvenient facts are ignored by the 'open and distributed' adherents of Open Innovation.

13. H. Chesbrough, *Open Innovation: The New Imperative for Creating and Profiting from Technology* (Harvard Business School Press, 2003).

14. See http://en.wikipedia.org/wiki/Open_innovation, last accessed March 21, 2019.

15. Michael Porter, *Competitive Strategy* (New York: Free Press), 1980; Michael Porter, *Competitive Advantage* (New York: Free Press), 1985.

16. Alfred Chandler, *Scale and Scope: The Dynamics of Industrial Capitalism* (Harvard University Press, 1990).

17. The entirety of chapter 1 of that book examines the experience of Xerox's Palo Alto Research Center, and offers a different interpretation of the root cause of Xerox's problems with PARC. Xerox was judged to be effective in utilizing PARC technologies that fit with Xerox's copier and printer business model. The failure was that Xerox could not conceive of an alternate business model through which to commercialize technologies that did not comport with that model. By contrast, the profile of IBM in chapter 5 showed a company that did reconceive its business model in response to a life-threatening crisis.

18. One paradox posed in Open Innovation was the surprising ability of Cisco to keep up with Lucent and its Bell Labs in the 1990s. As the 2003 book noted, 'Though they were direct competitors in a very technologically complex industry, Lucent and Cisco were not innovating in the same manner. Lucent devoted enormous resources to exploring the world of new materials and state of the art components and systems, to come up with fundamental discoveries that could fuel future generations of products and services. Cisco, meanwhile, did practically no internal research of this type.

   Instead, Cisco deployed a rather different weapon in the battle for innovation leadership. It scanned the world of startup companies that were springing up all around it, which were commercializing new products and services. Some of these startups, in turn, were founded by veterans of Lucent, or AT&T, or Nortel, who took the ideas they worked on at these companies, and attempted to build companies around them. Sometimes, Cisco would invest in these startups. Other times, it simply partnered with them. And more than occasionally, it would later acquire them. In this way, Cisco kept up with the R&D output of perhaps the finest industrial research organization in the world, without doing much internal research of its own' (p. xviii).

19. While comprehensive evidence of these points is elusive, some elements are already documented in the literature. Lemley (2001: 11–12) cites studies that report a large fraction of patents are neither used, nor licensed by firms. Davis and Harrison (2001) report that more than half of Dow's patents were un-utilized. Sakkab (2002) states that less than 10 percent of Procter & Gamble's patents were utilized by one of P&G's businesses.

20. See Lubica Hikkerovaa, Niaz Kammoun, and Jean-SébastienLantz, 'Patent Life Cycle: New Evidence', *Technological Forecasting and Social Change*, 88, October 2014, pp. 313–24.

21. These data are taken from H. Chesbrough, *Open Business Models* (Boston: Harvard Business School Press, 2006).

22. The quotation is from H. Chesbrough, *Open Business Models* (Harvard Business School Press, 2006), p. 201.

23. See Mark Johnson's book, *Seizing the White Space: Business Model Innovation for Growth and Renewal* (Harvard Business School Press, 2010), Alex Osterwalder's book, *Business Model Generation* (Wiley, 2010), and a special issue of *Long Range Planning*, 43 (2–3), 2010. that was dedicated entirely to academic articles on business models.

24. See Annabelle Gawer and Michael Cusumano's excellent book on *Platform Leadership* (2002), for an indepth analysis of what it takes to build and sustain leadership within a platform. Geoffrey Parker and Marshall VanAlstyne's *Platform Revolution: How Networked Markets Are Transforming the Economy and How to Make Them Work for You* (2016) updates this thinking for today's digital era.

25. H. Chesbrough, *Open Services Innovation: Rethinking Your Business to Grow and Compete in a New Era* (Jossey Bass, 2011).

26. Source: Henry Chesbrough, chapter 1, in Chesbrough, Vanhaverbeke, and West, *Open Innovation: Researching a New Paradigm* (Oxford University Press, 2006).

27. For details on these surveys, see Chesbrough and Brunswicker, 2013, and Brunswicker and Chesbrough, 2015. Our sample was restricted to firms with annual sales over $250 million, headquartered in either the US or Europe. So they cannot inform us about small firms' use of Open Innovation, nor the use of Open Innovation in other parts of the world.

28. See Laursen and Salter, 2006 and Du. Leten and Vanhaverbeke, 2014, for two excellent large sample analyses that show a statistically significant benefit to the use of Open Innovation in firms.

29. See K. Boudreau and K. Lakhani, 'How to manage outside innovation', *Sloan Management Review*, 2009 for a good discussion of the benefits of competition vs. the benefits of collaboration in innovation communities that propose solutions to problems.

30. See Hila Lifshitz-Assaf's excellent article on OI at NASA: 'Dismantling knowledge boundaries at NASA: The critical role of professional identity in Open Innovation', *Administrative Science Quarterly* 63.4 (2018): 746–82.

31. Ikujiro Nonaka and Hiro Takeuchi (1995) established the importance of managing knowledge by getting team members to engage with one another extensively. This was particularly needed for experiential, or tacit, knowledge.

32. A nice recent analysis of the role of teams in Open Innovation initiatives can be found in Amy Edmondson and Jean-Francois Harvey's 2017 book, *Extreme Teaming*. They were even kind enough to allow me to write the Foreword to this book!

33. Morten Hansen (2001) has done some excellent work on the importance of T-shaped managers. The base of the T refers to the person's deep expertise in some domain of knowledge. But the cross of the T refers to the ability of that manager to engage with other experts from other domains of knowledge, and find connections between the domains.

34. See Lifschitz-Assaf, 'Dismantling knowledge boundaries at NASA', 2018.

35. See Chesbrough and Chen, 2013.

36. See Ron Adner, *The Wide Lens* (2012) for an insightful discussion of the role of complementers in the ecosystem in promoting a successful innovation, or inhibiting the success of an otherwise promising innovation.

37. See https://www.tsmc.com/english/dedicatedFoundry/oip/index.htm, last accessed March 21, 2019.

38. See Henry Chesbrough, 'GE's ecomagination challenge: An experiment in Open Innovation.' *CaliforniaMmanagement Review* 54.3 (2012): 140–54.

39. The initial Blue Ocean proposals and recipients are described at http://blue oceangrants.com/, last accessed March 21, 2019.

3. From Open Science to Open Innovation

1. See Paul David's delightful history of early scientific institutions in Paul A. David, 'Understanding the emergence of "open science" institutions: functionalist economics in historical context.' *Industrial and Corporate* Change, 13.4 (2004): 571–89.

2. Ibid.

3. See   Robert K. Merton, *The Sociology of Science: Theoretical and Empirical Investigations* (University of Chicago Press, 1973).

4. See Opensciencegrid.org.

5. See https://rd-alliance.org/about.html for more about the origins and structure of the Research Data Alliance.

6. http://wlcg.web.cern.ch/

7. http://www.egi.eu

8. http://scoap3.org/

9. See Boisot, Nordberg, Yami and Incquevert, *Collsions and Collaborations: The Organization of Learning in the Atlas Experiment at the LHC* (Oxford University Press, 2011) for one detailed description of the institutions governing the science at CERN.

10. See, for instance, Atlas Collaboration: 'Observation of a new particle in the search for the Standard Model Higgs boson with the ATLAS detector at the LHC', *Physics Letters B* 716, 1 (2012): 1–29. doi:10.1016/j.physletb.2012.08.020. It is unclear at this point how helpful it is to each of the individual contributing scientists to be among the 6000 authors, in terms of personal recognition and prestige. Merton's CUDOS implies scarcity in academic credit yields prestige and recognition. When such credit is distributed across 6000 people, the social rewards to any one individual may be diluted.

11. One interpretation of the Horizon 2020 program, with its Flagship Initiatives, is that these are intended specifically to address the lack of industrial take-up of new scientific knowledge, by providing new resources to encourage such development.

12. In Eric von Hippel's latest book, *Free Innovation* (MIT Press), 2016 for instance, he ignores the need for business models, investment capital, and a financial return for that investment capital.

13. One example of such a successful commercial activity came out of the pioneering work done at CERN by Berners-Lee and colleagues around the underpinnings of the Web (such as the http and html protocols). The University of Illinois Champagne-Urbana's supercomputing center developed a browser (Mosaic) that allowed people to employ a 'point and click' user interface for these protocols. One of the students at UI, Marc Andreeson, met up with Jim Clark of Silicon Graphics in California, and formed Netscape. It was Netscape that really developed the first business model for the point and click user interface, by giving away the client browser for free, and charging content owners for the tools needed to publish their content on the web that was 'best viewed with Netscape'. Only then did the commercial use of the Internet begin to take off, because Netscape deployed the first real business model for the Internet, which previously was confined to scientific and technical uses.

14. Alfred North Whitehead. '*Science and the Modern World*' (London: Macmillan, 1925).

15. Consider the bitter protest of Professor Henry Rowland, who lamented the fame of 'tinkerers' like Edison relative to men of science such as himself. Addressing the American Academy for the Advancement of Science in 1883, he proclaimed:

> 'The proper course of one in my position is to consider what must be done to create a science of physics in this country, rather than to call telegraphs, electric lights, and such conveniences, by the name of science... When the average tone of the [scientific] society is low, when the highest honors are given to the mediocre, when third-class men are held up as examples, and when trifling inventions are magnified into scientific discoveries, then the influence of such societies is prejudicial.'

16. Kenneth Arrow, 'Economic Welfare and the Allocation of Resources for Invention', in *The Rate and Direction of Inventive Activity*, edited by Richard R. Nelson, (Princeton, NJ: Princeton University Press, 1962), 609–25.

17. 'Science: The Endless Frontier', a report to the President by Vannevar Bush, Director of the Office of Scientific Research and Development, July 1945.

18. Samuel Kortum and Josh Lerner, 'What is behind the recent surge in patenting?.' *Research Policy* 28.1 (1999): 1–22.

19. Indeed, one perhaps extreme contrast to Henry Rowlands comes from the just-retired President of Stanford University. John Hennessey is an acclaimed computer scientist, and the former Dean of the Engineering School at Stanford. But he has also taken three leaves of absence during his academic career to start up new companies, and sits on the board of Google and Cisco as of this writing. While Rowlands would be appalled, Hennessey is likely a new model for a university leader, who combines deep research knowledge with deep practical experience in applying that knowledge.

20. Henry Chesbrough, *Open Innovation: The New Imperative for Creating and Profiting from Technology* (Harvard Business School Press, 2003); table 3.1. See James Bessen's paper 'The Value of US Patents by Owner and Patent Characteristics' for more recent data: https://www.immagic.com/eLibrary/ARCHIVES/GENERAL/BOS_U_US/B061129B.pdf

21. See the Science and Technology Indicators report, Table 4-11 of the National Science Foundation for these data, https://www.nsf.gov/statistics/2018/nsb20181/report/sections/research-and-development-u-s-trends-and-international-comparisons/u-s-business-r-d (last accessed July 6, 2019).

22. www.imec.org

23. www.fraunhofer.de

24. www.eit.europa.eu

25. www.attract-eu.org

4. The Back End of Open Innovation

1. We will see these shared services, and their organizational challenges, again when we examine the role that open innovation can play with Lean Startup Processes in Chapter 5.

2. See Hila Lifshitz-Assaf, 'Dismantling Knowledge Boundaries at NASA', 2018. Her NASA work grew out of an executive education class that her advisor Karim Lakhani taught. The attendees included some people from NASA, and Karim was able to engage with them, and eventually insert his doctoral student, Hila, in a long term study of the organization. Hila first presented this work at our inaugural World Open Innovation Conference in Napa, California in 2014.

3. See Chesbrough and Brunswicker, 2013.

4. This definition is taken from Chesbrough, Vanhaverbeke, and West, *Open Innovation: Researching a New Paradigm* (Oxford University Press, 2006), p. 1. Alert readers might notice that this definition has since been updated, as discussed in Chapter 1 of this book. Unfortunately, that update happened after we'd conducted our survey.

5. I am grateful to my former students Sohyeong Kim, Maurice Hagin, Anna Roumiantseva, Jiayin Song, and Wolfgang Sachsenhofer for their assistance on this part of the chapter.

6. See the following link for more information on Github: http://www.howtogeek. com/180167/htg-explains-what-is-github-and-what-do-geeks-use-it-for/, accessed August 20, 2016. Microsoft acquired Github for $7.5 billion in June, 2018, though the hub continues to operate much as it did prior to the acquisition.

7. See Intel Labs case (Chesbrough, 1999) for a short history of Intel's organization of its research function. As shown in that case, although Intel was highly dependent on research breakthroughs for its business, it had negative experiences with separating research from development.

8. See the following link for an introduction to the Open Innovation 2.0 initiative. Note that the first author was the head of Intel's labs in Europe until summer 2016: http://ec.europa.eu/information_society/newsroom/cf/dae/document.cfm?doc_ id=2182

9. EMC was acquired by Dell in 2016 for $67 Billion. I cannot tell yet whether the EMC processes described here have survived the acquisition or not. I include them here because the shift within EMC's innovation unit from technology push to business unit pull is relevant for many companies.

10. See https://www.gore.com/innovation-center, led by Linda Elkins (Ms Inside) and Paul Campbell (Mr Outside). Last accessed February 15, 2019.

11. Most academic attention to open innovation appears to be concentrated in the least-used practices in companies, at least in large organizations. I invite academically-minded readers to ponder this finding. Are we as academics focused on the most important innovation issues that organizations face? Do we need to change our research priorities, in order to be more relevant to these organizations?

5. Lean Startup and Open Innovation

1. Eric Ries, *The Lean Startup* (New York: Crown Business, 2011).

2. Eric Ries was a student of Steve Blank, and also was involved in a company that Steve Blank invested in. Steve conditioned his investment on Eric taking his class, and exposed Eric to Steve's radically different thinking about startups. Eric then developed his own thinking about Lean, and Lean Startup emerged. So both Eric and Steve have made fundamental contributions to Lean Startup concepts, and it is hard to disentangle who started that ball rolling first!

3. See Steve Blank and Bob Dorf, *The Startup Owner's Manual* (K&S Ranch Publishing, 2012), where he puts forward these definitions.

4. Eric Schmidt, former Executive Chairman of Google, discussed this allocation of resources many times. Here's one example: https://www.forbes.com/sites/ quentinhardy/2011/07/16/googles-innovation-and-everyones/#4d3ef9ca3066 (last accessed Feburary 15, 2019).

5. My paper with Richard Rosenbloom (2002) discussed this issue at length in the context of Xerox and its Palo Alto Research Center (PARC). We show that PARC technologies were easily absorbed when they aligned with the copier and printer business model of Xerox. It was the 'misfit' technologies (also known as 'false

negative' technologies) that Xerox struggled to manage, precisely because they did not align with Xerox's business model.

6. While the Lean project leader might want to use the corporate brand to strengthen the value proposition of the new project to a prospective customer, the Chief Marketing Officer of the corporation will rightly resist. Brands take years or decades to build, and can be damaged quickly. Some flaky MVP might create a huge headache for the brand if something goes wrong. (Again, a startup doesn't worry about this.) One solution is to create sub-brands (e.g., Google Beta, or Google Labs) that signal the different character of the MVP prototype, while conveying the corporate backing of the brand. Another is to create a 'white box' brand, used for testing new ideas, while keeping separate the corporate brand.

7. For more information, see my guest posting on Steve Blank's website, available at this link: http://steveblank.com/2014/03/26/why-internal-ventures-are-different-from-external-startups/

8. See T. Weiblen and H. Chesbrough, 'Engaging with startups to enhance corporate innovation', Weiblein and Chesbrough, *California Management Review,* 2015.

9. See F. Piller, 'Open Innovation with Customers: Crowdsourcing and Co-Creation at Threadless' (October 5, 2010). Available at SSRN: https://ssrn.com/abstract=1688018 or http://dx.doi.org/10.2139/ssrn.1688018

10. See the Telefonica Lean Elephants case, by H. Chesbrough, https://hbr.org/product/telefonica-a-lean-elephant/B5863-PDF-ENG

11. http://www.tid.es/who-we-are.

12. The Internet of Things is the network of physical objects or 'things' embedded with electronics, software, sensors, and network connectivity, enabling these objects to collect and exchange data. https://en.wikipedia.org/wiki/Internet_of_Things.

13. A SIM card is a chip that securely stores the mobile subscriber number and other information that the mobile phone needs to use. This portable, exchangeable memory chip is used in some cell phone models, as well as in other electronics devices.

14. Susana Jurado and Maria Olano, 'Lean Elephants: Addressing the Innovation Challenge in Big Companies', Innovation and Research Telefonica, http://www.tid.es/sites/526e527928a32d6a7400007f/assets/53bfe9f128a32d6733001f37/Lean_Elephants.pdf, p. 13.

15. Ibid., p. 6.

16. Ian Small left Telefonica to become the CEO of Evernote in October of 2018.

6. Engaging with Startups to Enhance Corporate Innovation

1. An earlier version of the ideas in this chapter was published by Weiblen and Chesbrough (2015).

2. See Rita McGrath, *The End of Competitive Advantage* (Boston, MA: Harvard Business School Press, 2013), for a thoughtful discussion of why large

organizations can no longer expect to enjoy long periods of sustained competitive advantage. In a volatile, uncertain, complex, and ambiguous (VUCA) world, the best that companies may aspire to is a series of temporary competitive advantages, according to McGrath.

3. See the Yearbook of the NVCA, downloadable at www.nvca.org (last accessed February 15, 2019).

4. See the archives of the National Business Incubator Association, http://www. innovationamerica.us/innovation-daily/archives (last accessed February 15, 2019).

5. The NSF I-Corps was originated at UC Berkeley's Haas School of Business, under the leadership of Steve Blank and Andre Marquis. Each week (the duration typically runs eight–ten weeks), every startup must conduct at least ten customer interviews for the startup's idea. One early analysis of the results of this training found that, while typical SBIR applicants had an acceptance rate of 18 percent for the first phase awards, I-Corps graduates experienced a nearly 60 percent acceptance rate for SBIR grants, a three-fold improvement. Rhonda Shrader carries on the I-Corps program today. Hundreds of startup teams have been trained at Berkeley over the years, and more than one hundred universities have trained their own professors in this I-Corps methodology. When the startup teams that all of those professors have since taught are included, one can conservatively estimate that tens of thousands of startup teams have been through this rigorous, eight to ten week program.

6. It's a different situation in China. There, nearly half of all startup equity investment comes from corporations, particularly the Big 3 (Alibaba, Baidu, Tencent). https://techcrunch.com/2018/07/05/china-vc-has-overtaken-silicon-valley/ (last accessed February 15, 2019).

7. See Paul Gompers, 'Corporations and the Financing of Innovation: The Corporate Venture Capital Experience', in *Economic Review* (Federal Reserve Bank of Atlanta), Q4 (2002): 1–17.

8. A more detailed discussion of linking CVC investments with company strategies can be found in Henry Chesbrough, 'Making Sense of Corporate Venture Capital', *Harvard Business Review*, 80.3 (2002): 90–9.

9. See Haemin Park and Kevin Steensma, 'When Does Corporate Venture Capital Add Value for New Ventures?', *Strategic Management Journal*, 33.1 (January 2012): 1–22.

10. See the National Venture Capital Association's Pitchbook, https://files.pitchbook. com/website/files/pdf/3Q_2018_PitchBook_NVCA_Venture_Monitor.pdf (last accessed February 27, 2019). It reports that corporate venture capital investors participated in 1403 deals in 2017, for a total value of $36.3 billion dollars, which comprised 44 percent of all venture capital invested that year. Through the first three quarters of 2018, there were 1096 investments, amounting to $39.3 billion of capital, which comprised 47 percent of all venture capital invested.

11. See Henry Chesbrough (2002) for a history of Xerox spin-off companies, and how they were funded. Lucent's New Ventures program is discussed in detail in Chesbrough and Socolof (2000).

12. See https://www.bosch.com/stories/bosch-start-up-platform/, last accessed March 22, 2019.
13. See https://foundry.att.com/, last accessed March 22, 2019.
14. Andre Marquis and Manav Subodh, *Hypershift: How Established Companies can Work with Makers, Inventors and Entrepreneurs to Leverage Innovation, Enter New Markets, Establish Brand Leadership, and Unlock Value,* (Hypershift Advisory Press, 2014).
15. Annabelle Gawer and Michael Cusumano are a great introduction to platforms. See 'Industry Platforms and Ecosystem Innovation', *Journal of Product Innovation Management,* 31.3 (May 2014): 417–33, for a helpful summary of the body of their work. Another useful reference is Geoffrey Parker, Marshall VanAlstyne, and Sangeet Chaudory, *Platform Revolution: How Networked Markets Are Transforming the Economy and How to Make Them Work for You* (New York: Norton and Co., 2016).
16. There is an increasing amount of activity in the pharmaceutical industry that is creating paths out of the internal labs for unused or abandoned compounds. See H. Chesbrough and E. Chen, 'Recovering Abandoned Compounds Through Expanded External IP Licensing', *California Management Review,* 55.4 (Summer 2013): 83–102.

7. Open Innovation Results in Smart Cities and Smart Villages

1. See Richard Florida, *Cities and the Creative Class* (New York: Routledge, 2005).
2. See Melissa Lee, Esteve Almirall, and Jonathan Wareham, 'Open data and civic apps: first-generation failures, second-generation improvements', *Communications of the ACM,* 59.1, January 2016. An earlier, more hopeful assessment can be found in T. Bakici, E. Almirall, and J. Wareham, 'A Smart City Initiative: The Case of Barcelona', *Journal of the Knowledge Economy,* 4.2 (June 2013), pp. 135–48.
3. See Dambisa Moyo's penetrating critique, *Dead Aid: Why Aid is Not Working and How There is a Better Way for Africa* (New York: Farrar, Strauss and Giroux, 2009), p. 28. While she examines aid in Africa, her critique extends to rural villages in other underdeveloped economies as well, such as India.
4. Ibid, p. 28.
5. Ibid, p. 44. In Africa, Moyo writes, it is not uncommon for a working family member to support as many as fifteen relatives.
6. Ibid, p. 67.
7. Ibid, p. 28.
8. Ibid, pp. 44–5.
9. This chapter draws from a more extensive case study and teaching note by Solomon Darwin and Henry Chesbrough. See 'Prototyping a Scalable Smart Village to Simultaneously Create Sustainable Development and Enterprise Growth Opportunities', HBS case B5886-PDF-ENG, 2017.
10. Source: US CDC: https://www.cdc.gov/dengue/

11. Source: 'Reverse Innovation': GE Makes India a Lab for Global Markets, Knowledge@Wharton, http://knowledge.wharton.upenn.edu/article/reverse-innovation-ge-makes-india-a-lab-for-global-markets/

12. Source: Soil Quality Information Sheet, Soil Quality Resource Concerns: Salinization, United States Department of Agriculture Natural Resources Conservation Service, http://www.nrcs.usda.gov/Internet/FSE_DOCUMENTS/nrcs142p2_053151.pdf

13. The total budget of the town council in Mori Village is roughly $8,000 per year, far too little to support any investment in IT infrastructure.

14. See C. K. Prahalad's helpful analysis, *The Fortune at the Bottom of the Pyramid: Eradicating Poverty through Profits* (Wharton Publishing), 2006.

15. See Eric Ries, *The Lean Startup*, 2011, for an introduction to this approach in the context of high technology startup companies, as well as the discussion in Chapter 5 of this volume.

16. See http://smartvillagemovement.org/ for an example of one local NGO working to disseminate Smart Villages to other places, both in India and in other rural settings.

17. See Mark Kramer and Michael Porter, 'Creating Shared Value: How to Reinvent Capitalism—and Unleash a Wave of Innovation and Growth', *Harvard Business Review*, January–February 2011.

8. Open Innovation Best Practices

1. Larry Huston and Nabil Sakkab, 'Connect and Develop: Inside Procter and Gamble's New Model for Innovation', *Harvard Business Review*, March 2006, 58–67.

2. See H. Chesbrough, *Open Business Models: How to Thrive in the New Innovation Landscape* (Boston, MA: Harvard Business School Press, 2006), chapter 8, for a discussion of P&G's early experiences with Open Innovation in general, the Glad joint venture in particular, and the 'use it or lose it' policy towards internal IP.

3. This section is based upon a longer case study. See H. Chesbrough, 'GE's Ecomagination Challenge: An Experiment in Open Innovation', *California Management Review*, 54.3 (April 2012).

4. This section builds on a longer case study. See H. Chesbrough, 'Innovation @ENEL: From Monopoly Power to Open Power', Harvard Business School case # B5866-PDF-ENG, July 1, 2016.

5. See D. Hounshell and J. Smith, *Science and Strategy: Dupont 1902–1980* (Cambridge, UK: Cambridge University Press, 1988). Hounshell and Smith indicate how Dupont followed Bayer in the early years of setting up its first R&D facilities.

6. Source: David Tamoschus, Christoph Hiererth, and Monika Lessl, 'Developing a Framework to Manage a Pharmaceutical Innovation Ecosystem', Best Emerging Scholar Paper Award recipient at the World Open Innovation Conference Santa Clara, CA in December, 2015.

7. Ibid.

8. For a discussion of Quirky's model, see Cara Wrigley and Karla Straker 'Designing innovative business models with a framework that promotes experimentation', *Strategy & Leadership*, 44.1 (2016), pp. 11–19. For its bankruptcy, see https://www.nytimes.com/2015/09/23/business/the-invention-start-up-quirky-files-for-bankruptcy.html

9. One example of such bad ideas came from GE's ecomagination challenge. One idea submitted was to place electric eels into a pond, and then to insert a cord to extract the electricity they generated. Another was to place a windmill on the back of a truck, and capture the wind energy generated. (If you don't know why this latter idea was bad, consult a text on the second law of thermodynamics!)

10. In two large sample surveys I conducted with Sabine Brunswicker on the adoption of Open Innovation in large firms, crowdsourcing was the least used of ten different outside-in Open Innovation practices. This low level of usage suggests that many large companies recognize full well the limits of crowdsourcing, even if my academic colleagues do not.

11. This point was powerfully illustrated in Chesbrough and Rosenbloom (2002), in the context of Xerox and its many PARC spin-off technologies.

12. http://usersoffice.web.cern.ch/sites/usersoffice.web.cern.ch/files/pdf/Users-Stat/Users_Statistics_2017.pdf, last accessed December 27, 2018.

13. This approach to background and foreground IP has been shown to work effectively elsewhere. The International Micro Electronics Consortium (IMEC) is one such example at the University of Leuven, where these IP approaches have been in place for many years now. See *Interuniversity MicroElectronics Center (A)*, by H. Chesbrough, W. Vanhaverbeke, and L. Odusanya, Berkeley Haas Case Series, 2009.

14. See H. Chesbrough, 'NeuroTherapy Ventures: Catalyzing Neurologic Innovations,' HBS case 602124-PDF-ENG (2002) for an example of nonprofits looking to advance new therapies in ways that do not block the subsequent development of the technology.

15. See http://www.pgscience.com/home/connect_develop.html, last accessed February 27. 2019.

16. See https://hbr.org/2006/03/connect-and-develop-inside-procter-gambles-new-model-for-innovation, last accessed July 25, 2017.

17. A. G. Lafley and Ram Charan, *The Game-Changer: How You Can Drive Revenue and Profit Growth with Innovation,* (New York: Crown Business, 2008).

18. https://hbr.org/2011/06/how-pg-tripled-its-innovation-success-rate, last accessed July 25, 2017.

19. Source: each of these were listed in this order on this page, http://www.pgscience.com/home/connect_develop.html, last accessed February 27, 2019.

20. Visit by Ashok Chatterji, then P&G head of Connect & Develop, in my class in Berkeley, 2013.

21. Adapted from H. Chesbrough, The Era of Open Innovation, *MIT Sloan Management Review*, 44.3, Spring 2003.

9. Open Innovation with Chinese Characteristics

1. The ideas and evidence in this chapter have been inspired by a collaboration with Dr Sohvi Leih of the Berkeley Research Group, and Mei Liang of Peking University. An early version of the arguments in this chapter appeared in a conference paper submitted to the 5th annual World Open Innovation Conference, titled 'Open InnovationOpen Innovation with Chinese Characteristics'. I have also benefited from discussion with Fu Xiaolan. Her 2015 book, *China's Path to Innovation* (Cambridge, UK: Cambridge University Press), traces the development of China's innovation capabilities.

2. See S. Brachman (2015). Chinese support of indigenous innovation is problematic for foreign IP owners. *IPWatchdod* (April 9). http://www.ipwatchdog.com/2015/04/09/chinese-indigenous-innovation-problematic-foreign-ip-owners/id=56525/.

3. Elizabeth Economy's impressive book, *The Third Revolution* (Oxford University Press, 2018), documents the evolution of Xi Jingping's policies over time. She depicts a sobering trend of these policies moving away from globally integrated supply chains, towards a more indigenously-oriented approach. She argues that Xi Jinping's administration should be understood not as a continuation of Deng Xiaoping's policies, but instead as a 'third revolution' (Mao being the first, and Deng being the second).

4. M. Martina and P. Wen (2017), 'China enshrines "Xi Jinping Thought", key Xi ally to step down', Reuters. https://www.reuters.com/article/us-china-congress/china-enshrines-xi-jinping-thought-key-xi-ally-to-step-down-idUSKBN1CT0C9

5. See Xiaolan Fu (2015), *China's Path to Innovation,* for an authoritative account of China's innovation activities in the past forty years.

6. See R. Zhong and P. Mozur (2018), 'Tech Giants Feel the Squeeze as Xi Jinping Tightens His Grip', https://www.nytimes.com/2018/05/02/technology/china-xi-jinping-technology-innovation.html

7. This uneven pattern of innovation performance exists beyond these three specific industries. Chinese renewable energy technology has surged to the forefront of the world, as photovoltaic technology in China is now exported all over the world. In other industries, though, the innovation performance of Chinese companies lags behind the best of the world, in industries such as flat panel displays or pharmaceuticals.

8. This section is deeply informed by the work of Mei Liang, who was a postdoctoral student at the Haas School of Business at UC Berkeley for the year 2017–18. He returned to Tsinghua University, and is now on the faculty at Peking University. His paper at our 4th World Open InnovationOpen Innovation Conference received the Best Paper prize that year. Mei, Liang (2017), 'Navigating Open Innovation under institutional influence: Lessons from China high-speed rail industry', *4th World Open InnovationOpen Innovation Conference Paper.*

9. This section is heavily influenced by the work of Professor Li Xianjun and his students. Professor Li works in the automotive engineering department of Tsinghua University. Two of his students, Ke Xu and Meng Donghui, were visiting scholars here at UC Berkeley, where I had the opportunity to work directly with each of them.

10. For one account of this, see Xu, Ke, and Li, Xianjun (2014), 'Technological innovation from imitation in latecomer firms: evidence from China's auto firms', *Innovation and Development*, 4.1, pp. 161–73.

11. M. Schuman, August 29, 2017, 'China's Car Sector Needs a Shakeup', *Bloomberg*. https://www.bloomberg.com/view/articles/2017-08-29/china-s-car-sector-needs-a-shakeup-not-buyouts

12. See Professor Li Xianjun's research 'Industrial Value Migration, Path Innovation and Competitive Advantage: Empirical Analysis Based on China's Automotive Firms', http://en.cnki.com.cn/Article_en/CJFDTOTAL-ZGRK201001013.htm (last accessed March 1, 2019). Li's research shows that the larger the Chinese automotive company, the weaker its innovative capabilities.

13. K. Bradsher (2018), 'China Is Opening Its Car Market: But Not Enough, Say Auto Companies', *New York Times*, https://www.nytimes.com/2018/04/25/business/china-auto-trade.html

14. See D. Ma (2017), 'Can Chinese Industrial Policy Determine Winners or Just Stir up Froth?', *Macro Polo*, https://macropolo.org/can-industrial-policy-propel-chinas-ev-industry-just-stir-froth/, and also Schuman (op cit).

15. See Xu and Li (2014), 'Technological innovation from imitation in latecomer firms: evidence from China's auto firms'.

16. See my earlier study with David Teece: Henry Chesbrough, and David Teece (2005), 'The Globalization of R&D in the Semiconductor Industry, final report to the Alfred P. Sloan Foundation', New York, NY.

17. See my paper with Xiaolan Fu and colleagues, Fu, Xiaolan, Li, Jizhen, Hongru Xiong, and Henry Chesbrough, 2014. 'Open Innovation as a Response to Constraints and Risks: Evidence from China', *Asian Economic Papers*, 13.3, pp. 30–58.

18. See C. Ting-Fang (2018), 'China's upstart chip companies aim to topple Samsung, Intel and TSMC', *Nikkei Asian Review*.

19. See Henry Chesbrough and Liang, Feng Helen (2008), 'Return to R&D Investment and Spillovers in the Chinese Semiconductor Industry: A Tale of Two Segments'. 2008 Industry Studies Conference Paper. Available at SSRN: https://ssrn.com/abstract=1120024

20. See P. Clarke (2017), 'Top ten Chinese chip companies ranked', EE News. http://www.eenewsanalog.com/news/top-ten-chinese-chip-companies-ranked

21. See C. Cadell (2018), 'Chips down: China aims to boost semiconductors as trade war looms', Reuters : https://www.reuters.com/article/us-usa-trade-china-chips/chips-down-china-aims-to-boost-semiconductors-as-trade-war-looms-idUSKBN1HR1DF

22. Yasheng Huang documents the poor performance of many Chinese SOEs in his book, *Capitalism with Chinese Characteristics: Entrepreneurship and the State* (Cambridge, UK: Cambridge University Press, 2008).

23. George Yip and Bruce McKern capture these achievements nicely in their 2016 book, *China's Next Strategic Advantage* (Cambridge, MA: MIT Press).

24. M. Bey (2017), 'In China, Innovation Cuts Both Ways', *Stratfor*: https://worldview. stratfor.com/article/china-innovation-cuts-both-ways

Bibliography

Aad, G. et al. 'Observation of a New Particle in the Search for the Standard Model Higgs Boson with the ATLAS Detector at the LHC', *Physics Letters B*, 716.1 (2012), pp. 1–29: doi: 10.1016/j.physletb.2012.08.020

'About RDA'. *RDA*, rd-alliance.org/about.html. Last accessed April 17, 2019.

Adner, Ron. *The Wide Lens: a New Strategy for Innovation*. Portfolio/Penguin, 2012.

'AT&T Foundry'. *ATT Foundry*, foundry.att.com/. Last accessed April 25, 2019.

'Archives'. *Innovation America*, 2016, www.innovationamerica.us/innovation-daily/archives.

Arrow, Kenneth, 1962. 'Economic Welfare and the Allocation of Resources for Invention', NBER chapters, in: Richard Nelson, *The Rate and Direction of Inventive Activity: Economic and Social Factors*, pp. 609–26, National Bureau of Economic Research, Inc.

Baden-Fuller, Charles et al., (eds). 'Long Range Planning', 43.2–3 (April 2010), pp. 143–462.

Bakıcı, Tuba et al. 'A Smart City Initiative: the Case of Barcelona', *Journal of the Knowledge Economy*, 4.2 (2012), pp. 135–48., doi: 10.1007/s13132-012-0084-9.

Baldwin, Carliss, and Eric Von Hippel. 'Modeling a paradigm shift: From producer innovation to user and open collaborative innovation', *Organization Science*, 22.6 (2011), pp. 1399–417.

Bey, Matthew. 'In China, Innovation Cuts Both Ways', *Stratfor* (October 24, 2017), worldview.stratfor.com/article/china-innovation-cuts-both-ways.

Blank, Steve. 'Steve Blank: Why Internal Ventures Are Different from External Startups', *Steve Blank*, March 26, 2014, steveblank.com/2014/03/26/why-internal-ventures-are-different-from-external-startups/.

Blank, Steve, and Bob Dorf. *The Startup Owner's Manual: the Step-by-Step Guide for Building a Great Company*. K&S Ranch Publishing, 2012.

Bogers, M., A. K. Zobel, A. Afuah, E. Almirall, S. Brunswicker, L. Dahlander, L. Frederiksen,, A. Gawer, M. Gruber, S. Haefliger, and J. Hagedoorn, 2017. 'The open innovation research landscape: Established perspectives and emerging themes across different levels of analysis', *Industry and Innovation*, 24.1, pp. 8–40.

Boisot, Max, Markus Nordberg, Said Yami and Bertrand Niquevert. *Collisions and Collaboration: the Organization of Learning in the Atlas Experiment at the LHC.*, Oxford University Press, 2011.

Boudreau, Kevin J., and Karim R. Lakhani. 'How to Manage Outside Innovation', *MIT Sloan Management Review*, 50.4 (2009), pp. 69–76.

Boudreau, Kevin J., and Karim R. Lakhani. 'The confederacy of heterogeneous software organizations and heterogeneous developers: Field experimental evidence on sorting and worker effort', *The Rate and Direction of Inventive Activity Revisited*. University of Chicago Press, 2011, pp. 483–502.

Brachmann, Steve. 'Chinese Support of Indigenous Innovation Is Problematic for Foreign IP Owners.' *IPWatchdog.com|Patents & Patent Law*, September 28, 2015: www.ipwatchdog.com/2015/04/09/chinese-indigenous-innovation-problematic-foreign-ip-owners/id=56525/.

Bradsher, Keith. 'China Is Opening Its Car Market: But Not Enough, Say Auto Companies', *The New York Times*, April 25, 2018: www.nytimes.com/2018/04/25/business/china-auto-trade.html.

Brown, Bruce, and Scott Anthony. 'How P&G Tripled Its Innovation Success Rate', *Harvard Business Review*, July 24, 2017: hbr.org/2011/06/how-pg-tripled-its-innovation-success-rate.

Brown, Korbin. 'What Is GitHub, and What Is It Used For?' *How*, How-To Geek, September 6, 2017: www.howtogeek.com/180167/htg-explains-what-is-github-and-what-do-geeks-use-it-for/.

Brunswicker, Sabine, and Henry Chesbrough. 'A Fad or a Phenomenon?: The Adoption of Open Innovation in Large Firms', *Research-Technology Management*, 61., (December 28, 2015), pp. 16–25: doi: 10.5437/08956308X5702196.

Brynjolfsson, Erik, and Lorin Hitt. 'Paradox Lost? Firm-Level Evidence on the Returns to Information Systems Spending', *Management Science*, 42.4 (April 1, 1996), pp. 541–58: doi: 10.1287/mnsc.42.4.541.

Brynjolfsson, Erik, and Lorin M. Hitt. 'Beyond the Productivity Paradox', *Communications of the ACM*, 41.8 (August 1998), pp. 49–55.

'Section 2: Views of Long-Term Future, Past', Pew Research Center for the People and the Press: www.people-press.org/2011/01/20/section-2-views-of-long-term-future-past/. Last accessed September 18, 2018.

Cadell, Cate. 'Chips down: China Aims to Boost Semiconductors as Trade War Looms', *Reuters*, Thomson Reuters (April 20, 2018): www.Reuters.com/article/us-usa-trade-china-chips/chips-down-china-aims-to-boost-semiconductors-as-trade-war-looms-idUSKBN1HR1DF.

'CERN Accelerating Science', *WLCG*, wlcg.web.cern.ch/. Last accessed April 25, 2019.

'CERN Users by Institute and Nationality', European Organization for Nuclear Research, 2017. http://usersoffice.web.cern.ch/sites/usersoffice.web.cern.ch/files/pdf/Users-Stat/Users_Statistics_2017.pdf. December 27, 2018.

Chandler, Alfred Dupont. *Scale and Scope: The Dynamics of Industrial Capitalism*. Harvard University Press, 1994.

Chesbrough, Henry W. *Intel Labs (A): Photolithography Strategy in Crisis*. Harvard Business School Case, 600–032, October 1999.

Chesbrough, Henry. 'Making Sense of Corporate Venture Capital', *Harvard Business Review*, 80.3 (2002).

Chesbrough, Henry. *NeuroTherapy Ventures: Catalyzing Neurologic Innovations*. HBS No. 602124-PDF-ENG. Boston, MA: Harvard Business Publishing, 2002.

Chesbrough, Henry. "Graceful exits and missed opportunities: Xerox's management of its technology spin-off organizations." *Business History Review* 76.4 (2002): 803–837.

Chesbrough, Henry W. *Open Innovation: the New Imperative for Creating and Profiting from Technology*. Harvard Business School Press, 2003.

Chesbrough, Henry. 'The Era of Open Innovation', *MIT Sloan Management Review*, 127.3 (April 15, 2003).

Chesbrough, Henry William. *Open Business Models: How to Thrive in the New Innovation Landscape*. Harvard Business School Press, 2006.

Chesbrough, Henry. *Interuniversity MicroElectronics Center (A)*. Case Study. Berkeley. Berkeley Haas Case Series, 2009.

Chesbrough, Henry William. *Open Services Innovation: Rethinking Your Business to Grow and Compete in a New Era*. Jossey-Bass, 2011.

Chesbrough, Henry. 'GE's Ecomagination Challenge: An Experiment in Open Innovation', *California Management Review*, 54.3 (April 1, 2012), pp. 140–54.

Chesbrough, Henry. *Telefonica Lean Elephants Case*. HBS No. B5863-PDF-ENG. Boston, MA: Harvard Business Publishing, 2016.

Chesbrough, Henry. *Innovation @ENEL: From Monopoly Power to Open Power*. Case Study. Berkeley. Berkeley Haas Case System, 2016.

Chesbrough, Henry, and Eric L. Chen. 'Recovering Abandoned Compounds through Expanded External IP Licensing', *California Management Review*, 55.4 (2013), pp. 83–101: doi: 10.1525/cmr.2013.55.4.83.

Chesbrough, Henry and Liang, Feng. 'Return to R&D Investment and Spillovers in the Chinese Semiconductor Industry: A Tale of Two Segments', *2008 Industry Studies Conference Paper*. Available at SSRN: https://ssrn.com/abstract=1120024 or http://dx.doi.org/10.2139/ssrn.1120024

Chesbrough, Henry, and Richard S. Rosenbloom. "The role of the business model in capturing value from innovation: evidence from Xerox Corporation's technology spin-off companies." *Industrial and corporate change* 11.3 (2002): 529–555.

Chesbrough, Henry W., and Stephen J. Socolof. "Creating new ventures from Bell Labs technologies." Research-Technology Management 43.2 (2000): 13–17.

Chesbrough, Henry and David Teece (2005), 'The Globalization of R&D in the Semiconductor Industry, final report to the Alfred P. Sloan Foundation', New York, NY.

Chesbrough, Henry William., Wim Vanhaverbeke, and Joel West. *Open Innovation: Researching a New Paradigm*. Oxford University Press, 2006.

Chesbrough, Henry, Wim Vanhaverbeke, and Joel West. *New Frontiers in Open Innovation*. Oxford University Press, 2014.

Clarke, Peter. 'Top Ten Chinese Chip Companies Ranked', *EeNews Analog*, December 19, 2017, www.eenewsanalog.com/news/top-ten-chinese-chip-companies-ranked.

Cohn, D'Vera, and Paul Taylor. 'Baby Boomers Approach 65: Glumly', *Pew Research Center's Social & Demographic Trends Project*, April 10, 2014,: www.pewsocialtrends.org/2010/12/20/baby-boomers-approach-65-glumly/.

Cohen, Stephen S., and J. Bradford DeLong. *Concrete Economics: the Hamilton Approach to Economic Growth and Policy*. Harvard Business Review Press, 2016.

'Connect + Develop', *PG Science*, www.pgscience.com/home/connect_develop.html. Last accessed April 25, 2019.

Crichton, Danny. 'China VC Has Overtaken Silicon Valley, but Do Aggregate Numbers Tell the Whole Story?' *TechCrunch*, techcrunch.com/2018/07/05/china-vc-has-overtaken-silicon-valley/. Last accessed July 5, 2018.

Darwin, Solomon and Henry Chesbrough. *Prototyping a Scalable Smart Village to Simultaneously Create Sustainable Development and Enterprise Growth Opportunities*. HBS No. B5886-PDF-ENG. Boston, MA: Harvard Business Publishing, 2017.

David, Paul A. 'Understanding the Emergence of 'Open Science' Institutions: Functionalist Economics in Historical Context', *Industrial and Corporate Change*, August 1, 2004: academic.oup.com/icc/article/13/4/571/718486.

'Dengue | CDC', *Centers for Disease Control and Prevention,* www.cdc.gov/Dengue/. Last accessed March 17, 2019.

Diamandis, Peter H. *Abundance: the Future Is Better than You Think*. Simon & Schuster, 2015.

Du, Jingshu, et al. 'Managing Open Innovation Projects with Science-Based and Market-Based Partners', *Research Policy*, 43.5 (2014), pp. 828–40: doi: 10.1016/j.respol.2013.12.008.

Economy, Elizabeth C. *The Third Revolution: Xi Jinping and the New Chinese State*. Oxford University Press, 2018.

Edmondson, Amy C., and Harvey Jean-François. *Extreme Teaming: Lessons in Complex, Cross-Sector Leadership*. Emerald Publishing, 2017.

'EGI Advanced Computing Services for Research', *EGI*, www.egi.eu/. Last accessed April 25, 2019.

Euchner, James A. 'Two Flavors of Open Innovation', *Research-Technology Management*, 53. 4 (2010), pp. 7–8: doi: 10.1080/08956308.2010.11657634.

Florida, Richard L. *Cities and the Creative Class*. Routledge, 2005.

Fu, Xiaolan. *China's Path to Innovation*. Cambridge University Press, 2015.

Fu, Xiaolan, et al. 'Open Innovation as a Response to Constraints and Risks: Evidence from China', *Asian Economic Papers*, 13.3 (2014), pp. 30–58: doi: 10.1162/asep_a_00289.

Gawer, Annabelle, and Michael A. Cusumano. *Platform Leadership: How Intel, Microsoft, and Cisco Drive Industry Innovation*. Harvard Business School Press, 2002.

Gawer, Annabelle, and Michael A. Cusumano. 'Industry Platforms and Ecosystem Innovation', *Journal of Product Innovation Management*, 31.3 (2013), pp. 417–33: doi: 10.1111/jpim.12105.

Gompers, Paul A. 'Corporations and the Financing of Innovation: The Corporate Venturing Experience' *Economic Review*, 87.4 (2002).

Gordon, Robert J. *The Rise and Fall of American Growth: the U.S. Standard of Living since the Civil War*. Princeton University Press, 2016.

'Gore Innovation Center', *Gore*, www.gore.com/innovation-center. Last accessed April 25, 2019.

Hansen, Morten T. "Introducing T-shaped managers. Knowledge management's next generation." *Harvard Business Review* 79.3 (2001): 106–16.

Hardy, Quentin. 'Google's Innovation: And Everyone's?' *Forbes Magazine*, August 18, 2011: www.forbes.com/sites/quentinhardy/2011/07/16/googles-innovation-and-everyones/#33c2084b3066.

Helsel, Mike. Personal interview. October 15, 2014.

'Hi, We Are Research & Development', *Telefonica Research and Development*: www.tid.es/who-we-are. Last accessed April 25, 2019.

Hikkerova, Lubica, et al. 'Patent Life Cycle: New Evidence', *Technological Forecasting and Social Change*, 88.C (October 2014), pp. 313–24: doi: 10.1016/j.techfore.2013.10.005.

'Home', *ATTRACT Project*, attract-eu.com/. Last accessed April 25, 2019.

Hounshell, David A., and John K. Smith. *Science and Corporate Strategy: Du Pont R and D, 1902–1918*. Cambridge University Press, 1989.

Huang, Yasheng. *Capitalism with Chinese Characteristics: Entrepreneurship and the State*. Cambridge University Press, 2008.

Huston, Larry, and Nabil Sakkab. 'Connect and Develop: Inside Procter & Gamble's New Model for Innovation', *Harvard Business Review*, February 7, 2006: ,hbr.org/2006/03/connect-and-develop-inside-procter-gambles-new-model-for-innovation.

'IMEC Login', *IMEC Login*, imec.org/. Last accessed March 17, 2019.

'Internet of Things', *Wikipedia*, Wikimedia Foundation, April 12, 2019: en.wikipedia.org/wiki/Internet_of_things.

Johnson, Mark W. *Seizing the White Space: Business Model Innovation for Growth and Renewal*. Harvard Business Press, 2010.

Jurado A., Susana, et al. 'Lean Elephants: Addressing the Innovation Challenge in Big Companies', Innovation and Research Telefonica: http://www.tid.es/sites/526e527928a32d6a7400007f/assets/53bfe9f128a32d6733001f37/Lean_Elephants.pdf.

Kortum, Samuel, and Josh Lerner. 'Stronger Protection or Technological Revolution: What Is Behind the Recent Surge in Patenting?' *Research Policy*, 28.1 (January 12, 1999), pp. 1–22: doi: 10.3386/w6204.

Kramer, Mark R., and Michael Porter. "Creating shared value." *Harvard Business Review* 89.1/2 (2011): 62–77.

Lafley, Alan G., and Ram Charan. *The Game-Changer: How You Can Drive Revenue and Profit Growth with Innovation*. Crown Business, 2008.

Lakhani, K. R., K. Hutter, S. Healy Pokrywa, and J. Fuller, 'Open Innovation at Siemens', *Harvard Business School*, Case 613, 100, (2013).

Laursen, Keld, and Ammon Salter. 'Open for Innovation: the Role of Openness in Explaining Innovation Performance among U.K. Manufacturing Firms', *Strategic Management Journal*, 27.2 (November 21, 2005), pp. 131–50: doi: 10.1002/smj.507.

Lee, Melissa, Esteve Almirall, and Jonathan Wareham. 'Open Data and Civic Apps: First Generation Failures, Second Generation Improvements', *Communications of the ACM*, 59.1 (2015), pp. 82–9: doi: 10.1145/2756542.

Li, Xianjun. 'Industrial Value Migration, Path Innovation and Competitive Advantage: Empirical Analysis Based on China's Automotive Firms', www.cnki.com, 2010: en.cnki.com.cn/Article_en/CJFDTOTAL-ZGRK201001013.htm.

Liang, Mei. 'Navigating Open Innovation Under Institutional Influence: Lessons from China's High-Speed Rail Industry', December 2017. World Open Innovation Conference, student paper.

Lifshitz-Assaf, Hila. 'Dismantling Knowledge Boundaries at NASA: The Critical Role of Professional Identity in Open Innovation', *Administrative Science Quarterly*, 63.4 (2018), pp. 746–82.

Lohr, Steve. *Go To*. BasicBooks, 2001.

Ma, Damien. 'Can Chinese Industrial Policy Determine Winners or Just Stir up Froth?' *MacroPolo*, October 9, 2018: macropolo.org/can-industrial-policy-propel-chinas-ev-industry-just-stir-froth/.

Marquis, Andre and Manav Subodh, 'Hypershift: How Established Companies Can Work with Makers, Inventors and Entrepreneurs to Leverage Innovation, Enter New Markets, Establish Brand Leadership and Unlock Value, Hypershift Advisory Press, 2014.

Martina, Michael, and Philip Wen. 'China Enshrines "Xi Jinping Thought", Key Xi Ally to Step Down', *Reuters*, Thomson Reuters, October 25, 2017: www.Reuters.com/article/us-china-congress/china-enshrines-xi-jinping-thought-key-xi-ally-to-step-down-idUSKBN1CT0C9.

McGrath, Rita. 'Transient Advantage', *Harvard Business Review*, 91.6 (2013), pp. 62–70.

McGrath, Rita. 'The End of Competitive Advantage', Harvard Business Review Press, 2013

Merton, Robert K., and Norman W. Storer. *The Sociology of Science: Theoretical and Empirical Investigations*. University of Chicago Press, 1973.

Moyo, Dambisa. *Dead Aid: Why Aid Is Not Working and How There Is a Better Way for Africa*. Farrar, Straus and Giroux, 2009.

'National Venture Capital Association', *NVCA*, nvca.org/. Last accessed March 17, 2019.

Nelson, Richard R. *The rate and direction of inventive activity: Economic and social factors*. Princeton University Press, 2015. (originally published in 1962)

'News Release', 'P&G Sets Two New Goals for Open Innovation Partnerships', |P&G News| Events, Multimedia, Public Relations, October 28, 2010: news.pg.com/press-release/pg-corporate-announcements/pg-sets-two-new-goals-open-innovation-partnerships.

Nonaka, Ikujiro and Hirotaka Takeuchi, The Knowledge-Creating Company: How Japanese Companies Create the Dynamics of Innovation, Oxford University Press, 1995.

Oecdecoscope. 'The Best vs. the Rest: The Global Productivity Slowdown Hides an Increasing Performance Gap across Firms', OECD ECOSCOPE, January 25, 2017: oecdecoscope. blog/2017/01/25/the-best-vs-the-rest-the-global-productivity-slowdown-hides-an-increasing-performance-gap-across-firms/.

Open Innovation', *Wikipedia*, Wikimedia Foundation, en.wikipedia.org/wiki/Open_innovation. Last accessed March 21, 2019.

'Open Innovation Platform', *Taiwan Semiconductor Manufacturing Company Limited*, www.tsmc.com/english/dedicatedFoundry/oip/index.htm. Last accessed April 25, 2019.

'Open Science Grid', *Open Science Grid*, opensciencegrid.org/.

O'Reilly, Tim. 'Do More! What Amazon Teaches Us About AI and the "Jobless Future"', From the WTF? Economy to the Next Economy, June 8, 2017: medium.com/the-wtf-economy/do-more-what-amazon-teaches-us-about-ai-and-the-jobless-future-8051b19a66af.

Osterwalder, Alexander, and Yves Pigneur. *Business Model Generation: a Handbook for Visionaries, Game Changers, and Challengers*. John Wiley & Sons, 2010.

Park, Haemin Dennis, and H. Kevin Steensma. 'When Does Corporate Venture Capital Add Value for New Ventures?' *Strategic Management Journal*, 33.1 (2011), pp. 1–22: doi: 10.1002/smj.937.

Parker, Geoffrey G., Marshall, VanAlstyne, and Paul Choudary Sangeet. *Platform Revolution: How Networked Markets Are Transforming the Economy—and How to Make Them Work for You*. W. W. Norton & Company, 2016.

Piller, Frank T. 'Open Innovation with Customers: Crowdsourcing and Co-Creation at Threadless', *SSRN Electronic Journal*, 2010: doi: 10.2139/ssrn.1688018.

'PitchBook: Venture Monitor', National Venture Capital Association: https://files. pitchbook.com/website/files/pdf/3Q_2018_PitchBook_NVCA_Venture_Monitor.pdf. February 27, 2019.

'Plenty of Room for Creativity', *Bosch Global*, www.bosch.com/stories/bosch-start-up-platform/. Last accessed April 25, 2019.

Porter, M. E. *Competitive Strategy: Techniques for Analyzing Industries and Competitors*. New York: Free Press, 1980.

Porter, M. E. *The Competitive Advantage: Creating and Sustaining Superior Performance*. New York: Free Press, 1985.

Prahalad, Coimbatore K. *The Fortune at the Bottom of the Pyramid: Eradicating Poverty Through Profits*. Wharton School Publ., 2006.

'"Reverse Innovation": GE Makes India a Lab for Global Markets', *Knowledge@Wharton*, May 20, 2010: knowledge.wharton.upenn.edu/article/reverse-innovation-ge-makes-india-a-lab-for-global-markets/.

Ries, Eric. *The Lean Startup: How Today's Entrepreneurs Use Continuous Innovation to Create Radically Successful Business*. Crown Business, 2011.

Schuman, Michael. 'China's Car Sector Needs a Shakeup', *Bloomberg.com*, August 29, 2017: www.bloomberg.com/view/articles/2017-08-29/china-s-car-sector-needs-a-shakeup-not-buyouts.

'SCOAP3: The Sponsoring Consortium for Open Access Publishing in Particle Physics', *SCOAP3 RSS*, scoap3.org/. Last accessed March 17, 2019.

'Smart Village Movement', *Smart Village Movement*, smartvillagemovement.org/. Last accessed April 25, 2019.

'Soil Quality Resource Concerns: Salinization', United States Department of Agriculture Natural Resources Conservation Service: http://www.nrcs.usda.gov/Internet/FSE_DOCUMENTS/nrcs142p2_053151.pdf

'Startseite Fraunhofer-Gesellschaft', *Startseite*, www.fraunhofer.de/. Last accessed March 17, 2019.

Tamoschus, David, et al. 'Developing a Framework to Manage a Pharmaceutical Innovation System', December 2015. Best emerging Scholar Paper Award, World Open Innovation Conference, student paper.

Teece, David J. 'Profiting from technological innovation: Implications for integration, collaboration, licensing and public policy', *Research Policy*, 15.6 (1986), pp. 285–305.

Teece, David J. 'Explicating dynamic capabilities: the nature and microfoundations of (sustainable) enterprise performance', *Strategic Management Journal*, 28.13 (2007), pp. 1319–50.

Teece, David J., Gary Pisano, and Amy Shuen. 'Dynamic capabilities and strategic management', *Strategic Management Journal*, 18.7 (1997), pp. 509–33.

Ting-Fang, Cheng. 'China's Upstart Chip Companies Aim to Topple Samsung, Intel and TSMC', *Nikkei Asian Review*, April 25, 2018.

United States, Office of Scientific Research and Development, 'Science: The Endless Frontier', *United States Government Printing Office, Washington*, by Vannevar Bush, July 1945: https://www.nsf.gov/about/history/nsf50/vbush1945.jsp.

Van de Vrande, J., P. J. De Jong, W. Vanhaverbeke, and M. De Rochemont, 'Open innovation in SMEs: Trends, motives and management challenges', *Technovation* 29.6–7 (2009), pp. 423–37.

Von Hippel, Eric. 'Lead users: a source of novel product concepts', *Management Science*, 32.7 (1986), pp. 791–805.

Von Hippel, Eric. *Democratizing Innovation*. MIT Press, 2005.

Von Hippel, Eric. 'Open user innovation', *Handbook of the Economics of Innovation*. Vol. 1. North-Holland, 2010, pp. 411–27.

Von Hippel, Eric. *Free Innovation*. MIT Press, 2016.

Weiblen, Tobias, and Henry W. Chesbrough. 'Engaging with Startups to Enhance Corporate Innovation', *California Management Review*, 57.2 (2015), pp. 66–90: doi: 10.1525/cmr.2015.57.2.66.

'Welcome to the European Institute of Innovation and Technology', *European Institute of Innovation & Technology (EIT)*, eit.europa.eu/.

West, Joel, and Marcel Bogers. 'Leveraging external sources of innovation: a review of research on open innovation', *Journal of Product Innovation Management*, 31.4 (2014), pp. 814–31.

West, Joel, and Scott Gallagher. 'Challenges of open innovation: the paradox of firm investment in open-source software', *R&D Management*, 36.3 (2006), pp. 319–31.

West, Joel, and Karim R. Lakhani. 'Getting clear about communities in open innovation', *Industry and Innovation*, 15.2 (2008), pp. 223–31.

Whitehead, Alfred N. *Science and the Modern World*. Macmillan, 1925.

Wladawsky-Berger, Irving. 'The Current State of AI Adoption', *The Wall Street Journal*, Dow Jones & Company, February 8, 2019: blogs.wsj.com/cio/2019/02/08/the-current-state-of-ai-adoption/?guid=BL-CIOB-14751&mod=hp_minor_pos4&dsk=y.

Wrigley, Cara, and Karla Straker. 'Designing Innovative Business Models with a Framework That Promotes Experimentation', *Strategy & Leadership*, 44.1 (2016), pp. 11–19: doi: 10.1108/sl-06-2015-0048.

Xu, Ke, and Xianjun Li. 'Technological Innovation from Imitation in Latecomer Firms: Evidence from China's Auto Firms', *Innovation and Development*, 4.1 (2014), pp. 161–73: doi: 10.1080/2157930x.2014.886815.

Yip, George S., and Bruce McKern. *China's next Strategic Advantage: from Imitation to Innovation*. The MIT Press, 2016.

Zhong, Raymond, and Paul Mozur. 'Tech Giants Feel the Squeeze as Xi Jinping Tightens His Grip', *The New York Times*, May 28, 2018: www.nytimes.com/2018/05/02/technology/china-xi-jinping-technology-innovation.html.

Zobel, Ann-Kristin. 'Benefiting from open innovation: A multidimensional model of absorptive capacity', *Journal of Product Innovation Management* 34.3 (2017), pp. 269–88.

Zobel, A. K., B. Balsmeier, and H. Chesbrough. 'Does patenting help or hinder open innovation? Evidence from new entrants in the solar industry', *Industrial and Corporate Change*, 25. (2016), pp. 307–31.

Index